HER BEST SHOT

. . .

WOMEN AND GUNS
IN AMERICA

LAURA BROWDER

THE UNIVERSITY OF NORTH CAROLINA PRESS

CHAPEL HILL

. . .

HER BEST SHOT

Set in Scala and Madrone types

by Tseng Information Systems, Inc.

Manufactured in the United States of America

This volume was published with the generous assistance of the
Greensboro Women's Fund of the University of North Carolina Press.
Founding Contributors: Linda Arnold Carlisle, Sally Schindel Cone,
Anne Faircloth, Bonnie McElveen Hunter, Linda Bullard Jennings,
Janice J. Kerley (in honor of Margaret Supplee Smith), Nancy Rouzer May,
and Betty Hughes Nichols.

The paper in this book meets the guidelines for permanence and durability
of the Committee on Production Guidelines for Book Longevity of the
Council on Library Resources.

Library of Congress Cataloging-in-Publication Data

Browder, Laura, 1963–

Her best shot : women and guns in America / by Laura Browder.

p. cm.

Includes bibliographical references and index.

ISBN-13: 978-0-8078-3050-5 (cloth : alk. paper)

ISBN-10: 0-8078-3050-x (cloth : alk. paper)

1. Women—United States—History—Miscellanea. 2. Firearms owners—
United States—History. 3. Women outlaws—United States—History.
4. Women soldiers—United States—History. 5. Women radicals—United
States—History. 6. Women in popular culture—United States—History.
7. Firearms—Social aspects—United States. I. Title.

HQ1410.B76 2006

305.48'96920973—dc22   2006010730

10 09 08 07 06   5 4 3 2 1

For my parents,

ANDY AND ANNA BROWDER

CONTENTS

ILLUSTRATIONS

My first inkling of the central place guns would come to occupy in my thoughts came the first New Year's Eve I spent in my apartment in the heart of Richmond, Virginia. Had I looked across the street to the porch of the old folks' home, I would have seen my elderly neighbors sitting on rockers, cradling shotguns and rifles. As it was, I was not prepared for the barrage of shots that went off at midnight, from weapons of every caliber and description, all in the service of welcoming in the new year. A few years later I was so acclimated that I completely forgot to warn our northern houseguests, who were standing on the deck enjoying their champagne toast when the shooting began. Within minutes, the electrical transformer on the corner had been destroyed by machine-gun fire, plunging the neighborhood into darkness—something that happened, according to the power company repairmen who came to fix the damage, every New Year's in some part of the city.

I had spent my life in New England until I moved to Virginia in my early thirties. Although it had never seemed to me that I led a particularly sheltered existence, I soon discovered how ignorant I was about much of American life—especially with regard to guns. I realized that I had never, up to this point, known a gun owner—or at least I didn't think I had known one. In retrospect, I am sure I had a mistaken impression, but, still, it took me awhile to grasp how common gun ownership was in my new environment—and how pervasive gun culture was. Whether it was my next door neighbor shooting possums in our alley with a .45 or the radio ads I heard for the gun shows that came to Richmond every other weekend, weapons seemed to be everywhere. Although this book had its genesis in intellectual questions, I became aware that writing it was also a way of making sense of my new home—and of its thriving gun culture.

And once I began to research the book, I discovered that guns were even more prevalent than I had imagined. When I brought my two-year-old to a local Hannukah party, I mentioned my research—and all the fathers there were quick to tell me about the .357s and the 9 millimeters they kept in their homes. My research assistant told her liberal parents about her work on this project—and they proceeded to show her the seven guns, treasured family heirlooms, that they kept in closets and drawers throughout their house.

When I discussed my research with my sophomore English class, one of my students, a former Marine and a sharpshooting instructor at Quantico, volunteered to take me to gun stores and gun shows, and to teach me how to shoot weapons ranging from a black powder rifle to an AK-47.

There were times early on, especially the afternoons spent at self-defense classes or gun shows, surrounded by weapons of every description, survivalist manuals, and young couples with baby strollers, that I felt completely out of my element and considered abandoning the project. I was uneasy when my toddler daughter began talking about bullets and pistols, and I talked to her about how guns were not toys, how they hurt people. The effect of this speech was undercut when she found a photograph of me cradling a submachine gun and clearly having a good time: after all, it really had been fun learning to shoot. Still, my life as the mother of small children seemed unrelated to those afternoons spent blasting away with an AR-15 at a worn-out target in the woods. Over time, I came to appreciate not only the complex interplay between popular ideas of womanhood and gun ownership in the United States but also the way that maternity and gun use have been related in popular culture over the centuries. In 2000, the Million Mom March took the national spotlight with its attention-grabbing insistence that mothers need to band together to stop gun violence; nothing seemed more natural. And yet those million moms are only part of a long, complicated American story, one that begins with women who cross-dressed and fought in the Revolutionary War and continues through a cavalcade of Wild West stars, gangsters, revolutionaries of the right and left, and gun-owning housewives, all the way up to the female soldiers fighting in Iraq today.

ACKNOWLEDGMENTS

It is a great pleasure to thank the many people who helped in many different ways with this book. I have to start with Carol Summers, for getting me to think about women and guns in the first place, and the past and present members of my writing group—Abigail Cheever, Dorothy Holland, Carol Summers, Sydney Watts, and Janet Winston—whose encouragement, incisive (and tireless) readings of many drafts and whose marvelous suggestions made this a much better work.

Many thanks to my former student Greg Carlson, for introducing me to a wide range of gun enthusiasts, taking me to gun shows and gun stores, and teaching me how to shoot. Thanks to Nicole Anderson Ellis, for all of her great research assistance, and to Jessica Munsch, for her image research. I am grateful to the many friends and colleagues who read drafts and offered suggestions and images: Tom De Haven, who pointed me to striking pictures of armed women and provided crucial encouragement early on; Lucinda Kaukas Havenhand; Eve Raimon; Susan Barstow; Nick Frankel; Barbara Burton; and Jim Wehmeyer. Thanks to David Latane for the great gun ads and to Tom Doherty for the gangster girl photos. Thanks to Noel and Jeff Yegian for their wonderful hospitality in Colorado. Thanks to Rachel Price for her help in North Carolina and to Andy Browder for assistance in tracking down images in Rhode Island.

Thanks to Mark Potok at the Southern Poverty Law Center for his help on the subject of militia women. Thanks to Meg Sweeney and Jan Radway for their very useful advice early on. Thanks to Paul Wright for all the books about guns and those who love them.

At Virginia Commonwealth University, thanks to my department chair, Marcel Cornis-Pope, for offering both moral support and concrete encouragement in the form of release time and graduate student assistance. Thanks to my deans, past and present, Stephen Gottfredson and Bob Holsworth, for their research support. A 2001 Faculty Grant in Aid helped enormously, as did last-minute funding facilitated by Frank Macrina and Bob Holsworth. Members of the 2003 interdisciplinary faculty seminar offered wonderful suggestions and ideas. Thanks to Ginny Schmitz and Margret Schluer for their skillful assistance and to Michael Keller for all his technical help.

Thanks to Joyce Antler, who has been a great friend and inspiration for many years.

Thanks to Nina and Leo: Nina was a toddler when I began work on this project; Leo was born halfway through the writing process. With their presence, completing this work became much more eventful and much more fun. My husband, Allan Rosenbaum, made it all possible with his love, generosity, and boundless energy. If it weren't for him, this book would never have been finished.

It has been a delight to work with UNC Press once again. Kate Torrey was a dream editor, offering encouragement and expert guidance in just the right proportions. Thanks also to Ron Maner for all his help in shepherding the manuscript through the production process, to Paul Betz for his boundless patience, to Vicky Wells for her assistance with permissions, and to Rich Hendel for the book's design. Many thanks to Alan Trachtenberg for his very helpful early comments, and to the two anonymous readers commissioned by the Press, whose comments greatly improved the final work.

Thanks to Susann B. Cokal for her heroic intervention at the eleventh hour.

Early versions of some chapters were presented as papers at meetings of the American Studies Association; I am grateful to all in attendance who offered constructive suggestions and posed probing questions.

Many thanks to the interlibrary loan office staff at Virginia Commonwealth University, particularly Jeannie Scott; to the always helpful staff of the Library of Virginia; to the gracious and helpful archivists at the Denver Public Library's Western History Department, especially Barbara Walton and Colleen Nunn; and to Frances Clymer, Nathan Bender, and Pat Baumhover at the Buffalo Bill Historical Center, whose ideas, insights, and generous assistance made my work there particularly exciting and productive. I am equally appreciative of the efforts of Kristina L. Southwell at the Western History Collections of the University of Oklahoma and of Debbie Newman at the Arizona Historical Society. At the Wisconsin Historical Society, John Nondorf was of considerable help with photo research, and Dee Grimsrud provided knowledgeable assistance. I am also grateful to the staff at the Library of Congress.

Finally, a big thank you to my parents, Anna and Andy Browder. This book is for them.

HER BEST SHOT

Threⁱ he armed woman has held, and continues to hold, enormous symbolic significance in American culture. In the
pages that follow, I will explore the ways in which she
anchors popular debates about women's capacity for full citizenship—and
women's capabilities for violence. Throughout much of American history,
the gun has served as a recurrent symbol that links violence and masculinity. For over two centuries, there have been women who have escaped
conventional gender roles by picking up guns. In doing so, they became
armed icons. Paradoxically, to succeed with the public, these famous armed
women have had to embrace female stereotypes and expectations. Iconic
women with guns have challenged and yet reinforced the masculinist ideal
of America—that guns are inextricably tied to both masculinity and American identity. Public discussions of these women reflect the discomfort that
they have produced in American culture.

In the late 1980s, the media began reporting on a new trend in women's
involvement with guns. "Firearms Industry Woos Women Who Dress to
Kill" was the title of a 1986 story that described bras, garters, and belly
bands designed to hold concealed weaponry.[1] Other stories discussed the
National Rifle Association's decision to gear ads toward women, which were
placed in such magazines as *People, Family Circle, Ladies' Home Journal,* and
Redbook. The NRA created a women's issues division in 1990.[2] The press also
covered Smith & Wesson's introduction of its new LadySmith handguns,
the brochure for which, depicting a fur coat, a yellow rose, and a LadySmith
handgun, bore the caption "just possibly an ideal answer to a very contemporary need."[3] *Armed and Female,* a 1989 book by former actress turned gun
industry spokeswoman Paxton Quigley, became a publishing phenomenon
by selling more than 200,000 copies as of 2004.[4] Many stories noted the
growing popularity of *Women & Guns* magazine, founded in 1989, as it hit
the newsstands in 1991, with advertisers such as Feminine Protection, a
Dallas-based purveyor of concealed-carry handbags and other accessories,
and the American Huntress Bang Bang Boutique in Fort Lauderdale.[5] Most
of the media stories were positive, though many also contained quotes from
representatives of the gun-control movement questioning the wisdom of

having women arm themselves. Thus some articles bore titles in the vein of "NRA Is Defending as Educational Its Campaign Targeting Women," a 1993 headline in the *Wall Street Journal*.[6]

The coverage was not confined to the general interest media. Gun industry publications included such articles as "Targeting a New Market for Firearms (Women Buyers)," which began with a little handgun humor: "Women as targets! Not as targets for handgun practice (although most husbands probably harbor a thought like this from time to time) but women as targets for handgun marketing and sales." On a more serious note, the article's author warned that "the female market is growing quickly, and if you don't become a part of it soon, you may be left behind."[7] Indeed, the 1997 SHOT Show, an annual industry exposition hosted by the National Shooting Foundation, featured a seminar titled "Selling to the Fast Growing Women's Market."[8] *Women & Guns*, whose circulation had reached 20,000 by the mid-1990s, was joined in January 2003 by the NRA's new glossy magazine *Woman's Outlook*, a development that suggested this new marketing phenomenon was continuing to grow.

Of course, not every observer agreed with the NRA's assessment that gun ownership among women was increasing dramatically and that by the mid-1990s 12 to 20 million women owned guns. A 1995 article in the *Journal of Criminal Law and Criminology* pointed out that while "this claim has been accepted by most journalists and repeated in dozens of stories about the feminization of gunnery . . . pro-gun groups and the media have greatly exaggerated the rate of gun ownership among women." The article's authors, Tom W. Smith and Robert J. Smith, analyzed data presented by the University of Chicago's respected National Opinion Research Center, concluding that neither women nor men were more likely to own a handgun in 1995 than they had been in 1980. The Smiths asserted that "through the circulation of statistics of dubious reliability and accuracy, pro-gun groups have successfully created the impression that gun ownership by women has increased appreciably and has reached unprecedented levels. Most of the media have accepted the claims of increasing ownership and have sometimes even mangled and exaggerated these claims."[9] Indeed, despite statistical evidence to the contrary, industry supporters and most reporters agreed that although, as one journalist put it, "most women are taught from childhood that guns are for men,"[10] there was a strange new phenomenon in the United States. Whether fueled by women's fear of crime or by the gun industry's advertising blitz, women were becoming gun owners, seemingly for the first time.

In fact, the armed woman was hardly news. From the Revolutionary era to the present day, the armed woman has served—and continues to serve—as a locus for popular debates about women's capacity for violence, as well as women's capability to defend—or engage in insurrection against—the state.

Much of this history has been forgotten, as have earlier commercial images of women with guns. Yet for the pundits of the 1980s and 1990s commenting on the "new" phenomenon of women and guns, a glance at the magazines of a century ago might have proved illuminating. An 1891 ad for Stevens Special Firearms, published in *Forest and Stream*, depicts a series of tableaux of trapshooters: first two women in Victorian dress, then two men together, followed by a man and a woman, all shooting in different directions; and, finally, a fourth image of Annie Oakley standing alone. The text, which describes the rifles and pistols depicted, includes a mention of the Stevens Ladies' Rifle—"the proper rifle for ladies. It is wonderfully accurate and has no recoil."[11] Another ad for the Stevens Lady Model Rifles, from the year before, begins, "Here we are again with the same notice, which proved so popular last month that we have decided to try it again. . . . Have you any idea how many fine *Lady Shots* there are in this and other countries? *We have*, as we are supplying them with what has proved *the most popular* arm ever made for this purpose with both the *Ladies and Gentlemen* who do not care or are not able to use a heavy arm."[12]

Rather than suggesting that women needed guns to ward off undesirable men, some ads suggested that guns would attract suitors. "Armed with a Marlin repeater," runs one 1891 ad, "the Summer Girl is always surrounded by admirers." The ad portrays a fashionably dressed woman leaning the butt of her rifle on the ground with one hand as she shows off her target—and shooting skill—to a crowd of admiring men.[13]

Perhaps the most surprising ads from this period are the ones that feature gender-neutral copy yet depict female shooters. Most ads do not assume that women need men in order to hunt. A 1903 poster for Iver Johnson Sporting Goods shows a woman in full skirt climbing over a fence, dog in attendance, in order to retrieve the fox she has just shot.[14] In a Winchester poster from 1909, a woman prepares to load up her canoe with supplies—while holding her .22 caliber repeating rifle.[15] A 1915 ad for Winchester repeating shotguns, from *Leslie's Illustrated Weekly Newspaper*, shows a woman alone in the wilderness with her hunting dog for company, holding a shotgun. There is nothing in the ad that comments on her sex.[16] Similarly, a 1916 ad for the Ross rifle, which promises that the gun "paralyzes

ARMED WITH A

MARLIN

REPEATER

the Summer Girl is always surrounded by admirers.

Nothing you can take on your vacation will give you as much pleasure for as little money as a Marlin 22 calibre. Our 1897 Model, Take-Down, using short, long and long-rifle cartridges in the same gun, is the finest pleasure arm made. Ask your dealer. 198-page illustrated book of arms and ammunition free, if you will send stampts to pay postage to **The Marlin Fire-Arms Co., New Haven, Ct.** *Send 15c. for sample tube of Marlin Rust-Repeller.*

An 1898 Marlin ad from *Field and Stream* suggests that women with shooting skills will have an easy time attracting beaux—and that the fashionable markswoman need not surrender her femininity in order to shoot. Buffalo Bill Historical Center, Cody, Wyoming; Gift of Roy Marcot; Tucson, Arizona; MS111.12.36.

This Marlin 20-gauge repeater ad, which appeared in *Popular Mechanics* in 1914, is an early example of advertising linking a gun and a beautiful woman. Unlike the sturdy outdoorswoman who generally appeared in ads of the period, the model here gazes coyly at the viewer. Buffalo Bill Historical Center, Cody, Wyoming; Gift of Roy Marcot, Tucson, Arizona; MS111.12.106.

with a single shot," features a woman with an ammo belt slung casually around her skirted hips, aiming her rifle. Many Stevens ads also did not refer to women in the copy. One from 1905 had the caption "The story of the Stevens Tersely Told: Chapter 1 'Aim' [illustrated by a woman raising her rifle], Chapter 2 'Game' [showing the same woman with rifle lowered accepting a dead bird from her hunting dog]."[17] Clearly, a woman with a gun was such an unexceptional sight that it did not require comment.

Guns were presented as being so unthreatening that they were safe for young girls, as well as for women. An 1891 calendar for the Union Metallic Cartridge Company shows a girl, who cannot be more than four or five years old, surrounded by eight hunting dogs and carrying a rifle.[18] Sometimes girls were used in even more provocative images. A 1903 ad for Iver

This Stevens ad from 1907, which appeared in the *National Sportsman*, shows a practically dressed woman fully intent on her target. Buffalo Bill Historical Center, Cody, Wyoming; Gift of Roy Marcot, Tucson, Arizona; MS111.18.44.

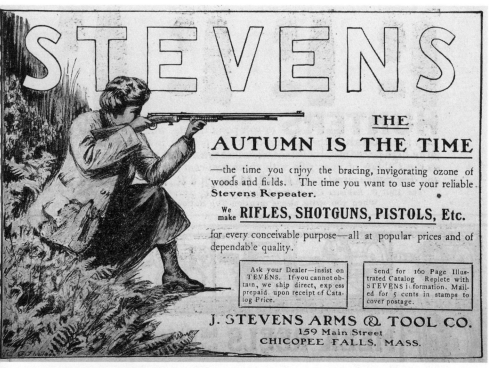

The copy in this 1905 Stevens ad does not make reference to its subject's gender; instead, it showcases her hunting abilities. Buffalo Bill Historical Center, Cody, Wyoming; Gift of Roy Marcot, Tucson, Arizona; MS111.18.40.

Johnson safety hammer automatic revolvers, for example, shows a little girl in a nightgown holding a revolver that she has pointed right at her face. The caption, written in childish script across the picture, reads, "'Papa says it won't hurt me.'" The main text advises readers that "an Iver Johnson revolver can lie around the house."[19]

While the women in these ads were portrayed as competent hunters, other magazine ads highlighted their accomplishments as trapshooters. Through the 1920s and even into the 1930s, ads featuring trapshooting regularly starred women champions. A 1921 ad for Ithaca Guns showed three-time trapshooting champion "Mrs. Harry Harrison." The sensibly attired Mrs. Harrison "says that any woman can break more targets with an Ithaca."[20] This particular ad ran in the magazine *National Sportsman*; clearly, women were considered readers of that publication—and the presence of women in the ads was not perceived to turn off male readers. A

Some early advertising images, like this one from a 1903 issue of *McClure's Magazine*, seem particularly alarming. The text written across the photo reads, "Papa says it won't hurt me." The "gentlemen" addressed in the ad are encouraged to leave the Iver Johnson revolver lying around the house. Buffalo Bill Historical Center, Cody, Wyoming; Gift of Roy Marcot, Tucson, Arizona; MS111.7.5.

1929 ad for Ithaca guns shows an unglamorous woman aiming her rifle. "Mrs. 'Bunny' Arnold Sanders won the ladies' championship of West Virginia with an Ithaca," the text tells us. "Her father, mother, husband and brothers are crack shots over traps or afield. Mrs. Sanders' family believe[s] Ithaca lock speed helps."[21] Here, shooting is not just a family sport but also one that involves generations of women. And it was no less suitable for single women to hunt or shoot traps: another Ithaca ad presents "an Iowa lass, Miss Alice Finkel."[22]

Interestingly, although ads from the 1880s through the turn of the century featured many images of women hunting, often alone, these images later vanished, to be replaced by more domestic scenes of gun use. Advertisements from the era of the First World War tended to show men teaching their wives to shoot as a means of protecting the home and children while the husband was away at war.

Over time, though, those ads disappeared as well. Generally speaking, the only women who appeared in weapons ads of the 1940s, 1950s, and 1960s were mothers and daughters participating, often somewhat vicariously, in the family sport of BB gun target shooting. An ad for the Winchester .22 from 1953 shows a picnicking group: two men and a boy engaged in target shooting while the two women happily unpack the picnic basket.[23] From the late 1960s to the present day, women in firearms ads have tended to be scantily dressed models posing with ultramasculine weapons. Women's sexuality has been used to enhance the appeal of these guns.

During the 1980s, however, a curious development became evident. The new gun ads promoted the notion that good mothers and responsible single women needed to carry handguns to ensure their own safety and the safety of their families. Housewives, lovingly tucking their children into bed, kept a revolver on the nightstand; ads featuring women without children played on fears of urban crime. Gun manufacturers had rediscovered women as potential firearms consumers and were anxious to redefine the image of the woman with a gun. These ads may represent only what gun manufacturers wished their customers to see, but they nonetheless serve as a cultural barometer: they reveal what manufacturers considered attractive to women and to the spouses, boyfriends, or fathers who would buy them guns.

The difference in content between the ads of the early twentieth century and the 1980s is suggestive in several important ways. The early ads featuring women and guns showed guns to be safe tools to be used as equipment for healthy recreation; one 1909 Winchester ad asserted that the gun "makes an outing outfit complete." However much we might now recoil at the picture of a little girl pointing a gun at her head, the manufacturers who produced this image clearly intended it to demonstrate just how safe and innocuous guns were. Indeed, many early ads showed idyllic scenes of little girls and boys asleep in the fields, cuddled next to their rifles, surrounded by hunting dogs. The message was that guns were not only safe; they were an important part of developing a healthy relationship to nature. As we shall see in the chapters that follow, outdoor recreation, which included acquiring hunting skills, was considered by political and social leaders to be key to building a racially strong nation filled with vigorous, fertile white women. Urban life, many worried, made women sickly and incapable of producing many children. In short, using a gun in the ways suggested by the ads was a part of good citizenship.

By contrast, weapons ads since the 1980s have encouraged women to buy guns not as part of an explicit nation-building effort but as a defense against anonymous violence, a task that the government is clearly not up to. No longer touted for use in a friendly forest, firearms for women are meant to ward off urban menace. Perhaps not surprisingly, in the gun manufacturers' world, the police are nowhere to be found; it is up to a woman alone to ward off the sexually threatening "predators" of the city. Over the course of a century, a dramatic difference has developed in what gun ads imply about the relationship between women, weaponry, society, and the state.

In *Her Best Shot*, I consider the ways that the gun has been a crucial symbol, over time, both to prominent armed women and to commentators seeking to define women's relation to the state. Throughout much of American history, the gun has stood not just for American citizenship but also for the linkage between violence and masculinity. Iconic women with guns challenge and yet reinforce the connection between firearms and (masculine) American identity. Consequently, public discussions of such women reflect the discomfort that they produce in American culture. Of course, words like "women," "citizenship," "violence," and "sexuality" demand close attention: our cultural fascination with the armed woman sometimes makes it easy to gloss over the many contradictions contained within these key terms. What is the relationship between citizenship and violence? How does the gun defend, express, or redefine a woman's sexuality? How does the gun serve as a charged symbol that has enabled white women to gain privileges by emphasizing their racial identity and freeing them from gender strictures?

The armed female celebrities I discuss have foregrounded sometimes their racial identity and at other times their gender identity in their use of firearms. Turn-of-the-twentieth-century female hunters and trapshooters found in the gun a means to uphold "whiteness" against the threat of racial degeneration. Both black and white women activists of the 1960s and 1970s used the gun as a bid for equal power within their often sexist movements, as well as a tool meant to dismantle the state apparatus. This book traces the development of racialized and gendered ideologies by looking at how armed celebrities fashioned their public image and at how such an image could in turn be re-created and disseminated throughout popular culture.

The social meanings of the armed woman, depicted within a single period, depend heavily on race and class, even, and especially, when there seems to be little variation in who is represented as an icon. The firearms ads of the late 1800s and early 1900s that seem surprisingly advanced in

Women and girl with hunting trophies at the Stone Ranch, circa 1890.
Wyoming State Archives, Department of State Parks and Cultural Resources.

their attitudes toward gender equality are decidedly less so in their representations of race and class. Almost uniformly, the ads depict well-to-do white women.[24] Yet photographs and illustrations from the period represent a wide range of experience. The ubiquitous ads from the 1870s and 1880s showing women of leisure trapshooting at a resort appeared along with such images as an 1877 *Harper's Weekly* cover picturing working-class women making cartridges in a factory. Photos of the self-consciously western Annie Oakley, in her girlish outfits, carefully posed to do trick shooting, were produced at the same time as a photograph of a mother, her preschool-aged daughter, and a teenage girl posed in front of a Wyoming ranch building, all three of them armed and holding the rabbits they have presumably just shot—animals that seem clearly destined not for the trophy shelf but for the stewpot.[25] While my focus is on iconic, mainstream images, these other images haunt the margins of u.s. culture during the late nineteenth century.

Although almost all the images from this period are of white women, their racial status was not always secure. The Wild West show performers who became the era's most famous armed women needed to take special care that both their femininity and their whiteness were unimpeachable, since their popularity depended on successfully representing civilization in opposition to the encroachments of nonwhite barbarity. Annie Oakley was a model of contained sexuality: she incorporated both her husband and their pet dog into her act, highlighting her status as a family-focused woman. In one famous image she dressed up in a dramatic Indian feather headdress, but her usual costume, which she sewed herself, was genteel and girlish, and decidedly not exotic. On the other hand, Wild West show performers who either were suspected of behavior that was too masculine, such as swearing or promiscuity, or were seen as racially ambiguous quickly found their performing careers derailed.

By the 1920s and 1930s, the social anxieties that focused on armed women demonstrate how unstable a category "woman" can be, even the category of "white woman." The promotion of armed (white, respectable) womanhood in the late nineteenth century depended on divorcing guns from the possibility of violence. Yet the weapons brandished by the urban gun molls of the 1920s highlighted for commentators dangerous linkages between these women's sexuality and their attraction to violence, and suggested as well the dangers posed by women's participation in urban working-class culture. These women with guns were not upholding the race; rather, they were using weapons to spread disorder and to further erode traditional gender roles. The "Brooklyn gungirls" who so transfixed newspaper readers during the 1920s were clearly threats to the urban social order.

Womanhood is, after all, linked closely to sexuality; and guns—and the possibilities of violence they promise—in the hands of women whose sexuality is unregulated or unorthodox have seemed especially dangerous to conservative commentators, who have often equated criminal gun use, degeneracy, and feminism. "Strange Phase of Modern Feminism Keeps Whole of the Police Department Guessing Hard" read a headline in the *New York World*, which reported on Celia Cooney, the infamous "bob-haired bandit" of the 1920s and the best known of the Brooklyn gungirls of the period. J. Edgar Hoover, writing about the bandits of the thirties, blamed American criminality on domineering women. He was appalled by the popular appeal of Bonnie Parker, the criminal who successfully managed her own media image by portraying her relationship with Clyde Barrow in a traditionally romantic vein. Parker, who published poetry about her affair with Barrow and who seemed to fully understand the importance of a domestic image even as she engaged in acts of criminal violence, was aghast when some gag photos Clyde Barrow took of her holding guns and smoking a cigar became public. Those pictures threatened to change public perceptions of her from a star-crossed lover to a sleazy, masculinized gun moll.

The images of Cooney and Parker illustrate the difficulties of separating out messages of gender empowerment and the exploitative use of sexuality: is the armed woman a powerful force or a seductive fantasy? Even as some women, like Parker, attempted to control the sexual message conveyed in how they were portrayed to the public, a thriving market developed in sexualized images of gun-toting women—in movies, detective magazines, and comic books. Such women were clearly posed for the titillation of male viewers: detective magazine covers often featured women pulling guns out of their garter belts or their generous cleavage. Although they might require energetic physical subjugation by the male protagonist of the story, their threat was always containable—they were more thrilling to the male viewer than menacing to society at large.

A similar efflorescence of sexualized images followed the next publicly decried outbreak of female armed violence, in the late 1960s and well into the 1970s. Just as commentators in the 1920s and 1930s had linked women's violence and feminism, the emergence of a large number of armed women prompted *u.s. News & World Report* to ask in 1974: "From car thieves to murderers, female outlaws are in the headlines—raising the question: are they influenced by 'women's lib'?"[26] Yet as the women portrayed in the article—Patty Hearst, the Manson girls, and the radical bank robber Susan Saxe—began to fade from the headlines, a new genre of softcore porn was born: posters and videos of women firing big guns, generally assault weapons. Even more clearly than in the detective magazines and comics of a previous era, these women are presented as a means of sexualizing weaponry. As the historian James William Gibson describes the videos, "Each [female fashion] model is introduced along with the weapon she will fire. A graph shows the gun's technical features on one side, with the model's height, weight, and breast, hip, and waist measurements on the other . . . the camera shows each model's body moving from recoil as she fires long bursts of 20 to 40 rounds. Models hold the weapons at their waists so that the camera can focus on their breasts."[27] Here, the armed woman is rendered unthreatening through objectification: as a mere accessory to her gun, she fires her weapon as instructed. There seems no danger that she would use her gun to reconfigure the social order.

While fewer iconic images of African American women with guns exist —and virtually no widely disseminated images before the late 1960s—they carry a different charge for viewers schooled in the semiotics of the armed

G. Gordon Liddy's popular "Stacked and Packed" calendar accessorizes a model's cleavage with assault weaponry, a hand grenade, and a crucifix. Photo by Mark Swisher. Courtesy of G. Gordon Liddy Network Productions.

woman: these images generally suggest insurrection rather than criminality. Until the late nineteenth century, American gun laws, especially in the South, used racial ideology to limit ownership of firearms (the infamous *Dred Scott* decision was, among other things, a case about the right of African Americans to own guns).[28] Given the long history of racialized gun laws, it is not surprising that the Black Panthers, most notably, claimed gun ownership for African Americans as a necessary element of American identity.[29] However, male Panthers also saw weaponry as a symbol of successful black manhood, leaving women Panthers to disrupt the symbolism by using the gun as a means to gain power within the movement as well as in a larger political framework. Although Bonnie Parker was a popular icon for many white women on the left, black women revolutionaries—as well as white radicals who were consciously trying to dismantle the basis of white supremacy—generally ignored earlier American models of armed womanhood and looked, instead, to third world exemplars such as the women of Vietnam and the Puerto Rican nationalists Lolita Lebron and Blanca Canales. Radical journals such as *Red Star* celebrated armed motherhood, invoking the example of the peasant women of Naxalbari, India, who joined in a 1967 uprising, fighting with children strapped to their backs.[30] These armed mothers did seem to echo, to some extent, American icons from an earlier era. Nevertheless, the image of the Prairie Madonna, widely represented at the turn of the twentieth century as a pioneer mother, rifle in one hand, baby on a hip, settling the West as part of a nation-building effort, was replaced here by the image of an armed mother intent on overthrowing the state.

The female guerrilla fighter may have been celebrated only on the left during the 1960s, but the combat-ready woman soldier has been a figure of controversy since the founding of the United States. Given the strong historical linkage between citizenship and the right and obligation to fight in wars, the female soldier has been a particularly contested figure in United States history. Both feminists and antifeminists in the years leading up to the Civil War saw military service as the ultimate outcome of the women's rights movement—and as the ultimate test of women's patriotism. Women's rights advocates of the 1840s pointed to actual Revolutionary War soldiers such as Deborah Sampson Gannett as proof that women were capable of martial valor and thus should gain access to the full privileges of citizenship, while readers snapped up cheap novels featuring rough, ready, and sometimes bawdy cross-dressing female soldiers.

Because the female soldier suggests a sexual ambiguity that conflicts with conventional expectations, the women who cross-dressed as soldiers in the Civil War and then published memoirs about their experiences had to portray themselves as almost ludicrously respectable and committed to upholding traditional gender roles if they were to succeed in reaching a wide audience. Belle Boyd, the most famous Confederate cross-dresser, claimed that she shot her first Union soldier because he used disrespectful language to her mother: the murder was framed as an attempt to protect her genteel status. Sarah Edmonds, author of a best-selling memoir about her service in the Union army, not only omitted mention of her years of cross-dressing before the onset of the war but also barely alluded to her soldierly disguise, burying her references to it beneath a welter of patriotic and Christian language. On the other hand, Loreta Velazquez, the Confederate author of *The*

Woman in Battle, described her military service primarily in terms of the pleasure it gave her to cross-dress and to outfight, outlove, and outswagger the male soldiers with whom she fought. Her memoir, as might be expected, was roundly denounced by commentators, who charged that she had besmirched southern womanhood.

Besides suggesting potentially troubling aspects of female sexuality, the idea of women in combat implicitly raised the possibility that, having fought on the battlefield, they would expect equal rights in other aspects of life. Although women no longer need to engage in cross-dressing to serve as soldiers, the relationship between armed patriotism and feminism continues to be contested to this day. Female soldiers were featured in a 2003 photo spread in the NRA magazine *Woman's Outlook*. However, in a caption accompanying the photo of Airman Rossana Ojeda—who is in uniform but wearing pink lipstick—Congresswoman Heather Wilson (R-N.M.) offers a nonfeminist rationale: "Women in combat is not about equity or equal opportunity. The point is National Security."[31]

The tensions surrounding women's armed patriotism are nicely contained by the fictional female soldier who remains the most famous of all American armed women. According to the legend, which was late in developing, Molly Pitcher was a Revolutionary War soldier's wife who took over her husband's artillery position when he fell in battle. As historians have pointed out any number of times, Molly Pitcher was a composite of several Revolutionary-era women.[32] Thus, Linda Grant De Pauw writes, "The woman memorialized on posters, postage stamps, and a rest stop on the New Jersey Turnpike was not a real woman at all but a mythic figure constructed by artists and writers many years after the war." Molly Pitcher had not been identified as anything more than "Captain Molly" until 1848, when Nathaniel Currier produced the first print of her; the first written mention of Molly Pitcher did not appear in a book until 1859.[33] But after 1876, when a Carlisle, Pennsylvania, man published a genealogy identifying a local woman as "the heroine of Monmouth," the Molly Pitcher cult grew and grew. Molly Pitcher was never pictured as a cross-dresser; instead, she was portrayed as a properly feminine—though heroic—helpmate. Margaret Corbin and Mary McCauley, the women on whom the character of Molly Pitcher was purportedly based, were far from being models of feminine deportment: Corbin was known as "Dirty Kate" and "died a horrible death from the effects of a syphilitic disease" after the war, and McCauley was remembered as "a very masculine person . . . [who] could both drink whiskey and swear."[34] However, the idealized Molly Pitcher—who grew more

Molly Pitcher, the fictional female soldier who remains the most famous of all American armed women, was always pictured as very feminine, never as a cross-dresser. In this engraving, a number of men stare at her exposed breast as she loads the cannon. Engraving by J. C. Armytage after Alonzo Chapel. National Archives and Records Administration.

perfect over the years—had none of the sexual ambiguity or unseemly independence of actual female Continental soldiers.

From Molly Pitcher to the present, a stunningly broad range of images and performances suggest the ways in which women's associations with guns have both shaped and reflected American notions of femininity and citizenship. In researching this book, I read early nineteenth-century autobiographical pamphlets, the proceedings of nineteenth-century women's rights conventions, best-selling novels of the Civil War era, gun advertisements from the 1890s to the present day, detective magazines of the 1930s, revolutionary feminist handgun manuals of the 1970s, and twenty-first-century magazines marketed to gun-owning women, as well as mainstream newspapers, magazines, and popular autobiographies. These sources offer something that a public-policy approach does not, and that is access to the realm of American imaginings about armed women. Looking at a range of subjects, from female Civil War soldiers to gangsters such as Bonnie Parker, from Wild West stars to Patty Hearst, I explore the self-fashioning of these armed female icons and their cultural meaning as a way of looking closely at questions of gender, power, and citizenship.

Because armed women celebrities—and their interpreters—have often looked to a stock of iconic American images, such as the pioneer woman, in creating their characters, I am able to trace these images and their metamorphoses over two centuries. The authors of female soldier autobiographies in the early nineteenth century had a limited range of antecedents and images to which to refer and on which to model themselves: Joan of Arc, the Maid of Saragossa, and perhaps Revolutionary War heroine Deborah Sampson Gannett. However, the evolution of mass-mediated culture has given armed women today an enormous library of images from which to draw, and with which to negotiate their place in American life. And the icons of the past are often used by female gun owners and gun-industry supporters in different, and contradictory, ways. For instance, how is armed citizenship interpreted by the women who make elaborate period costumes, invent "frontier" names for themselves (under which they write imagined autobiographies), and spend their weekends at Wild West re-enactment shooting events? What is the community they imagine themselves to be re-creating? Are they harking back to an individualistic model of citizenship? For them, are guns a means of escaping a contemporary version of female identity that seems uncongenial? As Dianne Gleason, a well-known Calamity Jane impersonator and shooting champion whom I met (in her buckskins) at the Buffalo Bill Historical Center, told me when I asked her about her decision to embark on this role, "I ain't no Doris Day." For her, choosing an identity as Calamity Jane—branded in her time as criminal, drunk, and racially degenerate—was a means to personal freedom. Gleason's first character, she told me, had been an imagined servant girl who had shot the employer who raped her. For Gleason, a Wild West identity seemed to be a way of asserting both female strength and rage. Yet to the writers for gun magazines, women's shooting reenactments are primarily a way to make guns seem "fun" and historical—and, thus, an effective way to soften the opposition of gun-control advocates.

In the past decades, a vast scholarly literature on citizenship has emerged, with many writers focusing on the complex interplay between gender, race, and nationhood.[35] This book follows on this body of research to examine what is perhaps the most charged symbol of American citizenship. The gun, after all, suggests the close connection between violence and citizenship, as well as the ongoing debate over who should have access to firearms, and how they should be used in relation to the state—to defend it, literally (in the case of soldiers) or figuratively (in the case of Wild West show women), to dismantle it (in the case of left- and right-wing revolutionary women) or to take over the functions of an ineffectual government (which the "Armed Citizen" column in the NRA magazine *American Rifleman* regularly details, recounting the successful attempts by homeowners to resist criminal break-ins). Citizenship, after all, entails more than the rights and obligations of full political participation in the nation. It also involves the chance to partake in the imagined life of the nation—to enter into the mythologies of nation making and nation building. Perhaps that is, most of all, what cowgirl reenactors are doing when they claim their place on the frontier during weekend shooting events.

Commentators on the right, most notably the NRA, have drawn a direct line between gun ownership and citizenship, claiming that any laws controlling gun ownership abrogate the rights of citizens. Commentators on the left, of course, interpret the Second Amendment in a different way. It is not necessary to take sides on this issue, however, in order to agree that Americans care deeply about guns, both as symbols and as actual objects. The NRA can regularly rally its 4.3 million members to defeat laws limiting the availability of assault weapons, laws limiting the ability of gun-show attendees to skip background checks, and laws limiting the purchase of multiple handguns at gun shows.[36] The extent of the NRA's success has led to an absence of gun regulations and to widespread ownership—and, critics on the left argue, to levels of gun violence that are without parallel in other industrialized nations. In fact, the NRA's rhetoric has aroused widespread revulsion only when it has most bluntly urged gun ownership for citizens worried about the encroachment of the state on their individual rights—such as when NRA executive vice president Wayne LaPierre referred in an infamous 1994 fund-raising letter to the "jack-booted government thugs [who] take away our constitutional rights, break in our doors, seize our guns, destroy our property, and even injure and kill us."[37] Guns are everywhere in the United States; today, about 200 million of them are in private hands. According to recent estimates, between 35 and 45 percent of American households contain guns, and the number of firearms owned by individuals has been on the rise in the past few decades.[38] But even more important for the purposes of this book, gun mythologies abound.

"Figurines II" (1998). The contemporary artist Cynthia Consentino uses images of prepubescent girls with handguns and rifles to continue and transform the sentimental figurine tradition: the guns suggest both violence and self-protection.
Courtesy of Cynthia Consentino.

Because the range of cultural images of women and guns is so wide, I have been selective in my approach. Although this study is chronological, I have chosen to focus each chapter on a particular question. The first chapter looks most closely at the relationship between citizenship and the right —or obligation—to fight in wars. The second chapter examines the complex racial politics of armed womanhood, as seen in frontier expansion and the move away from militarism to spectacle. The portrait of armed women in coffeehouse ballads of the late eighteenth century and the best-selling novels and popular memoirs of the Civil War era morphed into the Wild West show performance, which offered its stars, most notably Annie Oakley, unprecedented opportunities for international celebrity. While armed women from the Revolutionary era through the Civil War were generally portrayed as white soldiers fighting alongside and against other white soldiers, the Wild West shows stressed racial and ethnic conflicts—most obviously, those between European settlers and Native Americans. The third chapter highlights the linkage between women's violence and women's sexuality and explores how the armed woman has triggered social debate about women's capacity for lawlessness. The fourth chapter concerns left-wing women who saw in the gun a means of redefining or—in the most extreme cases—dismantling the state. The fifth chapter looks at the ways women on the far right in the 1980s and 1990s made guns the basis for discussing the relationship between femininity, violence, and the nation and for redefining the idea of armed citizenship from a white supremacist perspective. The final chapter delves into twenty-first-century gun magazines for women and considers the complex and contradictory ways that the gun lobby today uses the image of the woman with a gun.

Our national fascination with guns shows no signs of diminishing, and neither does the passionate investment by those on the right and on the left in the place guns have held in our nation's history.[39] Although images and narratives of women and guns have shocked and titillated Americans since the nation's founding, they can provide us with far more than entertainment. The images of armed women that have appeared throughout American history have always been contradictory and difficult to contain; they have challenged the boundaries of gender definitions and the multiple meanings of the gun itself as an American icon.

1

MILITARY HEROINES

NARRATIVES OF FEMALE
SOLDIERS AND SPIES IN
THE CIVIL WAR

The first Currier and Ives print of Molly Pitcher appeared in 1848, the same year that Elizabeth Cady Stanton and other feminists met at Seneca Falls for the first women's rights convention. The "Declaration of Sentiments and Resolutions" passed by the delegates at the convention called for women's enfranchisement as "this first right of a citizen." Perhaps it was no accident that Molly Pitcher emerged as a celebrated figure when issues of individual rights were in ferment; by the time of the Civil War and immediately thereafter, the discussion linking citizenship to the bearing of arms in battle was particularly intense in the United States. During this period, the female soldier, both real and fictitious, became a focus for popular discussion about women's rights and women's obligations. In popular culture the figure of Molly Pitcher stood, sometimes awkwardly, alongside celebrity female Civil War soldiers such as Belle Boyd and Sarah Edmonds, as well as novelist E. D. E. N. Southworth's fictional armed heroine Britomarte, the Man-Hater.

How did popular cultural representations of armed women become a way to talk about women's emancipation, as well as women's violence and sexuality? The warrior woman had been a popular literary figure in American narratives since the early nineteenth century, and she had featured in Anglo-American balladry dating back to the mid-seventeenth century. However, with the onset of the Civil War, these fictional representations took on greater weight, raising questions about women's enfranchisement and its relationship to women's putative nature. In this chapter I will discuss how representations of armed women involved in the Civil War revised popular notions of female patriotism, how actual women who took up arms represented themselves in their bids for celebrity, and why their autobiographies succeeded or failed with the public.

The feminists who demanded equal rights at Seneca Falls were doing so within the context of a long tradition linking military service to the idea of citizenship. Linda Kerber has traced this trajectory from the Spartan ideal of the warrior-citizen through the work of Machiavelli and has highlighted the importance that American revolutionaries of the eighteenth century attached to the political theories of eighteenth-century English writer James Burgh, who described the "possession of arms [as] the distinction between a freeman and a slave." As Kerber writes, in the early American republic, the "connection between the republic and male patriots—who could enlist— was immediate. The connection between the republic and women—however patriotic they might feel themselves to be—was not."[1] Although not all male citizens would be called on to serve in battle, women were considered physically and mentally unsuitable for combat, and thus for the obligations and rights of full citizenship. Military service was at the heart of arguments for women's disenfranchisement, for during times of war men's valor and strength and their service to the nation was given especially great importance.

Both feminists and their opponents understood the literal nature of the body politic. When only white males were considered full citizens, commentators often noted that women's bodies rendered them unsuitable for the vote. One popular satire of women's emancipation suggested that if women were granted equal status to men, they might give birth in the pulpit, while discharging their duties as physicians, or "in a raging tempest of battle, and then what is to become of the woman legislator, the female captain of the ship, or the female general of the army. The idea is ludicrous beyond measure."[2] An abolitionist journal reported in 1853 that a Cincinnati woman who dressed like a man in order to vote was sentenced to twenty days in prison.[3] While some advocates of bloomers recommended that women dress in male attire simply for reasons of comfort, the notion of a cross-dressing woman was obviously threatening to many—if a woman could appear to be a man, how could her inherent feminine weakness be detected? As a writer for the southern periodical *De Bow's Review* wrote mockingly of women's rights advocates, "At this rate, ladies, it is time to throw aside your kid gloves, and accustom yourselves to something even more manlike than your satin and muslin Bloomer equipments. Your fair hands must harden themselves to the management of Colt's revolvers, of bombs, grenades, and whatnot?"[4] This suggestion was clearly sarcastic—after all, southern courts had affirmed that, legally speaking, even self-defense in the home was an action to be taken only by the male head of household.[5]

The humorous discussions of women's physical ability to handle tasks of public responsibility had serious implications, for feminists as well as antifeminists tied their ideas about women's citizenship to military service. Women's rights advocates used a number of strategies to question the ideal of the male citizen-soldier, ranging from pointing out that soldiers sometimes made less than ideal citizens, to championing women's pacific nature and questioning the need for warfare, to finally, and most provocatively, pointing to historical examples of female soldiers.

First, feminists stressed there were many reasons for men to go to war, many of which had nothing to do with civic virtue. As H. H. Van Amringe pointed out at the 1850 Woman's Rights Convention held in Worcester, Massachusetts, military service was undertaken by men for a number of reasons, including "a passion of ambition, a love of glory, a desire for carnage, and as a means of subsistence."[6] In other words, the traits of good soldiers did not necessarily make for the best citizens.

Other feminists went further in rejecting the model of the citizen-soldier by claiming that women's enfranchisement would mean the end of all wars. Speaking in 1849, Lucretia Mott asserted that although many women throughout history had fought in wars, "more noble, moral daring is marking the female character at the present time, and better worthy of imitation. As these characteristics come to be appreciated in man too, his warlike acts, with all the miseries and horrors of the battlefield, will sink into their merited oblivion."[7] Thus, Mott looked to women's enfranchisement to redefine the meaning of citizenship and to sever the connection between martial valor and full civic participation.

However, the ideal of the citizen-soldier remained well entrenched in American culture. Because of this, the female soldier was the most charged of symbols in a republican ideology that stressed male valor as the basis for citizenship. At the Syracuse Woman's Rights Convention of 1852, a speaker noted that women had fought in every war, ably playing men's roles at every rank and taking positions of leadership.[8] Some feminists pointed all the way back to biblical times in order to invoke a long history of female soldiers as a justification for women's rights. If women could engage in warfare, there was no reason, so this argument went, to deny them full civic rights. During a time of active public debates about women's suitability for full citizenship, the Civil War provided an opportunity for feminists and antifeminists to rethink the nature of women's patriotism. Specifically, it offered a chance for women to use the gun to redefine their role in society.

The image of the woman armed with a gun was particularly resonant during the Civil War, when mass production made firearms much more reliable and mass marketing made them much more widely available. As William Hosley notes of the Civil War era, "Never before or since has American society embraced guns with such a vengeance."[9] Contributing to an increase in national consciousness of the gun's role in shaping America's identity was its crucial function in subduing "savage" peoples and in making Manifest Destiny possible in the years leading up to the Civil War; the gun was also considered to be a "peacemaker" that could prevent wars through deterrence. Moreover, guns did not demand great strength to operate, and they enabled one to kill quickly, efficiently, and from a distance—no direct contact with the victim was required. Thus, the use of the gun in combat meant that women could less persuasively be debarred from wartime service on account of physical weakness. It offered the chance for women to write themselves into the history of war as soldiers, as well as for novelists to write women into war as violent actors. Although it may be tempting to view women soldiers of the Civil War as mere curiosities, their memoirs and the fiction written about them in fact speak to the central issues regarding women's status as patriots and as citizens.

THE LITERARY TRADITION OF THE FEMALE SOLDIER

Although the public's fascination with the female soldier intensified during the Civil War era, when issues related to patriotism and women's rights were in the forefront of the nation's consciousness, the armed woman had interested Americans since Revolutionary War times.[10] Early depictions of the female soldier include seventeenth- and eighteenth-century "warrior woman" ballads featuring adventurous lovers in drag, Revolutionary-era fiction about female patriots and autobiographies of female soldiers, and early and mid-nineteenth-century narratives proposing that cross-dressing and taking up arms were the means of personal liberation. By the time of the Civil War, the female soldier even appeared in gothic guise in a series of popular dime novels. Although not all of these fictional female soldiers were concerned with the rhetorical construction of the female citizen, taken as a whole, they provided a rich context for armed Civil War–era women to draw on for their autobiographical self-presentations. As we shall see, the figure of the female soldier was often deployed for entertainment or titillation, but in times of national crisis it became a more charged, contested character. Moreover, the actual female soldiers who published autobiographies and embarked on stage tours often modeled their narratives on those of their fictional counterparts.

ORIGINS

The figure of the female soldier was well established internationally by the time it became popular in the American colonies. However, early representations focused on female soldiers as lovers, rather than as patriots. At the turn of the seventeenth century, ballads featuring female warriors first appeared in print in Britain, where they soon became popular and established a genre: 100 new female warrior ballads were printed between 1700 and the middle of the nineteenth century. As folklorist Dianne Dugaw notes, one of the earliest of these, *Mary Ambree*, was "the equivalent in her time of *Ain't She Sweet* in the 1920s, *Blowin' in the Wind* in the 1960s."[11] The British ballads soon made their way across the Atlantic, and by the eighteenth century broadside publishers in Boston, Providence, and Philadelphia were issuing American editions. One can gauge how well these songs were liked by the fact that an imprisoned American sailor's journal of the Revolutionary War era included handwritten versions of two of them.[12]

The British ballads were not concerned with the legal foundations of women's rights: the typical protagonist was motivated by romantic considerations to don sailor's or soldier's clothing and follow her lover into battle. The early bawdy ballads, featuring tough women whose imposture was detected only when they became pregnant, gave way to more sentimental ones. But the focus of the ballads remained on the construction of gender; politics and citizenship were not at issue.

THE REPUBLICAN CONTEXT

The charged debates of the Revolutionary era over the suitability of women for citizenship, given their inability to fight in battle, gave rise to representations of female soldiers that directly engaged these questions of rights and responsibilities. Within the American context, the figure of the female warrior was early identified not just with love and glory but also with patriotism and feminism.

The earliest American representation of the female soldier was fictional. In his 1799 novel, *Ormond*, Charles Brockden Brown included the character of Martinette de Beauvais, an American Revolutionary War veteran who follows her husband into battle. The sympathetically portrayed Martinette, a Frenchwoman, was a very different type than the female soldiers depicted in ballads. Perhaps Brown reckoned that a violent, feminist Frenchwoman would seem less threatening or unappealing to readers than an American woman of a similar personality. As she explains to the novel's heroine, Constantia, "My soul was engrossed by two passions, a wild spirit of adventure, and a boundless devotion to [my husband]. I vowed to accompany him in every danger, to vie with him in military ardour; to combat and to die by his side." Thus, Martinette's military service is motivated by competition as well as love: her "boundless devotion" is not, in her mind, incompatible with her desire to "vie" with her husband on the battlefield. Soon it becomes clear that cross-dressing and military services are means for her to transform herself completely: "I delighted to assume the male dress, to acquire skill at the sword, and dexterity in every boisterous exercise. The timidity that commonly attends women, gradually vanished. I felt as if embued by a soul that was a stranger to the sexual distinction."[13] If her very soul can be altered by the process of fighting in warfare, what then is the basis for "sexual distinction"? Martinette not only succeeds in boisterous exercises but also rescues her husband "more than once . . . from death by the seasonable destruction of his adversary" (202).

Martinette is a transitional figure in the history of the female warrior—she starts off as a lover but becomes a patriot—one who, moreover, delights in inflicting violence on her political enemies. It is not her love for her husband that keeps her on the battlefield; after his death from a wound, she travels to Paris, where she fights in the revolution. When Constantia asks her, "How can the heart of women be inured to the shedding of blood?" she replies with a passionate speech: "Have women, I beseech thee, no capacity to reason and infer? . . . My hand never faultered when liberty demanded the victim. If thou wert with me at Paris, I could show you a fusil of two barrels, which is precious beyond any other relique, merely because it enabled me to kill thirteen officers at Jemappe" (206). Her devotion to the cause—and her ability to kill "when liberty demanded the victim"—is proof of women's "capacity to reason and infer." Finally, she disputes the idea that hers is an exceptional case. As she tells Constantia, who is shocked at the idea that Martinette might have fought in the ranks, "Hundreds of my sex have done the same. Some were impelled by the enthusiasm of love, and some by a mere passion for war; some by the contagion of example; and some, with whom I myself must be ranked, by a generous devotion to liberty" (207).

While Charles Brockden Brown had the fictional Martinette express herself freely about her enthusiasm for patriotic violence and for the freedom given her by cross-dressing, an actual woman combatant of the Revolutionary era, negotiating republican unease with the idea of the female soldier, found it necessary to write with a great deal more reserve. Deborah Sampson Gannett was an American woman who cross-dressed and fought in the American Revolution under the name Robert Shurtliff. After the war she made a living giving stage performances, under her married name, Gannett, in which, dressed in an infantry uniform, she first delivered a text based on her experiences and then carried out manual exercises with a musket. In her performances, transcribed for publication in 1802, and in a 1797 memoir, *The Female Review*, she portrayed herself as demure by nature, but compelled by such an overwhelming devotion to liberty that she surmounted her feminine modesty and took up arms.[14]

It is hard to imagine a more apologetic female warrior than Gannett. When in her stage performance she takes up her wartime experiences of cross-dressing and fighting, she claims that "I indeed recollect it as a foible, an error and presumption, into which, perhaps, I have too inadvertently and precipitately run; but which I now retrospect with anguish and amazement." She continues, "And yet I must frankly confess, I recollect it with a kind of satisfaction, which no one can better conceive and enjoy than him, who, recollecting the *good intentions* of a *bad deed*, lives to see and to correct any indecorum of his life." Indeed, Gannett anticipates a kind of revulsion on the part of her listeners about her wartime deeds: "They are a breach in the decorum of my sex, unquestionably; and, perhaps, too unfortunately ever irreconcilable with the rigid maxims of the moralist; and a sacrifice, which, while it may seem perfectly incompatible with the requirements of virtue—and which of course must ring discord in the ear, and disgust to the bottom of sensibility and refinement, I must be content to leave to time and the most scrutinizing enquiry to disclose."[15] Throughout the performance Gannett attempts to disarm potential critics by insisting that only the extraordinary oppression suffered by the American colonies led her to consider British tyranny: "Perhaps nothing but the critical juncture of the times could have excused such a philosophical disquisition of politics in woman, notwithstanding it was a theme of universal speculation and concern to man" (10). And, she says, she proceeded from thought to deed only because "poverty, hunger, nakedness, cold and disease had dwindled the *American Armies* to a handful . . . not merely for the sake of gratifying a facetious curiosity" (12).

After all of these caveats, Gannett ends her performance by reaffirming the importance of distinct gender roles: "as we readily acquiesce in the acknowledgment, that the *field* and the *cabinet* are the proper spheres assigned for our Masters and our Lords; may we, also, deserve the dignified title and encomium of Mistress and Lady, in our *kitchens* and in our *parlours*" (29). Gannett's wartime service, as well as her years-long battle to win a pension from Congress based on her status as a disabled soldier, certainly took a great deal of perseverance and moxie. Yet her fighting spirit was the last thing she chose to highlight in public performance. It is fair to say, though, that she made a radical statement simply by appearing on stage during a period when performing in public was not widely viewed as acceptable for women.

The Female Review; or, The Memoir of an American Young Lady attracted a great deal of attention when it appeared. It is not a memoir so much as a moralizing biography, for unlike the most famous self-made man of her era, Ben Franklin, Gannett did not tell her own story. To have done so would have violated female codes of modesty, and, besides, she was far from being a practiced writer. Herman Mann, the book's "as-told-to" author, who also wrote the text of Gannett's stage performance, took care to distinguish Gannett's story from a mere entertainment, as well as to dismiss suggestions that Gannett was a self-promoter. Mann's preface informs readers that "the Female, who is the subject of the following Memoirs, does not only exist in theory and imagination, but in reality."[16] However, Mann also stresses Gannett's reluctance to publicize herself, "though it has become more fashionable in these days of liberty and liberality, to publish the lives of illustrious persons" (vii). Not only was biography an enormously popular genre in the nineteenth century; it was, as Scott Casper notes, a cultural force: "Biographers and critics and readers alike believed that biography had power: the power to shape individuals' lives and character and to help define America's national character."[17] So although Mann insists on the authenticity of *The Female Review*, and refers readers to an authenticating appendix, he acknowledges that "I have taken liberty to intersperse, through the whole, a series of moral reflections, and have attempted some literary and historical information" (ix). (Mann also took the liberty, as Gannett's biographer, Alfred F. Young, points out, to plagiarize from a number of other works on female warriors, especially *The Female Soldier; or, The Surprising Life and Adventures of Hannah Snell*, published in London in 1750).[18]

In implicitly contrasting Gannett to the female warriors of ballads, with which his audience was presumably quite familiar, Mann insisted on Gannett's chastity throughout the memoir; he also felt obligated to append a "Resolve of the General Court, January 30, 1798," commenting on Gannett's petition to be granted an army pension, which speculated not only about whether Gannett had sex but even about her choice of locations: "It is hear-say that Mrs. Gannett refuses her husband the rites of the marriage bed. She must, then, condescend to smile upon him in the silent alcove, or grass plat; as she has a child, that has scarcely left its cradle. . . . For her nearest neighbors assert, there is a mutual harmony between her and her companion; which, by the bye, is generally the reverse of those deprived of this hymenial bliss" (*The Female Review*, 256–57). In other words, she was neither sexually out of control nor unnaturally asexual: Gannett's soldierly duties did not result in an inability to perform her womanly duties adequately. It is possible that Mann felt especially compelled to stress Gannett's virtue since he spent some time in her memoir detailing the romantic confession made to Robert Shurtliff by a seventeen-year-old girl.

Deborah Sampson Gannett was packaged by Mann, her publisher and promoter, as an avatar of virtue. Perhaps one mark of her success was the 1792 resolve by the Massachusetts legislature granting her back pay, on the grounds that "the said Deborah exhibited an extraordinary instance of female heroism by discharging the duties of a female soldier, and at the same time preserving the virtue and chastity of her sex unsuspected and unblemished, and was discharged from the service with a fair and honorable character."[19] Thus, Gannett managed to carefully balance her display of patriotism, virtue, and regret for her unwomanly actions.[20]

GENRE FICTION AND THE NINETEENTH-CENTURY FEMALE WARRIOR

However, a spate of American narratives that appeared in the first half of the nineteenth century laid much more emphasis on thrilling situations than on patriotic sentiment. Like the "breeches roles" popular on the nineteenth-century stage, in which women cross-dressed to play male roles,[21] fictional representations of the female soldier in the first half of the nineteenth century seemed designed to titillate audiences even as they purported to teach moral lessons. The creation of male authors, these ostensibly autobiographical accounts of female soldiers highlight the romantic and sexual aspects of their impostures. The focus of the narratives often becomes the delight their heroines take in the act of cross-dressing; one would be hard pressed to find much patriotic sentiment evinced by the protagonists, much musing on the differences between the sexes, or even much speculation on the essential qualities of each sex.

An excellent example of this genre is a publication from 1815, *The Female Marine: An Affecting Narrative of Louisa Baker, a Native of Massachusetts Who, in Early Life Having Been Shamefully Seduced, Deserted Her Parents, and Enlisted in Disguise, on Board an American Frigate as a Marine.* Lucy Brewer, also known as Louisa Baker, was a creation of itinerant Boston bookseller Nathaniel Coverly. *The Female Marine* was an enormously popular narrative, which went through at least nineteen editions.[22] As the subtitle of the "memoir" suggests, its protagonist narrates the story of being seduced and abandoned, and details her years working in a brothel. Her escape from the brothel and into the role of a marine becomes a means of rebirth into virtue. This character never has a bad word to say about her stint as a male, fighting as a marine on the USS *Constitution* in the War of 1812, spending time in brothels and lifting a cheerful glass. Eventually, her virtue redeemed, she rejoins her parents. It is as though being treated with respect, and distinguishing herself with bravery, has been enough to make her comfortable once more in her role as a dutiful daughter.[23] Brewer's interest in transvestism endures after she has been revirginated by her battle experiences, and it always proves a profitable one for her. Even after rejoining her parents, she continues to cross-dress on occasion. While in drag, she is chivalrous toward a wealthy girl, whom she protects against boorish men, and that eventually enables her to meet and marry the girl's brother. In Lucy Brewer's case, military service and transvestism, far from unsexing her, actually make her successful as a woman.

The enthusiastic cross-dresser remained a fictional staple well into the nineteenth century. An 1851 text, *The Female Volunteer; or, The Life and Wonderful Adventures of Miss Eliza Allen, a Young Lady of Eastport, Maine,* by Eliza Allen Billings, offers impersonation in war as a flight into romance. Allen, who follows her fiancé to fight in the Mexican-American War, seems a much more successful male than her hapless lover—more attractive to women, better able to earn money, stronger in every way. She strikingly remarks that even after all their tribulations, when they are finally together, "I was constantly returning to my former appearance, which as much interested the one I was now so happy with, as myself."[24] Thus, she, like Lucy Brewer, continues to thrive as a cross-dresser once her military service is over.

THE PATRIOTIC WOMAN WARRIOR

The Civil War period produced a number of fictional female soldiers whose reasons for fighting in the war were political, rather than romantic or sexualized, and who generally fought as women, rather than assuming male attire. However, these heroines were far from ordinary women. The chief creator of the genre, Charles Wesley Alexander (writing under the name of Wesley Bradshaw), dealt with the problems of representing armed woman-hood by imbuing his female soldier characters with magical powers, making them so markedly different from actual women that it was impossible for readers to take these characters as role models. Alexander, a pulp fiction writer, was extremely prolific in his depictions of female soldiers and spies, such as those in *Pauline of the Potomac* (1862), *Maud of the Mississippi* (1863), and *General Sherman's Indian Spy* (1865).[25]

Although Alexander generally confined himself to describing the exploits of Union heroines, he portrayed in *The Picket Slayer* a demonic young Englishwoman who fights on the other side. Alexander described her actions on behalf of the Confederacy in Manichaean terms: "She was a child of sin, doomed from the moment of her birth to perdition, and destined, while she remained on earth, to be the enemy of everything good."[26] As she tells the Confederate president, "My mission hither, President Davis, is to render your cause assistance, not because it is holy, as you hypocritically say, but because it is the most diabolical that could be conceived of" (30). Able to appear and vanish at will, possessed of supernatural strength and cunning, the picket slayer is evil incarnate—hardly the jolly, love-besotted cross-dresser the public had come to expect. But, then again, she was a Confederate sympathizer, and Alexander was a Union partisan and a writer hardly given to subtlety.

Alexander's female soldiers were different from ordinary white American women not only by virtue of their supernatural powers; they were also distinct because of their ethnicity or nationality. Surprisingly enough, none of Alexander's heroines was, by the standards of the time, American. As General Sherman's spy Wenonah tells him when she signs up for a career as his spy, "General, I would help the good pale faces. I love the pale faces. Pale face blood and Indian blood, Tecumseh's blood, runs in my heart together, like brother and sister."[27] Wenonah, although she is certainly capable of shooting Confederates in self-defense, does not see herself as a fighter: "A woman," she tells Sherman, "makes but a poor warrior" (21). However, her Indian attributes ("the eagle's eye and the fox's ear" [21]) make her an excellent spy. And, like the picket slayer and Pauline of the Potomac, Wenonah has access to supernatural means: she is able to put guards to sleep with a "strange moving of her hands" (22). At times, she appears to others to be racially ambiguous; thus, one drunken would-be rapist tells her, "—— me ef I ken tell yer frum an Injun or a nigger?" (27). Wenonah is capable of exploiting her interlocutor's racist beliefs to her advantage; as she tells the drunk when he asks her to run off with him, "Oh! I go! I go! You give me plenty pretty blankets, plenty shiney [sic] money, plenty pretty beads" (28). Yet she is entirely limited by her ethnic identity. She is an object of lust rather than veneration; when a Confederate lieutenant falls deeply in love with her, "this love was not that of a pure heart, but merely an ardent passion" (31). And while she reacts to a threat of execution with "the stoicism of her race" (43), she is incapable of an equal relationship with Sherman: she speaks to him "like a child, confiding in a beloved father" (59). When she finally dies in battle, Alexander eulogizes her: "Poor child of the wilderness. Pure as the air of her prairie home, beautiful as the rose, brave as the warrior from whom she was descended, and gentle as the dove" (63). Exoticized, magical, and dead, Wenonah is a tragic Indian maiden, and Alexander's last words about her encourage readers to pity her, rather than imagine themselves in her place.

While half-breed Wenonah is presented as a primitive, the heroine of *Pauline of the Potomac* (who in a sequel takes on the identity of Maud of the Mississippi) is portrayed as a superwoman, far outside the mainstream of white American middle-class femininity. As one would expect of an Alexander protagonist, she is not an American; having fled the Revolution of 1848 in France, she is an émigrée. Although she originally planned to enter a convent upon her father's death, she agrees to the deathbed wish he makes after draping her with the American flag: "Pauline, my child, I devote you to America, the land of our adoption . . . This starry flag, the standard that Washington loved . . . is the veil that you now take."[28]

Pauline is a gift to America, but she is crucially different from American women and not a character with whom readers are expected to identify, as the narrator makes clear: "Doubtless many might consider the course of Miss D'Estraye as rather masculine or at least outside of the established line of conduct for a female and a refined lady; but we beg leave to remind our readers that Miss D'Estraye was French, and that what would seem indecorous to American women, is by no means so regarded by the gentler sex in France" (49). Thus, Pauline does not hesitate to threaten her would-be Confederate captor: "One more movement . . . and I blow your traitorous brains from your skull, and trample your vile carcass into the earth" (53). She goes beyond mere words, however, and is more than willing to take action, as she demonstrates when recollecting an incident in which she was threatened by rape: "Whipping out one of my revolvers, I discharged it directly at the villain on my right, and, without waiting to see its effect, immediately after leveled and fired at the one on my left" (85). The distance between Pauline and her readers is not simply one of national identity. Although she does not have access to Indian magic, she has training in special skills, which she received from a family friend who was a wizard or necromancer. Able to remember, from childhood, descriptions of a folding boat, she designs and has built such a boat so that she can run the batteries at Vicksburg. For energy on her perilous and exhausting journeys, she keeps about her "a small bag of the *Coacoa* leaf, so highly prized by the natives of South America."[29]

Alexander's female warriors are violent, but the Union sympathizers among them discharge their weapons only in defense of their chastity; although they defend the nation, they do so from an outsider position, as Europeans or Native Americans. Thus, Alexander managed to sidestep questions of citizenship entirely. The armed women he created were so outlandish that his books about them could be enjoyed as patriotic entertainment, rather than taken as the substance of debate.

FEMALE PATRIOTISM AND FEMALE SOLDIERING

Women who attempted to forge careers based on their exploits as soldiers in the Civil War had a broad range of popular culture models of the female soldier available to them, from the bawdy female soldiers of traditional ballads to the helpmate Molly Pitcher to the supernaturally gifted heroines of Alexander's popular texts. Yet with all of these models on which to draw, they had to tread a minefield of hazards to their public images: they needed to be acceptable yet interesting.

For example, despite the popularity of Molly Pitcher, the generation of the 1840s found the memoir of her nonfictional counterpart Deborah Sampson Gannett to be unpalatable, and Gannett herself was considered to be a sympathetic yet somewhat misguided character. Elizabeth Ellet, in her 1848 work, *The Women of the American Revolution*, notes of Gannett's memoir that this "half tale, half biography . . . [was] not in any measure reliable, and that the heroine had repeatedly expressed her displeasure at the representation of herself, which she 'did not at all recognize.'"[30] Although Ellet admires her enthusiasm, "the ignorance and error mixed with this enthusiasm, should increase our sympathy without diminishing the share of admiration we would bestow, had it been evinced in a more becoming manner" (123).

Molly Pitcher—who did not cross-dress, who was never portrayed as attracting the romantic attentions of other women, and who acted only as an extension of her husband—seemed to many to be a much more appealing representation of true womanhood. However, no matter how popular the dutiful Molly Pitcher was, there remained a great public interest in spicier narratives: stories that were more violent, more romantic, more frightening, and more titillating. Female Civil War soldiers who sought celebrity used a variety of rhetorical strategies, which reflected differences based in large part on their regional affiliations.

It is not altogether clear how many women participated in the Civil War as combatants and armed spies. One contemporary commentator put the number of cross-dressing soldiers at over four hundred.[31] In fact many scholars today suggest that even more women entered the fray, estimating that as many as four hundred soldiers fought on the Union side and two hundred and fifty on the Confederate side.[32]

The "military heroine" was both ridiculed and extolled in newspapers: ridiculed because of her unwomanliness; extolled because her extreme devotion to the Union or the Confederacy led her to take extraordinary action. Working-class single women were generally treated humorously by the press. "A Rejected Recruit," a typical item in the *Liberator*, recounted the story of "a middle-aged person of Irish birth," who upon being handed over to the police "was suffered to depart, with the hint that the war could be prosecuted without her aid as a soldier."[33] The *Savannah Republican* described one Minnesota female soldier as so intimidating that a man who recognized her "became shockingly frightened at her threats of vengeance upon him if he exposed her, and he decamped."[34] However, middle-class married women who enlisted to stay with their spouses were often described by the press as true patriots. As Lee Ann Whites notes, the women who did go so far as to enlist with their husbands were generally applauded in newspaper accounts. The *Chronicle and Sentinel* of Augusta, Georgia, described local citizens who called upon one such visiting female soldier as "highly delighted with her agreeable manners and her heroic purpose."[35] A group of women in La Grange, a small Georgia town, formed a military company during the Civil War, which they named after Revolutionary heroine Nancy Hart. They drilled, practiced their marksmanship, and patrolled the streets of their town, while taking time out to nurse wounded soldiers and perform other womanly duties.[36]

While there were many women who attempted, successfully or otherwise, to enlist, a much larger number of women expressed the desire to do so, whether to friends or in their journals. Even women who had not previously expressed the desire for emancipation found themselves newly conscious of the limitations placed on them by their feminine roles. Drew Gilpin Faust has detailed the many discussions, letters, and diary entries of hitherto genteel southern women who felt useless in their societal roles at the onset of the war. For example, Alice Ready, a young woman in Tennessee, wrote in her diary, "I never before wished I was a man—now I feel so keenly my weakness and dependence. I cannot do or say anything—for it would be so unbecoming in a young lady—How I should love to fight and even die for my country. . . . [W]hat a privilege I should esteem it, but am denied because I am a woman."[37] Caught between the imperatives of patriotism and their inability to take an active role in fighting the war, many women became enraged at the enemy, at themselves, and at their roles: "I am angry so much now and use so many harsh expressions" (20), continued diarist Alice Ready. This anger may have contributed to a desire on the part of many women to pick up the gun.

Although women soldiers were sometimes the subjects of humorous or even admiring newspaper articles, anger and the violence it produced were not widely accepted as desirable aspects of female patriotism. After the war, as the nation struggled to come to terms with the conflict that had torn it apart, the many books that memorialized female courage did not easily accommodate the armed female patriot. As the era of nostalgia began, these volumes, chiefly on the Union side, extolled the heroines of the war and defined the ideals of female patriotism. For example, L. P. Brockett and Mary C. Vaughn's 1867 book, *Woman's Work in the Civil War: A Record of Heroism, Patriotism and Patience*, underscored feminine virtues that were clearly in line with domestic ideologies of the period. The authors celebrated the "effect of patriotism and self-sacrifice in elevating and ennobling the female character," honoring the women they profiled for their "gentle and patient ministrations" and endurance.[38] These female patriots hardly seemed to challenge prevailing gender roles and stereotypes.

Yet Brockett and Vaughn managed to cast in a nostalgic light even women whose service as soldiers would seem to fall outside the conventional categories of female patriotism, such as nurse or aid worker. The chapter devoted to "military heroines" begins with the acknowledgment that "the number of women who actually bore arms in the war, or who, though generally attending a regiment as nurses and vivandières, at times engaged in the actual conflict was much larger than is generally supposed, and embraces persons from all ranks of society" (770). However, the chapter does not dwell on the unladylike exploits of those who abandoned all claims to respectability.

The military heroines cited by Brockett and Vaughn fought not in contradiction to but rather in support of their identities as traditional wives: Madame Turchin, who took over command of her colonel husband's volunteer regiment when he fell ill; Bridget Divers, who attached herself to the First Michigan Cavalry in which her husband served as private; and Mrs. Kady Brownell, who accompanied her husband into battle with the Fifth Rhode Island Infantry and who "became as skillful a shot and as expert a swordsman as any of the company of sharp-shooters to which she was attached" (773). These were female soldiers at their most domesticated.

In fact, the most successful of the memoirs by female Union soldiers was written by a woman who represented herself as so thoroughly respectable that it is almost impossible to tell from her narrative when she was actually cross-dressing and fighting. The autobiography of Sarah Emma Edmonds, who fought in the Civil War from 1861 until her desertion in 1863, is both very Christian in tone and extremely patriotic. Although Edmonds was a farm girl who had begun cross-dressing well before she entered the Union army under the guise of "Franklin Thompson," she does not mention this in her text. In fact, though her 1864 memoir first appeared under the title *Unsexed; or, The Female Soldier Revealed*, it was reissued a year later as the more neutral-sounding *Nurse and Spy in the Union Army*. Edmonds is vague about when she was cross-dressing and even what gender her interlocutors assumed her to be. She describes her motivations as purely patriotic, and she donated the profits from her book—which sold 175,000 copies—to agencies concerned with the welfare of soldiers. Her patriotism was irreproachable; her cross-dressing and violence were downplayed.

Yet Edmonds's patriotic memoir was a singular success. There were only a few female soldiers whose exploits were lauded by the authors of gift books, and just a few women tried to make money from their wartime experiences by taking to the stage or writing memoirs. The texts of these women's endeavors reveal the ruptures and fissures in their self-representations as that impossible entity, the female soldier. The best-known of these memoirs include two by Confederates: the genteel armed spy Belle Boyd and the swashbuckling Loreta Velazquez, who not only confounded public expectations of southern womanhood but also occupied a territory somewhere between truth and fiction. Another narrative of note is the pro-Union text by the actress Pauline Cushman, who posed as a Confederate sympathizer in order to spy for the Union. These female soldiers moved, in the postwar era, from engaging in bloody conflict to involving themselves in performance art. In addition to publishing autobiographies, Cushman and Boyd toured the stages of the United States, reenacting their dramatic exploits.[39] Unlike the modest, patriotic, charitable Edmonds, these women attempted to make a living off their self-representations as soldiers, and their careers as public women militated against their general acceptance as models of female patriotism.

Cushman, Boyd, and Edmonds offered their stories up to an American public that was enthralled with tales of female patriotism; they used the form of autobiography to write their way both into and out of a long fictional tradition. However, their stories did not always fit easily into popular conceptions of how women should support the war effort. Some, like Sarah Edmonds, expressed frustration with the expectations of female soldiers created by the melodramatic fictions popular during the war. Others, like Pauline Cushman, modeled their narratives after these fictions. It is clear that all of the women whose autobiographies are discussed here were keenly aware of the traditions of the female soldier—in song, drama, and fiction—and of the paradoxes embodied by the armed female patriot. Some chose to deal directly with the paradoxes, while others smoothly sidestepped them. Yet all of their narratives speak to the issues of their time, engaging questions of women's patriotism and bravery, capacity for violence, and fitness for the duties of citizenship.

While both southern and northern women fought as soldiers, the records they left of their military performances (and the reception accorded their books and theatrical tours) were flavored by the distinctly different life experiences and underlying ideologies of northern and southern white womanhood prior to the war.[40]

Received wisdom has it that in the antebellum era, in the North as well as in the South, a public man was considered to be an engaged citizen, while a "public woman" was another term for a prostitute. An outpouring of recent scholarship has made it clear that the picture was much more complicated than that; in fact, women on both sides of the Mason-Dixon line were involved in party politics before the Civil War, as well as in other forms of social activism, such as working for benevolent societies.[41] Yet the complex realities of women's participation in public life went largely unacknowledged in the discourse of the time.

As Nancy Isenberg has noted, although northern women were not excluded from the literary public sphere, by "conjuring images of chaos and disorder resulting from the presence of public women, male writers branded them, like drunkards, as the most unlikely candidates for political leadership or professional office."[42] However, southern women were more explicitly confined to their homes than their northern counterparts, due to the preeminence of the household as a political and social unit in the South, and were more clearly subject to the rule of the male head of household.[43] In the urban North, work had largely been reorganized away from home by the middle of the nineteenth century, and middle-class women and men occupied separate spheres.

In both the North and the South, rhetoricians often tied the case for women's rights to the issue of slavery. In the largely rural South, life revolved around the household, which was headed by a man. Southern society was hierarchically organized, and proslavery ideologues made their case on this basis. As George Fitzhugh, a leading defender of slavery, wrote,

> Slavery in the general, slavery in principle, is right, natural, and necessary. Right, natural, and necessary, because it has been universal, because there is no so-called free society in the world in which four-fifths of the people are not slaves, governed and controlled, not by mere law, but by the will and ipse dixit of superiors. . . . By mere force of nature, by intuitive necessity, the strong protect and control the weak, the weak serve and obey the strong; but the property in each case is mutual. The husband is, by nature as well as law, master of wife and children, and bound to provide for, protect, and govern them; they are his property, but he is equally theirs.[44]

Given this ideology, which tied women's subordination to support for the institution of slavery, what could it mean for a woman to fight for the Confederacy? How could a woman in need of protection remain a lady while brandishing a pistol?

Belle Boyd, a Confederate spy from Martinsburg, West Virginia, wrestled with the meaning of her violent actions in her 1865 autobiography, and she couched all of her military behavior in terms of protecting southern womanhood. That is implied in how she describes her first assault on a Yankee soldier, someone who attempted to bring a Federal flag into her home and who responded to her mother's refusal with insults: "I could stand it no longer; my indignation was roused beyond control; my blood was literally boiling in my veins; I drew out my pistol and shot him. He was carried away mortally wounded, and soon after expired."[45] Boyd's ladylike self-depiction ensured the success of her 1865 memoir, which later formed the basis for her dramatic monologue, "Perils of a Spy." Although Boyd attracted a great deal of negative as well as positive publicity, she was able to continue her theater tour, presenting her "Memories of the War," until her death fourteen years later.[46]

During a war that was fought, in great part, about the meaning of the body politic, cross-dressing soldiers engaged in performances that fascinated the public because they so directly addressed current social questions about women's capacity for citizenship. For women on both sides of the Mason-Dixon line, successful military imposture highlighted gender as a performance, rather than as an essential quality. If women's nature was retiring, timid, and dependent, and if women's bodies were feeble, how could women act as soldiers while remaining women? When actress Pauline Cushman pledged her Confederate loyalties from the stage in order to become a more successful spy for the Union, or when, after the war, Belle Boyd took to the stage in a feminine version of a Confederate uniform to recount her exploits, they were engaged in theater in a sense that everyone could recognize. But the act of fighting as a male soldier must be recognized as theater as well, whether it is described vaguely, as in the way that Sarah Edmonds's memoir, *Unsexed*, is unclear about her apparent gender at any particular moment, or with great specificity, as in Loreta Velazquez's detailed descriptions of cross-dressing for the purpose of military or sexual conquest. Richard Schechner writes that "performances mark identities, bend and remake time, adorn and reshape the body, tell stories, and allow people to play with behavior that is 'twice-behaved,' not-for-the-first-time, rehearsed, cooked, prepared."[47] By taking the stage and demonstrating how they became (male) soldiers, the warrior women of the Civil War, by implication, presented their femininity as yet another performance.

THE THRILLING ADVENTURES OF PAULINE CUSHMAN

In light of the success of Charles Wesley Alexander's dime novels about glamorous female soldiers, it is not surprising that the narrative of actress Pauline Cushman promises readers an experience akin to reading popular fiction. A secret agent for the Union Army, Cushman won the trust of Confederates when she toasted Jefferson Davis from a Louisville stage. The title of her book gives the substance, as well as the flavor, of her account of her wartime career: *The Romance of the Great Rebellion; the Mysteries of the Secret Service; a Genuine and Faithful Narrative of the Thrilling Adventures, Daring Enterprises, Hairbreadth Escapes, and Final Capture and Condemna-*

tion to Death by the Rebels, and Happy Rescue by the Union Forces, of Miss Major Pauline Cushman.

Cushman was a spy, not a soldier on the battlefield. Nonetheless, her gun was important to her for symbolic as well as practical reasons. As Cushman reports, her boss in the Secret Service, Colonel Truesdail, "gave me a thoroughly serviceable six-shooter."[48] Yet she does not use it to kill her captors, though she is sorely tempted: "My rough companion rode on in front, quite carelessly, and time and again my hand was on the pistol I carried in my pocket. One good shot, and my reckless companion would trouble me no more, and my escape rendered almost certain. At length I had made up my mind to the fearful venture, when, just at the decisive moment, the Scout turned his face towards me and made some friendly remark. That, probably saved his life, for I was a cool, safe shot" (23). Cushman, though she toys with the idea from time to time, never shoots anyone. In fact, she writes that she preferred to rely on her "pocket pistol," "a good canteen full of the 'raal stuff'" (31). However, when she is captured by the Confederate general Bragg, she is anxious to prove her loyalty to the southern cause; she tells him that "should a doubt or suspicion still linger in your mind, give me a place in battle near you, and you will see me fight as vigorously and faithfully as any soldier in your army" (41). Her pistol, though she does not actually use it, plays a symbolically important role in her self-representation: it gives her the more distinguished aura of a soldier and serves to remove from her the taint of the spy.

Cushman, as an actress, had little claim to respectability. Moreover, her French and Spanish ancestry furnished her with an identity that, by the definitions of her era, was not quite white. An authorized biography published the year after her memoir appeared, *Life of Pauline Cushman*, by F. L. Sarmiento, provides a vivid example of how a woman who was skirting the edge of respectability might reassert her virtue through service as a female soldier—an updated version, perhaps, of Lucy Brewer, the fictional prostitute turned marine.

Throughout the text, Sarmiento has some difficulty in packaging Cushman as a role model. He describes her early move from the city of New Orleans, a place where racial and ethnic boundaries seem blurred, to the pioneer town of Grand Rapids, where "none could shoot the rifle more unerringly than she."[49] Though she associates for the most part with Indian children, Sarmiento makes clear that Cushman remains unambiguously white. A young brave falls in love with her, since "the maidens of his tribe

Although Pauline Cushman did not shoot anyone during her Civil War service, she used her pistol symbolically to give herself the more distinguished aura of a soldier, and to remove from herself the taint of the spy. Frederick Hill Meserve Collection, National Portrait Gallery, Smithsonian Institution.

pleased him no more. Their skins were dusky. In them flowed not the same blood that filled the veins of the daughter of the white man" (27). However, Cushman rebuffs him, saying that to him "it is left to sound on savage majesty through the clifts and rugged peaks of nature; but the 'Laughing Breeze' [Cushman's Indian nickname] is the breath of civilization. The Indian and the 'pale face' cannot mingle" (31).

Sarmiento strenuously insists on Cushman's respectability when he describes her move to New York and her ability to withstand the erotic temptations of the theater world in which she finds herself. He makes it clear that she is no ordinary actress: "Pauline Cushman was born an actress — but with the world for her stage — with the bloody drama of war as her piece, and her part that of a heroine whom future generations should look up to with wonder" (51). Indeed, Sarmiento has Cushman exclaim, "Let the spirit which burned in the breasts of Joan of Arc and the Maid of Saragossa be mine" (64). Throughout his account of her wartime career — with its elements of cross-dressing, spying, nearly murdering her captors, and stealing and lying when necessary — Sarmiento takes care to assure his readers that they should associate with Cushman none of "the obloquy which seems to attach to the very name of 'spy'" (122). Sarmiento even has General Morgan, when he captures her, but before he has become convinced of the charges against her, give her a "splendid silver-mounted pistol" and tell her that "we will . . . show the world what a female soldier can do; for, by heaven you are more of a soldier than half of my men" (250).

Cushman is more of a soldier, perhaps, than most men, but above all she is more of a true woman than most women. According to Sarmiento, she becomes an exemplar of female patriotism. "It is from soldiers' wives, soldiers' mothers, daughters and sweethearts that she has been hailed as a sister, and taken by the hand as a friend" (358). In fact, "we might say that she has become an apostle of womanhood in these degenerate days, when women are too much of the lady and too little of the wife or mother" (367). Of course, Cushman is neither wife nor mother. But that is of no consequence to Sarmiento: "We wanted some such type of true womanhood to exhibit to these dolls of fashion, while we teach them that it is neither unladylike nor inelegant to serve one's country, or to overstep the ordinary rules of conventionalism in behalf of our glorious Union and its brave supporters" (368). In quoting a letter that Cushman receives from a "sister-soldier" who fought at Antietam, Chancellorsville, and Gettysburg, Sarmiento says that it is "written with a true woman's heart" (363).

Thus, Cushman's noble deeds as a spy — redefined as those of a soldier —

end up cleansing her of the taint that attaches itself not just to spies but also to actresses and to women who are not quite American. In Sarmiento's portrait, though she is unquestionably white, she is able to benefit from the Indian skills she learned from her childhood friends: "Her rambles with the bold Indian youths and lasses had given her this unusual strength and quickness" (279) that facilitates her spying. Even her disdainful wave of her hand, which "seem[s] to say, What I have once promised I will perform," is linked to her unusual education: "There were many of the Indian associations of her youth still clinging to Pauline Cushman, and the action was full of the dignity of the forest and its red-skinned denizens" (113). Sarmiento's success in redefining Cushman as an armed patriot was remarkable. His biography was reprinted in many editions, and Cushman toured the country reenacting her exploits.

THE COUNTEREXAMPLE OF LORETA VELAZQUEZ

While Cushman used the gun to make herself respectable, another woman, Loreta Velazquez, failed utterly in creating a self-representation that audiences of her time found acceptable. When her memoir, *The Woman in Battle*, which purports to tell the story of her years fighting as a Confederate soldier and spy, appeared in 1876, it met with critical condemnation. Velazquez found her autobiography reviled for her critique of American manhood. In many passages in her book, she asserts the superiority of her own performance of masculinity to that of the soldiers with whom she fought, both in battle and in romance. The woman in battle portrayed by Velazquez was a reproach to the male soldiers for their lack of presumedly masculine qualities like courage and ambition.

Velazquez places herself in the ranks of female warriors, whose genealogy she traces all the way back to the biblical Deborah. Her interest in warfare seems to be tied up with both her love of cross-dressing and her desire for fame: "Many a time has my soul burned with a desire to emulate [Joan of Arc's] deeds of valor, to make for myself a name which, like hers, would be enrolled in gold among the women who had the courage to fight like men—ay, better than most men—for a great cause."[50] Unfortunately, she was publishing in an era in which the armed woman had become domesticated and the adventuresome, independent, somewhat sexually ambiguous female warrior had gone out of fashion.

It is not surprising that Loreta Velazquez's memoir, when it appeared in 1876, was greeted with skepticism, especially in light of Belle Boyd's still-popular stagings of ladylike southern armed womanhood. Two years later, the Confederate general Jubal Early was to remark that Velazquez seemed to him almost a Yankee-imagined creation; perhaps he was thinking of the lurid portrayals of Confederate women that were a feature of northern pulp fiction during and immediately after the war. In any case, Early angrily dismissed the protagonist of *The Woman in Battle* as "a mere pretender." Later critics have supported many of Velazquez's claims, however. The researcher Richard Hall has confirmed many details of her story, and Jesse Alemán, in his recent edition of *The Woman in Battle*, finds conflicting evidence, finally noting that "Velazquez's very existence, as with the narrative attributed to her, rests somewhere in between history and story."[51]

Other memoirists of the time claimed to fight in order to support men, or, at the very least, because they were so patriotic that they could overcome their distaste of cross-dressing. By contrast, Velazquez foregrounds her aggressiveness, her competitive nature, and her love of cross-dressing for its own sake: "I was especially haunted by the idea of being a man; and the more I thought upon the subject, the more I was disposed to murmur at Providence for having created me a woman. . . . It was frequently my habit, after all in the house had retired to bed at night, to dress myself in my cousin's clothes, and to promenade by the hour before the mirror, practising the gait of a man, and admiring the figure I made in masculine raiment" (42).

Velazquez takes no trouble to present herself as either virtuous or victimized: she coolly describes the way she plotted successfully to steal a schoolmate's lover and avoid a marriage her parents had arranged for her. When her husband goes to war, she determines to carry out her lifelong desire to cross-dress as a soldier and accompany him into battle. He assists her in cross-dressing to go out on the town for a night, simply so she can see "the least pleasing features of masculine life" (53). Velazquez's competitive nature asserts itself immediately as she surveys herself in the mirror: "I was immensely pleased with the figure I cut, and fancied that I made quite as good-looking a man as my husband" (53). When she dons a uniform for the first time, she is "ready to start on my campaign with as stout a heart as ever beat in the breast of a soldier" (69). She never represents herself as coy or dithering; rather, she seems to swagger through the pages of her memoir.

Velazquez refuses to engage in much ideological posturing. Rather, she tells us that she "longed for a war to break out" (49). And, although she pretends to agree with her husband when he tells her how dissatisfied he was with her performance as a cigar-smoking barroom habitué, she is eager to

MAKING A CHARGE.

In her autobiography, Loreta Velazquez stresses her valor in battle and her love of cross-dressing. Velazquez, in her guise as Lieutenant Harry T. Buford, is the goateed soldier gleefully brandishing her bayonet, as a fallen soldier aims at her with his pistol. "Making a Charge," illustration from Loreta Janeta Velazquez, *The Woman in Battle* (Richmond, Va.: Dustin, Gilman & Co., 1876). Documenting the American South (http://docsouth.unc.edu), The University of North Carolina at Chapel Hill Libraries.

prove him wrong when they next get together "and to show him that his wife [is] as good a soldier as he, and . . . bent upon doing as much or more for the cause which both [have] at heart" (56). Her competitiveness resurfaces both on the battlefield and in a contest for the affections of women. Seemingly predatory in her entanglements with women, she begins "to pride [herself] as much on being a successful ladies' man as upon being a valiant soldier." She even competes with her military comrades to see who can attract the most women.

Velazquez's love of warfare grew as she gained experience on the battlefield: "The skirmishes that I had thus far engaged only seemed to whet my appetite for fighting" (99). But, she recalls, at the battle of Bull Run, "the supreme moment of my life had arrived, and all the glorious aspirations of my romantic girlhood were on the point of realization" (100). She boasts that "no man on the field that day fought with more energy or determination than the warrior who figured as Lieutenant Harry T. Buford" (105).

Unlike most female soldiers who went on to write about their experiences, Velazquez neither downplays her violence nor expresses any regret about having taken her place on the battlefield. Rather, she views combat as an existential experience and a test of her personal valor.

Velazquez inevitably offended arch-traditionalists like Jubal Early, who could not contain his vitriol about someone he considered "no true type of a Southern woman." He complained that "the women she describes are not fair specimens of the pure devoted women who followed with their prayers the armies of the Confederate States through all their struggles and trials."[52] Velazquez failed to fit any of the nineteenth-century models of the female soldier: she was not especially patriotic, like Edmonds, nor was she acting out of love for a man (she barely mentions two of her four husbands during the course of her memoir). She reveled in her drag, in seducing women, in her successful masculinity: she was a swaggering cross-dresser. She did not cast herself as the heroine of a dime novel, like Cushman, nor could she by any stretch of the imagination be called a lady, like Belle Boyd. However, even the most successful of these celebrity female soldiers did not go so far as to directly engage the question of women's military service and its relationship to full citizenship. It would take a best-selling novel to bring that question to the fore.

BRITOMARTE, THE MAN-HATER

Although women's patriotism was a major topic of discussion in the South during the Civil War, only a few southern texts featured female soldiers as characters. A much more characteristic view of the Confederate female patriot appears in Augusta Jane Evans's immensely popular wartime novel *Macaria; or, Altars of Sacrifice*, in which the proud, strong heroine, before sending her father off to war, beseeches him, "If I were only a man, that I might go with you—stand by you under all circumstances. Couldn't you take me anyhow? Surely a daughter may follow her father, even on the battlefield?" Her father's response—light laughter and the comment that "If you were a boy, I swear you would not disgrace my name in any conflict"—is enough to keep her at home, tending the poor and the ill.[53] In fact, the very few southern authors who incorporated the female soldier did so in a rather lukewarm manner.[54]

Yet there is a southern novel, albeit one supportive of the Union cause, that does more than illustrate the many ways armed women might contribute to the war effort. It goes further by suggesting that the female soldier might not just gain full political rights but could even dramatically revise the institution of marriage. Mrs. E. D. E. N. Southworth's immensely popular Civil War novel *Britomarte, the Man-Hater* was serialized in the *New York Ledger* in 1864–65 and published in two volumes, *Fair Play* and *How He Won Her*, the following year. The fundamental question of the novel is phrased succinctly by Elfie, a farmer's daughter and one of the four young southern women whose fortunes the novel tracks; she finds herself asking what it means for women to be patriots during the war: "'I am sure I do not know,' she sobbed, 'why I or any woman should make any sacrifice for the sake of the country. What have *we* to do with the country? Why should *we* devote our time, labor, money, life, health and happiness to the country, as many of us *will* do, if this comes to a civil war? *We* have no share in the administration of the government, no voice in the election of its officers!'"[55]

Elfie's quandary directly addressed the question posed by women's rights advocates. And her solution was one proposed by both sides of the women's rights question, mockingly by antifeminists and seriously by some feminists: if citizenship depended on the ability to engage in military service, why should women not serve? In Southworth's novel, Elfie's vexed outburst on the subject of women's patriotism is followed by the next logical step: her attempt to enlist in the Union army. "She grew moody, silent and unsocial. She studied Casey's Tactics all day long, except for an hour in the morning, which she spent in drilling. She borrowed her father's rifle, and went through the exercises with it."[56]

In a passage that pointedly contrasts female bravery with male avoidance of military obligations, Southworth raises the question of why, after all, women should not be able to join the armed forces. When the enrolling officers come to her house, recording names of eligible soldiers, Elfie gives them the names of all the men in the house, who range from a seventy-year-old slave to those absent at sea or at war. Finally, she gives them her middle name, Sydney, telling them that "Sydney Fielding is at present at home, and not in the service, is white, is twenty years old, and sound in mind and body" (*HHWH*, 59), and awaits a draft notice. When her admirer protests that "women have enlisted, and have served; but always when disguised as men" (*HHWH*, 57), she sneers at him. And when Erminie, the "true woman" of the novel, insists that she should stop the practical joke, she asks why:

> I don't come under any one of the heads of exemption. I know that much. I am not an alien, nor an invalid, nor an idiot. I am not under eighteen

or over forty-five. I am neither the only son of my grandmother, nor am I the father of fourteen small motherless children, and one at the breast. In short, I cannot put in even the smallest of the numerous pleas by which the cowards cry off from serving their country. I am a native born citizen of the United States, aged twenty years, sound in mind and body, wind and limb, single, and with no one but my country depending on me for support. (*HHWH*, 61)

By highlighting the fact that men could and did avoid military service, Southworth raised questions about the absolute linkage between masculinity, military service, and citizenship. As Elfie says to the mustering officers when she reports for duty, "A healthy young woman is quite as able to perform military duty as most men are, and much more able than the mere boys they are constantly mustering into the ranks" (*HHWH*, 62). The next day, the newspaper carries an item headed "A Girl Drafted by Mistake and Insisting on Serving" (*HHWH*, 66).

Southworth, as a southern abolitionist, a sentimental novelist, and one of the best-selling authors of her time, provided for her female readership a portrait of the woman in battle that was perhaps the most radical of all the representations described in this chapter.[57] Her cross-dressing heroines are neither as coolly self-serving as Loreta Velazquez nor as piously mealy-mouthed as Belle Boyd. They do not rely on the magical practices of such fictional creations as Pauline of the Potomac and the picket slayer. Proudly patriotic, they use their participation in the armed services as a means of determining their obligations and rights as female citizens.

More than any other text of the time, fictional or nonfictional, *Britomarte* is devoted to working out all of the possible permutations of armed female service in battle. *Britomarte, the Man-Hater* features four southern girls, all but one of them Union sympathizers. The stories of three of these girls reflect and refract those of the protagonist, their friend. When the war comes, Elfie attempts to enlist: she is a patriot who seeks full citizenship. Britomarte, the eponymous feminist heroine described, on introduction to the reader, as someone who "like Joan . . . could have led armies without blenching" (*FP*, 29), may be the most vocal feminist of the group. Like the heroines of eighteenth-century ballads and early nineteenth-century "autobiographies," she cross-dresses to join her lover on the battlefield. However, her engagement in combat becomes a way of achieving a truly egalitarian relationship with him. Another of the belles, Alberta, becomes a guerrilla fighter along with her husband—she is the most sexualized and most violent of the characters. The last of the four, Erminie, does not fight; she is a model of conventional female patriotism.

We first encounter the four friends as Virginia schoolgirls, a few years before the outbreak of war. Britomarte begins the novel with a diatribe against marriage: she "rebelled against the fate that made her woman and the law that limited her liberty to man's sphere" (*FP*, 29). Although Britomarte may be exceptional, the narrator asserts that her strength is not: "She was coming upon years when the sternness of a Judith, the courage of a Joan and the devotion of an Agnes would be needed by every woman in the land" (*FP*, 29). Thus, from the beginning of the novel, this future female soldier is concerned with the laws that limit women, including the institution of marriage.

The narrator does not hesitate to tell us that, of the group of girls, Britomarte "represent[s] the Minerva, the goddess of wisdom and of war" (*FP*, 30); although the narrator identifies Erminie as "a true woman" and comments, "I fancy that she will be the favorite of my readers" (*FP*, 30), it is clear that Britomarte is the real center of the novel. Britomarte's cross-dressing and fighting in the Civil War are first portrayed seven hundred pages into the novel, but the thematic importance of these actions is also clear. Early on, Erminie exclaims, "I often think Britomarte might be the Joan of Arc in some future heroic war!" (*FP*, 109). Her assessment is echoed by almost everyone who meets Britomarte, including the sea captain who takes her on her ill-fated voyage to become a missionary. As he listens to her reading all the parts of *King Lear*, he disagrees with the ship's doctor, who remarks, "What a successful spy she would make in war time!" On the contrary, says the captain, "I cannot imagine her acting the part of a spy; there is something much too frank and noble about the girl! I can more easily imagine her, Joan-of-Arc-like, leading an army!" (*FP*, 223).

In Southworth's novel, female heroism and love are closely tied together. Britomarte's love interest, Erminie's brother Justin, becomes attracted to her when he hears her theme "The Civil and Political Rights of Women" read at the commencement exercises in the opening pages of the novel. The speech is read for her "because in that immaculate institution it was deemed unlady-like for a young lady to stand upon a platform before a mixed audience and read her own composition" (*FP*, 53). In many of its concerns, the novel echoes speeches given at women's rights conventions during this period. Very early in the narrative, which runs to almost 1,200 pages, Justin and Britomarte fall in love, but she does not consent to marry him until nearly the last page, despite being shipwrecked with him on a desert island for several years, among other adventures. She in fact questions the virtue of marriage, for as she declaims in the novel's opening paragraph, "God endowed woman with individual life—with power, will and understanding, brain, heart and hands to do His work; and if it were only in gratitude to him, she should never commit the moral suicide of becoming the nonentity of which man's law makes a wife!" (FP, 27).

Although the novel makes some nods to antifeminism, it undercuts itself. When Britomarte finds herself seasick during a gale, on the way to Cambodia to become a missionary, the narrator says that "at least a score of times she essayed to go above, but in vain! Her beautiful person was formed to delight the eyes and attract the hearts of the 'common enemy' whom she abhorred and renounced, rather than to rival their skill in such feats of masculine skill and marine gymnastics as were necessary to all who might attempt to tread with impunity that stormy deck" (FP, 233). Yet when Justin, once the gale has passed, challenges her feminist principle that women should not be barred from any form of employment, she invokes the example of Mary Patton, a sea captain's wife. Her husband fell ill as their ship was about to round Cape Horn, en route to California,

> and one of the mates was nearly useless from his ignorance of navigation, and the other was highly dangerous from his disposition to mutiny, and she had to contend not only with the frightful hurricanes and fatal water currents of that region, but also with an insubordinate crew, led on by the mutinous first mate, who wished to convert the merchantman into a pirate. What did she do? She put the first mate in irons; she suppressed the mutiny; and she, who had learned navigation from her husband as a mere pastime, carried the ship through all the storms around the cape, and up the Pacific coast, safely into the port of San Francisco. (FP, 237)

The content of this eloquent speech would have been familiar to any reader of women's rights tracts, or any attendee at a women's rights convention, because the example of Mary Patton was frequently invoked in the debates about rights. Positioned in the novel to follow Britomarte's bout with seasickness, the speech serves to undercut the conventional banalities of the narrator.

The narrator's antifeminist speeches are more than once contradicted by Britomarte's bravery and eloquence. On the desert isle, for instance, when Justin builds a house for Britomarte, the narrator interjects that "man loved, served and guarded women all over the Christianized world. And if he kept her from the field, the forum and the polls, it was more in tender care of her delicacy than in jealous fear of her rights. . . . If occasionally in the world a woman was enabled to stand alone, it was on the platform that man had already prepared for her. How helpless she was without this platform, how unable to stand quite alone" (*FP*, 527). Even the feminist Britomarte assents to this analysis, confessing to Justin that on the desert island "I found by experience how utterly helpless woman was without her brother man," that "in a wilderness, where nothing had been done—where there were no habitations, no manufactures, no planted crops—woman could not possibly exist without man; though he might live without her" (*HHWH*, 508). However, the valor that would seem to be necessary for citizenship falls, in this case, to Britomarte, who saves Justin from an assault by a pirate by knocking away his pistol arm with a cutlass.

Erminie, the "true woman" of the novel, is the only one of the four friends without martial ambitions. Rather, when it looks like hostilities are about to break out, and her father declares his intention to fight for the Union, Erminie declares that "I myself would strap the sword to your side and place the musket in your hand, and follow you to the field, if you would let me, to dress your wounds if you should be hurt, and nurse you if you be sick; and to risk my life with yours and die with you, if need should be!" (*FP*, 399). She spends the war visiting wounded soldiers in the hospital.

However, Elfie Fielding, the daughter of an affluent farmer, whose hair is "cut short, parted on the left side, and worn in crisp curls like a boy's" (*FP*, 31), is a somewhat comical contrast to Belle Boyd, who opens her autobiography with an account of shooting a Yankee soldier who dared to insult her mother after she refused to allow him to raise the Federal flag above their house. In Elfie's case, when local Confederate sympathizers object to her hoisting a homemade American flag and attempt to tear it down, she responds by blasting away at them with her father's double-barreled rifle, hitting one in the backside with a spent cartridge. She refuses to feel the remorse that Erminie expects of her—and refuses even to feel grateful that she did not kill him: "It would have been very shocking to a new recruit like me, just at the first go off; but, bless you! it would not have weighed on my conscience very heavily. I should have soon got over it, and been all the readier to pick off the next fellow that should insult the glorious flag" (*FP*, 410). When local secessionists return with weapons, Elfie joins her father in the gunfight, rejecting his pleas to leave the window: "'not while I have got a shot left to send at the enemy.' And so saying, she blazed away with her other barrel" (*FP*, 415). In other words, Elfie shoots to protect the flag, an abstraction of patriotism.

The violence that one of the four friends encounters and embraces as the wife of a guerrilla fighter is explicitly sexualized. In this, the novel prefigures the linkage of sexuality and violence in the 1920s that I discuss in chapter 3. Alberta, the wealthy Confederate girl, escapes from the convent to which her parents have consigned her and elopes with her Italian professor, whom she encourages to become a guerrilla. When she shows up at Erminie's house to try to get her husband out of prison, Alberta has shed the complacency she exhibits at the opening of the novel: now "that strange discordant laugh broke from Alberta's pallid lips, and jarred upon the ears of her hearers . . . Her face and form were still beautiful, but the 'glory' of their beauty was 'obscured.' Her once oval face was lengthened and hollowed, her perfect features pinched and sharpened; her fair complexion sunburned, her brilliant hair faded, her graceful form emaciated. Her whole aspect spoke of the hardships and exposures of the hunted and battling life she led by the side of the guerrilla chief" (*HHWH*, 86). Although she becomes a guerrilla for romantic reasons, and her husband takes the sexually suggestive nom de guerre of the Free Sword, she is rendered ugly by the experience.

Happy to be tasting tea for the first time in a year, Alberta explains to Elfie and Erminie that "I was always with my husband; he had an independent command, and was what *you* call a guerrilla chief; ours was a hunted life, a Cain's life; our hand was against every one, and every one's hand against us! Our home was the wildwood or the ruined farm-house; our occupation war, rapine, plunder" (*HHWH*, 89–90). Alberta, who incited her husband to join the guerrillas, has lost her femininity and has been almost driven mad by her engagement with violence.

Despite the experience of having "sometimes had to look on while hamlets were burning and spies hanging" (*HHWH*, 163), Alberta has the most romantic relationship of the four women: "We are all in all to each other. He is more than ever lover or husband was to woman before! I am more to him than ever was sweetheart or wife to man! We are one; we can never be divided. Nothing—no, nothing shall ever part us! not life, not death, not eternity! In all the gloom and horror of our downward course—and downward it is, Elfie—downward even to the depths of hell!—we have the one, great, deep joy of knowing that we go on together, inseparable forever! Yes, on earth or in hades, inseparable forever!" (*HHWH*, 165). Indeed, when the

Free Sword is gazing at the body of his beloved wife, after she has thrown herself in front of him to take a minié ball in the heart, he says to his comrades, "What do you suppose I really cared for the Confederacy? I am a foreigner. What are your civil wars to me? It was for *her* I drew my sword. She bade me draw it in the cause of the Confederacy, and I did it, as, if she had bid me draw it in the cause of the Union, or of the Lord, or of the Devil, I would have done it" (*HHWH*, 285). Appropriately, the Free Sword dies of a wound inflicted by the same minié ball that kills Alberta. The romance between Alberta and her husband makes for the most desperate relationship in the book. It seems inevitable that it will end in their violent deaths.

By contrast, Britomarte's relationship with her future husband, Justin, is based on comradeship, both on and off the battlefield. Although Elfie and Alberta take up arms as well, it is Britomarte who most fully uses her experiences in battle to establish a new form of marriage. When Justin joins the army, she bitterly regrets the principles that make marriage impossible for her and envisions an alternative relationship to him:

> But if it were possible that she could have followed him into battle, followed him through life, as his sister, that would have been the next best thing to being his wife; or better still, as his brother, for as his brother she might be beside him on the battle-field, in the midst of an engagement, when shot and shell were flying fastest, in the thickest carnage, where, as his wife, she would never be allowed to appear.
>
> A vehement, passionate desire to be all this to her beloved; to be to him more than wife, sister or brother had ever been to man before—more than all these combined could ever become—to be his brother-in-arms, his inseparable companion, his shadow, his shield, his guardian angel, in the tented field, in the pitched battle, in the rebel prison, or in the grave. (*HHWH*, 79)

The kind of relationship exemplified by Britomarte and Justin is presented by Southworth as being much more viable than either a more traditional or a more heatedly romantic alternative. Britomarte, who enlists without telling Justin and serves as his male orderly (soon promoted to adjutant), spends most of her time spying, saving Justin's life (three times in quick succession), and shooting enemies. She is the first to see the enemy's bayonets glittering in the darkness and to know when they have been ambushed; she is the person who can figure out what is making Justin's horse lame; she is the one who devises the most daring ruses, who kills the enemy without a second thought. Britomarte, as Adjutant Wing, becomes a captain in less than a year, promoted because, as a sergeant explains, "he has been under fire a score of times and never blenched. And I can tell you this, my comrades: When you *do* see him under fire, you see one who will not *drive* you like sheep, but *lead* you like men" (*HHWH*, 368). Indeed, when Britomarte advances as ordered with her company to take a battery, though "the order [is] a desperate one, and the duty well nigh a forlorn hope" (*HHWH*, 369), she does not hesitate: "Like an angel of destruction he rushed onward, followed by all his men" (*HHWH*, 370) to take possession of a rebel town. Britomarte's heroism is emphasized throughout the text, while Justin's, though unquestioned, is rarely discussed.

Britomarte's military comradeship with Justin makes their romantic relationship possible. When Justin is wounded in the battle of Cold Harbor and appears to be dying on the battlefield, he confesses to Britomarte that he recognized her from the beginning but has respected her decision to serve in the ranks undetected, for "to betray my knowledge of you would be to wound your delicacy and control your actions" (*HHWH*, 443). Justin is the ideal feminist partner. As he says, "There is not, Britomarte, in the universe a creature who understands and appreciates you and your motives as truly and justly as I can and as I do" (*HHWH*, 442). And she does not leave his side, even though it means incarceration in the dreaded Castle Thunder prison, where she languishes for almost a year.

Significantly, the one woman who does not take up arms and does not question her social role, Erminie, ends up with the most boring marriage, to a southerner twenty years her senior, who is one of the chief architects of a plot to overthrow the u.s. government. Even before she knows he is a traitor, the reader is led to dislike him as somewhat asexual and overly interested in his creature comforts. When he comes to stay with Erminie and her father after an absence, she sees "his look of appreciation and approbation as he glance[s] around the room before his eye [falls] upon herself" (*FP*, 360). Her father is put off by the lukewarm greeting—a compliment and a kiss of the hand—that the suitor gives Erminie: "That is all very high-toned, I dare say; but for my part, I had rather see him kiss her openly and heartily, as an honest sweetheart and betrothed husband should!" (*FP*, 360). Erminie's suitor is almost never around, since he is too busy conspiring, and seems generally inattentive and far from romantic. Of course, Erminie rejects him when she discovers that he has been using her home as the meeting place for the conspirators, and she only takes him back at the end of the book, when he is "pale, silent, sorrowful, mutilated" (*HHWH*, 494) (he has lost an arm in the war). He comes to repent his work for the Confederate cause: as he tells her, while she "[sits] down at his knee, as she had been accustomed to do in the early days of their betrothal" (*HHWH*, 495), "I am old and gray and broken and mutilated . . . I am a poor and penniless man . . . I have lost my right arm! And, worse than all, I have lost it in a bad cause! . . . my once spotless name is stained with reproach. Could you bear to wear it?" (*HHWH*, 496). Of course, she forgives him: "These two were reconciled, and this was but the forerunner of a deeper and broader reconciliation yet to come" (*HHWH*, 496). The women in the novel who have taken up arms seem to have passionate relationships with men. Erminie's relationship, by contrast, is muted and sad.

No matter how many times the narrator tells us to admire her, it is hard for the reader to feel that the pure, conventional Erminie has made a really wonderful marriage. Sitting at her lover's knee, having patiently waited and magnanimously forgiven all, she forms a contrast to the daring Elfie, who eventually marries a bold sea captain who has been promoted as a result of his bravery in battle. Even the misguided Alberta gets to die in a blaze of romantic glory. Most of all, Britomarte, who insists on comradeship, makes a great marriage. Finally, the novel suggests that women might use the gun, and engage in military service, not only to shoulder the burdens of citizenship but also to forge new relationships of full equality. In this, Southworth extended the claims of women's rights advocates—that women in combat could win the vote and other privileges of citizenship—to suggest that armed women might remake their private as well as their public lives. The novel, of course, is a form in which happy fantasy can run riot. The real women who attempted to remake their lives through publicizing their military service in the Civil War had a somewhat more difficult time in gaining public approval. And, as we have seen, those who did succeed did so through a complex and somewhat contradictory self-presentation.

The armed female celebrities who followed upon the generation of the Civil War combatants were the stars of Wild West shows. They were able to portray themselves as allies with white men in the battle for white nationhood, rather than as wartime combatants who were usurping men's positions in battle. By shifting the terrain from the military battlefield to the imagined frontier, and by fighting Indians and other nonwhite enemies, the armed women who succeeded in this next era were implicitly engaged in the battle for racial supremacy; they did not aim at gender equality.

LITTLE MISS SURE SHOT
AND FRIENDS, OR HOW
ARMED WOMEN TAMED
THE WEST

In 1876, visitors to the Philadelphia Centennial Exposition were captivated by the exhibit of the famed Coloradan hunter and taxidermist Martha Maxwell. Behind a placard that read "Woman's Work" were hundreds of animals arranged in tableaux. One of the most popular displays featured a group of stuffed monkeys sitting on stools around a table, playing cards. Another comic tableau showed a duckling and a squirrel coming out of a small wooden house atop a mountain. J. S. Ingram wrote in *The Centennial Exposition* (1876) that "it was beyond all comparison one of the most effectively arranged displays of the whole Exhibition."[1]

The tableaux, which were widely admired by the spectators who thronged the exhibit, were emblematic of the public image of Martha Maxwell herself. The arrangements were sweetly domesticated groupings of dead animals, killed by a woman who was seen by the press and by spectators as variously white, Native American, a hunter, a housewife, a lady, and an amazon. In short, Maxwell embodied many of the contradictions of the western woman. Her work with the gun in the wilderness caused her to share enough qualities with Indians and men that the public questioned both her whiteness and her femininity. Maxwell was popular during the 1870s, a time when the West was still widely perceived as being truly wild, and when the battles between the u.s. government and the Indians were not yet over: her exhibit was on display the same summer that General George Armstrong Custer made his last stand against the Sioux. Once the frontier had officially been closed in 1890 and the image of the Wild West became tinged by nostalgia, a new kind of armed celebrity came to the fore: the armed woman who could stake her place in the popular imagination as a helpmate in the struggle to tame the frontier.

While certainly not every woman who fought in the Civil War did so as an act of feminist protest, much of the debate surrounding armed women of the Civil War era centered on the gendered nature of citizenship (if women were to bear the same martial obligations as men, then they deserved equal rights as citizens). Armed women in the era following the Civil War used the gun to draw racial distinctions between conquering whites and the nonwhite peoples they conquered. Self-consciously crafting their public images, these women used western imagery to gain public attention. However, the most successful of them highlighted their whiteness and their gentility at the same time that they appropriated the symbols of the frontier, a region associated in the popular imagination with roughness and with its settlers' close interactions with members of many ethnic groups.

Although the frontier was multiethnic, the regulation of gun ownership had long had a basis in race, and often, as well, a basis in gender. Laws dating back to the seventeenth century, such as the 1648 Virginia law called An Act Preventing Negroes from Bearing Arms, limited the ability of nonwhites to own guns.[2] The Uniform Militia Act of 1792 required free, able-bodied white males between the ages of eighteen and forty-five to enroll in a militia, bearing their own arms and equipment, but it banned from service all slaves, freed blacks, and Indians.[3] Despite the laws prohibiting them from doing so, colonists continued to trade guns with Indians. Yet as Kathleen Brown writes of colonial Virginia, "Although efforts to restrict the availability of guns to English freemen and keep them out of the hands of enslaved Africans, Indians, and English servants were never completely successful, the exclusion of women from the community of gun owners and users seems to have been nearly universal."[4] Even so, late nineteenth-century historians and white women shooters retrospectively wrote the armed woman into colonial history—and even gave her a starring role.

The politics of white supremacy in the South, both before and after the Civil War, mandated that whites use guns as instruments of terror to control blacks and that blacks be forbidden from using firearms. The southern antebellum gun laws were upheld in the *Dred Scott* case, which specifically gave states the right to bar blacks, slave or free, from citizenship, and thus not allow them "to keep and carry arms wherever they went."[5] The Black Codes established in the South following the Civil War included gun-control measures aimed specifically at African Americans, such as a Mississippi law that kept blacks from owning or carrying any kind of guns.[6] Many more laws of this nature were enacted following the race riots of the late 1860s in Norfolk, Memphis, and New Orleans, in which newly enfranchised African Americans used firearms to defend their new rights. A black activist in Louisiana remarked, "As one of the disenfranchised race, I would say to every colored soldier, 'Bring your gun home.'"[7] Of course, most racialized gun violence was committed by whites in the South against blacks.

However, the South was not the only region in which whites and non-whites were involved in gunfights. As Richard Slotkin has pointed out, the *New York Herald* explicitly linked the race wars of the South to the armed confrontations between the u.s. Army and Indians in the West in its coverage of the July 1876 Hamburg Massacre of South Carolina, in which six black militia members were shot by an armed mob of whites. Most specifically, the *Herald*'s article pointed to Custer's Last Stand, which took place just days before the Hamburg Massacre. Slotkin comments, "The fact of the Last Stand was evidence of the need for transferring troops out of the South and into the West, to fight dark-skinned savages rather than 'oppressing' progressive southern whites."[8] While newspapers were documenting the dangers posed by armed blacks in the South and armed Indians in the West, white women shooters used the gun as a concrete symbol of their alliance with white men, implicitly against people of color.

When Martha Maxwell emerged as the most visible armed western woman of her day, the popular image of the western woman was still coalescing. Mary Dartt's 1878 narrative of Maxwell's life, *On the Plains, and Among the Peaks*, opens with a group of tourists and journalists in the Colorado Building of the 1876 Centennial Exposition in Philadelphia marveling at Maxwell's display of taxidermy:

> "'Woman's work!' What does that mean? Can it be possible any one wishes us to believe a *woman* did all this?"
>
> "Couldn't say—I'm pretty sure I shan't stretch my credulity so much —it would ruin the article!"
>
> "I should think so! Why one might think the ark had just landed here! —buffaloes, bears, birds, wild-cats, mice and who but Noah or Agassiz could name what else!"[9]

On answering a tourist's question, "Does that placard really mean to tell us a woman mounted all these animals?" the narrator finds herself besieged with inquiries:

> "How could a woman do it?"
> "What did she do it for?"
> "Did she *kill* any of the animals?" (8)

Audiences debated whether the taxidermist Martha Maxwell was a genteel artist, as her palette and brush suggest, or a Nimrod, as the rifle leaning against the table implies. Courtesy Colorado Historical Society (BPF F 33373) All Rights Reserved.

Dartt finds herself challenged by the tourists' curiosity about the disconnect between the sign on the exhibit reading "*Woman's Work*" and their conceptions of what women should be working at. The questions continue:

"Does she live in that cave?"
  "If she's married, why ain't it called *Mr.* Maxwell's collection?"
  "Is she good-looking?"
  "Is she a half-breed?"
  "Is she an Indian?" (9)

These questions provide the framework for Dartt's narrative, and they can orient our discussion as well. How did the image of the armed frontier woman play out in an eastern context? How did Maxwell, whose publicity photos show her sitting with a rifle next to her specimens, help viewers understand the relationship between womanhood and American identity?

Dartt's book traces the career of a woman unconstrained by conventional gender expectations. Maxwell, born in Pennsylvania, raised in Baraboo, Wisconsin, educated at Oberlin and at Lawrence University, married a widower twenty years her senior, who had six children of his own; she moved with him to Colorado in 1860 to seek a fortune at Pike's Peak. A self-taught taxidermist and naturalist, she invented taxidermic methods that would first come into widespread use twenty years later, and she arranged her specimens in groupings that prefigured the exhibit style used at the end of the century. A dedicated supporter of women's rights, she wrote a friend that "my next ambition is to build up a temple of science that shall be a credit to *our sex* and an acquisition to the world."[10] She was a friend of Julia Ward Howe, author of the "Battle Hymn of the Republic" (1862), and Helen Hunt Jackson, author of the best-selling novel *Ramona* (1884), admired Maxwell's collections. She discovered an owl, *Scops maxwelliae*, so named by the Smithsonian in her honor.

The reviews of Dartt's book reveal the tensions among conflicting ideas of womanhood, science, frontier identity, Americanness, and whiteness. Several of the reviews focused on the book's scientific theme; the *New York Independent* lauded it for being "full of valuable scientific observations on the natural history of Colorado." Yet most reviewers seemed to share the conclusion drawn by the *Philadelphia Press*: "The description of the animals in her collection is at once graphic and scientific, but to our taste Mrs. Dartt's history of how the little lady became a naturalist, a taxidermist, and a good shot, is the best part of the book." The *Keystone* recommended Dartt's narrative "as a brilliant sketch of a singular character—an Amazon in endurance and yet a lady in refined sensibility." The reviewer for the *Sunday Post* wrote, "We wonder that boys will be so eager after yellow-back literature of Western hunting when such a pure and sprightly book, full of lively incident, can be found as this."[11] In keeping with the journalistic interest in Maxwell's femininity, *On the Plains, and Among the Peaks* stressed the womanly nature of its subject. As Dartt told it, although Maxwell had first picked up a gun as a child in order to save the book's author from a rattlesnake bite, she did not want to make a point about her prowess: "So shy was she of any display of skill unusual to feminine fingers, that few people ever saw her fire a gun."[12] Nevertheless, it was not always easy for those writing about Maxwell to come to terms with what they saw as her multiple identities.

Martha Maxwell's scrapbook from her trip to the Philadelphia Centennial Exposition shows how journalists writing about her struggled to find a balance between her westernness, her role as a naturalist, and her femininity. Many saw her achievement as one of preserving her identity as a lady under all circumstances. As the writer for the *Daily News* of Denver, Colorado, put it, "She illustrates what a woman can do who is devoted to something, having a capacity for it, and a purpose to achieve it—can do and still be womanly."[13] Some journalists went out of their way to emphasize her femininity at the expense of her reputation as a hunter or a scientist. The reviewer for *Harper's Bazaar*, for instance, noted that

> the museum prepared by Mrs. Maxwell demonstrates that verve and pluck are as efficient helpers in the hands of woman as of man, and her course shows simply and very openly to the world what quiet determination and persistent effort can accomplish. . . . It will be pleasant to most readers to know that the full strength and richness of Mrs. Maxwell's life have not been given to her journeyings as a huntress, or absorbed in her after-labors in preparing for exhibition the animals she has brought down. As a wife, mother and householder she holds a happy and well-accredited record.

Like other writers, this one focused in the end on Maxwell's physical appearance and its contrast to readers' presumed expectations: "Mrs. Maxwell is a quiet little blue-eyed woman, shy and unassuming in mien, and not at all like the Amazon that one might expect to find in the Rocky Mountain huntress."[14]

Maxwell's exhibit caused critics and exposition attendees to rethink the meaning of women's work. The "Centennial Correspondence" of the

Lynn City Item noted that "this is the first International Exhibition where woman's work has received the distinct recognition that is its just due; but it is not among the wax flowers and fancy work of the Women's Pavilion that the tourist finds the exhibit indicating the most enterprise and executive ability by one of the fair sex." In lauding what Maxwell had done, the correspondent reassured readers that her killing thousands of animals did not evidence violent tendencies: "The work was not undertaken out of a thirst for sport and hunting, but was the labor of love of an enthusiastic naturalist, working purely in the interests of science." Yet science seemed, to this writer, to take second place to the genteel arts of the Women's Pavilion: "The animals are tastefully arranged around an elevation." Finally, the writer emphasized that Maxwell's work had not made her less of a lady: "The exposed life necessary for the accomplishment of her great work has not tinged her complexion, nor altered her appearance from that of any lady of culture and education."[15] (This view was not shared by all journalists; a piece in *Forest and Stream* alluded to "a face somewhat tanned by exposure.")[16]

The coverage of Maxwell included discussion of her increasing celebrity and the slanders of newspaper articles. As Olive Harper wrote in an article for the *Weekly Alta California and San Francisco Times*, "There are few persons who have not heard of the lady huntress of Colorado, who has her animals and birds here on exhibition. All the papers have had more or less regarding her in them, and some of them were so utterly ridiculous that it is no wonder that she felt hurt and vexed at them. By some she was reported to be a sort of cross between a Piute savage and a Dahomey Amazon, whereas she is a pretty and extremely lady-like and cultivated little lady. . . . She is anything but the unsexed Amazon people have fancied."[17] Yet even this sympathetic portrayal may have irritated Maxwell; as *The New Century for Women*, a publication of the Women's Centennial Committee, reported, "It is a source of no small annoyance to this lady, who is simply and sincerely a naturalist, who shrinks from destroying life as sensitively as would the most delicately reared metropolitan woman, that she should be called for, almost demanded as part of the exhibit, as 'the Rocky Mountain *huntress*.'" Obviously, if Maxwell had truly shrunk from destroying life, she probably would not have shot and killed thousands of animals, but this was not a point that the author of the article chose to dwell on. She was, the publication insisted, "so wholly different from the muscular, Amazonian Rocky Mountain combination, armed with a bow like Diana, and dressed like a miner, that . . . fancy had conjured."[18]

Again and again, newspapers referred to the contrast between what visitors initially thought they would see in Maxwell and what they actually encountered. The *Advance* reported that "as a general rule [tourists] expect to meet an Amazon in size and strength, clad in a suit of buckskin, with murder in her eye, a Sharp's rifle in her hands, and wearing a belt stuck full of revolvers and hunting knives. Instead, however, they find a petite little woman, dressed in a plain dark suit, slight of stature, with pleasant face, dark hair, and the manners of a thorough lady."[19] The writer for the *Philadelphia Times* was happy to discover that Mrs. Maxwell was not "a bold masculine looking woman, such as are quite common among the women of the frontier."[20] The most daring writers merged the image of the lady and the amazon. *Truth for the People* reported that "we admire the pluck of this little woman, who handles a Colts [sic] revolver with as much grace as some of our city belles would a croquet mallet."[21]

Yet amid the reports of Maxwell's celebrity—she was disappointed to miss P. T. Barnum, who had dropped by to see her, but happy to shake hands with Dom Pedro, the emperor of Brazil—there was at least one article that expressed dissatisfaction with Maxwell's achievements. The *People's Journal*, while noting that "Mrs. Maxwell is doubtless the *living* heroine of the Centennial exhibition," snarled that "this work is well done by woman, if she has or has not chosen wisely; but we are glad our chosen companion is not a mighty huntress—a female Nimrod, nor a Colorado taxidermist. More than rumor reports that her husband is in some ways worse than a stupid stick, that her married life has been a doleful disappointment, and it would seem that she has turned from brutal man to find greater attractions in less brutal beasts, and who shall blame her? Mrs. Maxwell is by no means a savage, for her hand shake, and smiles and speech show her culture, but her calling is curious, and her surroundings strange."[22] In this writer's view, Maxwell's gun became a substitute for a satisfying marriage.

Maxwell's studio portraits, which she had hoped to sell during her visit to the exposition, highlight the tension between her gun-toting identity and her claims to gentility. In one, she sits at a table in a demure black dress, hair in a neatly arranged bun, paintbrush in one hand and palette in the other. On the table are a stuffed fox and hawk, and a rifle leans against the fox. In another picture, she poses in hunting costume against a fake boulder, bloomers peeking out from beneath her skirt, hair loose beneath an androgynous hat, rifle in hand, a large dead animal at her feet.

The Philadelphia Centennial Exposition would prove to be the high point of Martha Maxwell's career; it certainly afforded her the greatest public visibility she was ever able to attain. The armed woman as scientist was not a figure that endured, for an intellectual woman hunter was an uncomfortable combination of things—too smart, too violent—for the public to assimilate. Yet even as Maxwell faded from public view at the end of the 1870s, a generation of women sharpshooters stepped forward to take her place in the public imagination as icons of armed femininity.

MILITARIZATION AS FEMINIZATION: THE NATIONAL RIFLE ASSOCIATION AND THE RISE OF THE FEMALE SHARPSHOOTER

Beginning in the 1870s and continuing well into the 1920s, women were active in the popular sport of trapshooting. Books on the sport published during this period featured illustrations of both women and men, and trapshooting for women was publicized by gun manufacturers as yet another feminine activity, not far removed from shopping or club work. How did riflery, first promoted by the National Rifle Association as a means of building a more effective army, become a sport for women? In pursuing the answer to this question, we can see how female shooters (as well as gun manufacturers and the NRA) manipulated popular associations of guns with war, marksmanship, and hunting.

The NRA developed in reaction to the lack of training given to soldiers in the Civil War; its founders aimed to militarize and professionalize the practice of riflery.[23] As Captain George W. Wingate of the New York National Guard, one of the two former Union officers who founded the NRA,[24] wrote, "The Civil War had demonstrated with bloody clarity that soldiers who could not shoot straight were of little value. This situation, and the general ignorance concerning marksmanship which I found among our soldiers during the Civil War appalled me, and I hoped that I might better the situation." Wingate, moreover, wanted American marksmen to resemble national icons: "I believed that if I could help dispel the prevalent ignorance about rifle shooting I might bring our American Rifleman nearer in actuality to his legendary status."[25] Thus, the NRA was incorporated to "encourage rifle shooting on a scientific basis."[26] In November 1871, New York State granted the organization a charter and allotted it money to build a rifle range. However, by 1892, an unsympathetic governor and a poor economic climate brought state sponsorship of the organization to a halt, and the NRA temporarily folded, to be reactivated with the support of President Theodore Roosevelt in 1900.[27]

The NRA's stated mission was particularly attractive to the state government of New York. Target shooting had enjoyed a vogue in New York City from the 1830s onward: it is estimated that in 1850 target companies in New York had 10,000 members.[28] Yet, by the late 1860s, target shooting was associated in the public imagination with rowdy, drunken behavior and the terrifyingly haphazard marksmanship of the former firemen and ex-soldiers who made up associations like the Chowder Club. Less frightening to observers were the German Schützenbünde, which flourished in cities with substantial German immigrant populations before the Civil War, such as Chicago, St. Louis, and New York; their members congregated for fancy meals followed by organized shooting at novelty targets, after which prizes were distributed. Not every member of the Schützenbünde was involved in target practice; entire extended families of German Americans, from senior citizens to small children, showed up at the festive events.[29] However, the members of these clubs could hardly be said to exemplify the American Rifleman that NRA founder George Wingate apotheosized. The Schützenbünde were considered so unthreatening that they were allowed to reorganize in the South almost immediately after the cessation of Civil War hostilities.[30]

The NRA Americanized target shooting. Although it was closely linked at its founding with military objectives and had state and federal support, the NRA paradoxically feminized target shooting by opening the door for women to participate in large numbers. As Russell Stanley Gilmore has written, "Control and repetition are essential in target shooting as in few other sports, and it affords little of the posturing and heroics shared by military life and hunting. . . . Partisans of riflery urged marksmanship for character building more often than sport, and the 'arm of precision' truly demanded Protestant virtues, including temperance—alcohol and tobacco interfered with success."[31] By disassociating riflery from the "posturing and heroics" of military life, and stressing instead the patience and temperance needed to succeed, the NRA made it possible for women to be on an equal footing in this arena. Military officers of the 1890s, entering into the debate about using rifles in wartime, were eager to point out just how unrelated sharpshooting skill was to military service: after all, many women were crack shots, but that did not make them soldiers.[32]

The rifle clubs of the 1870s and 1880s often welcomed both women and military organizations. For instance, an 1886 letter to the editor of the *Rifle*, a monthly published in Boston, from the secretary of the Capital Rifle Club, noted that "we are to have a special day or two devoted to military shooting, inviting nothing but organized military companies to participate, in which nothing but the regulation arm will be allowed. We also have a day set aside for the ladies' shoot, as we have a 'Ladies Rifle Club,' which is an auxiliary to Capital Rifle Club."[33]

However, the overall tone of the sport was not military, but increasingly feminine. An 1888 front-page article in the *Rifle*, titled "Ladies' Day at the Rifle Range," begins by noting that "it is not strange that with the amount of enthusiasm existing at the present time among gentlemen interested in rifle and pistol practice, their wives, sisters, and lady friends should partake of the interest in this pastime. . . . It is no uncommon sight to see ladies at the rifle range, and that many of them are becoming capital shots." The article goes on to say, "The skill of some of the ladies who occasionally visit the Walnut Hill and the Lynn (Mass.) rifle range is surprising; and it is a fact that they often surpass the efforts of some of the sterner sex." In the view of the author, what makes shooting such an appropriate sport for women? "Rifle and pistol shooting is recognized as one of the cleanest sports, and there are many reasons why a lady should learn to use a rifle and pistol. . . . Most of our readers know how the enthusiastic rifleman is inclined to decorate his sanctum with trophies of the chase and souvenirs of victories on the rifle range. The same mania has seized the markswomen of New England; and it is not uncommon to see, amid Kensington work, decorated pottery, and paintings, a handsome .22 or .32 caliber rifle, a Stevens pistol, or a Smith and Wesson revolver." Here, the gun has been rendered so genteel that it can appear in a middle-class parlor along with more conventional bric-a-brac. As the author concludes, "Ladies are rapidly becoming interested in rifle and pistol shooting, and why should they not?"[34]

Yet no matter how much writers linked shooting to other genteel feminine practices, it remained true that guns were implements of warfare, and this could pose some problems for the skilled female shooter. The case of Plinky Topperwein serves to illustrate this point. From 1903 until 1940, Elizabeth Servaty "Plinky" Topperwein traveled with her husband, Adolph, for the Winchester Repeating Arms Company as an exhibition shooter. In 1907, she held the world's record for trapshooting, with 1,952 hits out of 2,000 targets over a five-hour period.[35] She was a celebrity in her time, and as a promotional pamphlet that Winchester distributed notes, "The coming of the Topperweins, as a rule, means a veritable holiday in most towns; if it is during the school season, schools are closed in order to give young America an opportunity to turn out and witness these marvelous shooting stunts."[36]

Trapshooting was a popular sport for upper-class women at the end of the nineteenth century. Here, three members of the Women's Shooting Club, Alma, Wisconsin, circa 1889, pose with their "schuetzen-rifles." Courtesy of Wisconsin Historical Society, 9831.

Plinky Topperwein was a celebrity shooter on equal terms with her husband—until it came time to give shooting demonstrations for the u.s. Army. Buffalo Bill Historical Center, Cody, Wyoming; Gift of Garry Fellers; MS64.1.9.

The promotional materials for the Topperweins always made it clear that Plinky's shooting developed only as a result of her marriage to Ad. As another Winchester pamphlet noted, "Mrs. Topperwein says she did not know the difference between a shotgun and a rifle before her marriage. She became interested in the sport watching her husband's fascinating shooting, and under his coaching developed into a star of the first magnitude."[37] Plinky Topperwein appeared in advertising material not only for Winchester but also for the American Powder Mills, which boasted, in an ad that appeared in a 1907 issue of *Outdoor Life*, that "Mrs. Ad Topperwein, who is considered the greatest woman shot in the world, uses Dead Shot exclusively, for the maximum results it always gives."[38]

The Winchester promotional material insisted that "it has always been a debatable question as to which of the Topperweins is the better shot, Mr. or Mrs." Yet the company proved skittish about promoting Plinky over Ad when it attempted to have the Topperweins do exhibition shooting for soldiers during World War One. In a 1917 letter to Major Leonard A. Horner of the u.s. Army Signal Corps, the vice president of Winchester, Henry Brewer, wrote to offer the company's services in teaching trapshooting to the aviators. "We have in mind especially Mr. and Mrs. Topperwein, who have a nation-wide reputation as marksmen with the shotgun as well as with the rifle." Brewer went on to assure the major that his sharpshooters were sufficiently patriotic. "Topperwein's name would indicate that he is of German origin but he is certainly not of German sentiment. He is a husky Texan and his wife is a New Haven girl. Both of them are keenly patriotic Americans." The greater concern he foresaw was Plinky Topperwein's sex: "I rather hesitate to suggest Mrs. Topperwein for the reason that her position in military camps would perhaps be rather embarrassing for her. On the other hand, she is a very charming ladylike woman and a first-class shotgun and rifle instructor."[39] Horner responded enthusiastically, suggesting that "if it could be brought about, it would seem desirable to have Mr. Topperwein in the service and Mrs. Topperwein used for training men who would later assist in the schools."[40] The final correspondence between Brewer and the War Department concerned arrangements for Ad Topperwein to give an exhibition for the War Department with a Browning Light Machine Rifle at the Aberdeen Proving Grounds; there is no mention of Plinky Topperwein's inclusion in the event.[41]

Although Winchester may have felt constrained about promoting a woman sharpshooter in a military context, the gun industry as a whole marketed its products to women throughout the 1910s. In 1915, for example, the

E. I. Du Pont Nemours Powder Company published a manual titled *Diana of the Traps*, which was meant to reclaim the "hunting instinct" for women by invoking the ancient myth of Diana. The figure of Diana is not of a war goddess but rather of a huntress. She is intelligent, androgynous, and altogether a much more acceptable role model for twentieth-century women than the warlike amazon. Tellingly, the author of the pamphlet's preface, Harriet Whitford, emphasizes the mythic figure's femininity: "That the sportsmanship of the 'fair crowned queen of the echoing chase' was tempered with womanly attributes, is shown by the fact that the beautiful Cynthia [Diana] was not only huntress but guardian of wild beasts."[42] The pamphlet that follows provides practical instructions for duplicating the success of the first women's trapshooting club, organized by Harriet D. Hammond in Wilmington, Delaware, in 1913. An employee in the agricultural division of Du Pont, Hammond had suggested that the company offer shooting classes especially for women as part of its gun club. The classes went so well that a trapshooting club for women was established.[43] An adjunct of the Du Pont Trapshooting Club, the women's group was allowed to use the traps one afternoon a week, since "it was not feasible to give up one of [the main club's] traps to women on regular shooting days" (5). The photographs illustrating the pamphlet are of women in long dresses, and subchapters trumpet the success of women in competition with men ("Members of Nemours Trapshooting Club Carry off Five of the Eight Prizes").

Among the most interesting features of the pamphlet are the stories solicited by the sponsoring powder company from women trapshooters. Some narratives stress how much more feminine trapshooting is than hunting. According to Mrs. J. Fred Ebright, of El Dorado, Georgia, the apparel needed for hunting is simply not suitable: "Years of experience have taught me that the only fit costume to hunt in is a hideous cross. You've got to wear a man's coat and a vest loaded with a back-breaking weight of shells; and a skirt so short it shouts! And how are you going to sneak past scandalized persons, on your way to trolley or train, for a day's hunt, if the shoes you wear are stout and heavy enough to resist the rough going in the woods?" Trapshooting, however, eliminates those problems: "There is no fatigue, no killing, no need to wear cumbrous or unbecoming clothes, as when one hunts. Indeed, you can wear your prettiest and daintiest. A soft linen pad to slip over the gun stock would protect your shoulder from any chance grease" (44). A trapshooting woman can escape the unwelcome attentions of "scandalized persons" and look like a dainty lady even when practicing her sport.

Martha E. Dewey also extols trapshooting as a way of enjoying shooting while retaining femininity, for according to her a woman

> loves every flower that blooms in her pathway and every song bird that has left the wild and makes its home with us . . .
>
> She wishes to remain young and in sympathy with her own family circle and the coterie of friends who gather at her home.
>
> A woman's viewpoint is subject to her environment. Many of our outdoor pastimes are too strenuous for a woman. (27)

Trapshooting, then, is the perfect solution. Mrs. E. B. Belknap of Wyoming, New York, advises that "the woman having an indulgent brother, father or husband interested in the sport and appreciating the fact that a woman's life is naturally confining, stands a better chance of getting into the game" (31).

Not all of the trapshooters quoted in the pamphlet manage to completely divorce shooting from warfare. Jeannie P. Hirst writes of shooting that "it is typically an American sport in that Americans as a nation have an inborn desire to use firearms—the small boy's (or small girl's) affection for a pistol or anything that looks like one and will make a noise is proof of that. Perhaps it's the old soldier ancestry of most of us, or maybe just the remnant of the primitive" (23). Yet soon enough Hirst is assuring readers that "the quality of Mrs. A. Topperwein (the champion woman shot of the world), that captivated and charmed us all was not so much her wonderful shooting as her wholesome and unaffected womanliness" (25). Trapshooting, in fact, affords a range of opportunities for balancing one's gender instincts: "There is something, too, in learning to control the *unladylike* desire to use—well, emphatic expletives—and the *ladylike* inclination to cry when the birds are particularly stubborn, and learning to take it all like a man, or a gentleman, rather, as part of the game" (25).

Another contributor to the pamphlet, Ruth Alexander Pepple of Erie, Kansas, reaches back for precedents to the Revolutionary War: "On the 28th of June, at Monmouth, in the year 1778, when Mollie Pitcher, unmindful of the shot and shell, of the turmoil and tribulation surrounding her, took a firm stand at the breech of her martyred husband's cannon and helped save the day for the American forces—little thought she that her brave act established a precedent to be followed far down through the years to come by women of the nation she had so gloriously assisted" (33). For her, Pitcher's natural descendants are "women of to-day, who, having an inherent love for out-of-door recreation with the gun, have also had the moral courage and stamina to break loose from conventionalities and frivolities and lead the life of the even-balanced, calm and steady-nerved individual" (33). By claiming Pitcher as a foremother and exemplar, Pepple thus explicitly links armed women with warfare and the expression of patriotism.

When Pepple applauds the comradeship that can spring up between a husband and a wife who go shooting together, she finally adverts to the racial reasons for women to bear arms: "By making trapshooting the initial step toward strengthening mind and body, women may fire another shot that will be heard and recognized as the 'opening gun' of a campaign for a better, stronger, healthier and more influential race" (35). Even someone like Mrs. J. H. Martin, of Wilmington, Delaware, who confesses that "I do not make good scores," can still maintain that "I feel like I've spent my money to good advantage. . . . Nerves and neuralgia are no longer troubling me since I've learned to shoot" (42). In early twentieth-century America, nerves and neuralgia were generally understood to be race-weakening symptoms, typical of the overcivilized, urban woman.

Women were so visible in trapshooting at this time that some publicity treated them as honorary men. A 1918 pamphlet published by the Interstate Trapshooting Association opened with the headline "Smashing the clay birds—a real man's sport." Yet more than half of the trapshooters depicted were female. The pamphlet noted that the association was open to "any white man or woman."[44]

Although many women gravitated toward trapshooting, not every woman agreed that bloodshed was odious and hunting costumes too unflattering. Many saw clear eugenic advantages to hunting that outweighed any minor matters of wardrobe. Race and the topic of racial hygiene erupted into explicit discussions in the late nineteenth-century magazine articles on why women should hunt. For instance, a caption in a 1904 issue of *Outdoor Life* read, "The Gun an Important Factor in the Saving of the American Race." The accompanying photo showed a man and a woman, shotguns at the ready, in the woods, presumably on the verge of bagging some game. As Daniel Justin Herman notes, the vigor that Theodore Roosevelt promoted as a means of averting "race suicide" found its expression among many women in the sport of hunting.

Frontier women had been hunting for sustenance on the frontier since the eighteenth century. Daniel Boone's wife, for example, once shot a deer in his absence. Yet hunting for sport among upper-class American women was something new. By the late nineteenth century, it had become a staple of outdoor magazines.[45] The July 1896 issue of *Outing* magazine had an article by Mary Trowbridge Townsend, "A Night with the White Goats." The description in the table of contents read, "Comparatively few of our readers know anything about the curious white antelope-goat of the Western mountains. How one plucky woman scaled the barren peaks and secured her prize."[46] The December 1909 cover of *Recreation* magazine featured a woman in a sweater with a hunting gun slung over her shoulder. Outdoor magazines contained ads for hunting guns modeled by women. Strikingly, none of the ads called attention to the fact that they featured a woman rather than the more traditional male model. The women in these ads were not sex objects. Rather, they were sturdy, attractive middle-class women looking to enjoy a wholesome day in the out-of-doors.

Turn-of-the-century newspapers also noted the attraction that western hunting had for women. Theodore Roosevelt had strengthened popular associations of the West with wildness, freedom, and adventure, in opposition to the soul-deadening industrialization of the East. This, thought many commentators, made it an ideal place for women to engage in racially strengthening exercise.[47] A 1903 *Denver Post* article, "Monster Buck Trophy of Pueblo Huntress," reported that "the taking out of permits by women has lost its novelty in the office of the county clerk. Two weeks ago the officials had much ado to keep from gently laughing. There is no laughing now, for several of the buckskined [*sic*] Dianas who were scoffed at have sent in braces of grouse, saddles of venison and juicy bear steaks."[48] At times this activity was explicitly connected to Roosevelt's injunction that people engage in strenuous living. In 1905, the *St. Louis Globe Democrat* featured an article on the bear-hunting craze; its subtitle read, "Strenuous and Dangerous Form of Recreation Appeals to Many Dianas." As the article went on to point out,

> Many Eastern . . . women have turned to bear hunting in the Rocky Mountains as the most fascinating and health-giving of sports. Before the advent of the "athletic girl" women hunters of big game were almost unknown in the Rocky Mountains. But to-day they are to be seen in constantly increasing numbers. Society women from the East, whose health has been impaired by too great a devotion to social duties, or whose lungs are so weak as to necessitate the seeking of purer air, have succumbed to the glamour of the chase, and unite with President Roosevelt in declaring bear hunting "bully."
>
> The new sport for women seems to unite those health-giving and exciting qualities for which the girls of a strenuous age are looking.[49]

In a 1904 issue of *Outdoor Life* magazine, Mrs. Francis Trevelyan Miller emphasized how debilitating life in urban America had become: "Herded life stunts nature and dwarfs the character. The most appalling danger in modern Americanism is the tendency to accumulate in the cities and to neglect the greater country. This huddling is not only unsanitary, but deteriorating, the moral conditions not being conducive to the desired excellency in American habits."[50] The solution to the problem of herding, which "breeds pallid faces and weakened constitutions" (15), is suggested by the accompanying photograph of two women hunting, the caption for which reads, "The Gun an Important Factor in the Saving of the American Race." With the same air of romanticization that made Wild West shows popular and ensured the success of Owen Wister's *The Virginian* (1902), Miller writes that "it is the West that teaches the love of nature, the greatest of all life lessons" (16).

Finally, Miller uses martial metaphors to suggest the imperative that both genders commune with nature. While "it is the outdoor life that is making manhood, for he who lives close to the earth absorbs its generous virtue and strengthens the moral with the physical" (16), women's changing circumstances mandate their participation in the hunting sports. "Since woman entered the battle for mercantile supremacy, she, too, is driven by necessity to the great sanitorium of the woods, stretching herself for a little while upon the earth, that she may soon again return to the conflict to feel the thrill of its glad rush, to listen to its shoutings, to share its sweat and dust, and to give and take blows with the lustiest" (16). There is no suggestion that women should be anything but "thrilled" about going at it with the lustiest.

EASTERN SHOOTING, WESTERN IMAGERY

Of all the women shooters who became celebrities in the late nineteenth century and the first half of the twentieth, none could match the enduring public recognition of Annie Oakley, who performed in Buffalo Bill's Wild West.[51] Amid the dozens, if not hundreds, of female sharpshooters who became famous in Wild West shows, Oakley was an extraordinary phenomenon. Nevertheless, as a group, the women of the staged "Wild West," and the press reports about them, created a powerful archetype of the armed western woman as skilled at using firearms, yet not violent, exotically different in her western attire, yet emphatically white and domestic.

The mythology of the West that Theodore Roosevelt and Owen Wister helped to shape was centered on a simple, harsh land where easterners could be healed of the ill effects of overcivilization. This romantic realm was epitomized by the Wild West shows, which became popular in the 1880s. Eastern audiences could read about armed western women in nonfiction books about the settling of the West and in dime novels about the exploits of western heroes and heroines; they could see them in action by attending western-themed melodramas and Wild West shows. In these shows, which highlighted a multicultural West in which ethnic warfare was necessary for survival, the female shooter became a star. How did she surmount the contradictions of her position? Given the ubiquity of armed dime-novel heroines with questionable sexual and racial backgrounds, as well as of western celebrities with even more dubious morals, such as Calamity Jane, how was it possible for Wild West show women to reenact life on the frontier while remaining cute and feminine?

The white armed woman in the Wild West show needed to negotiate a complex array of public expectations about white womanhood, feminism, and the feared rise of nonwhite people. As Louise Michele Newman notes, from the 1870s through 1920, observers writing in such periodicals as *Harper's*, *Atlantic Monthly*, and the *Nation* tied the growth in public roles for white women and their demands for political equality to troubling racial questions: How was the declining birthrate among white women linked to the increase in the populations of people of color? Did increased rights for white women mean a loss for the white race and a gain for other races?[52] Even as the woman's movement gained more publicity and influence in the 1870s and 1880s, the armed women in the Wild West shows had to provide an exemplar of dutiful femininity in order to succeed with the public.

The women of the Wild West shows performed against a cultural backdrop of popular paintings, profiles, and dime novels focused on the armed female settler, who was variously represented as "Prairie Madonna," as race mother, and, in less palatable form, as bad woman. Annette Stott has pointed out that the paintings and prints of early westward expansion tend to portray women as Prairie Madonnas—gentle, submissive, pious exemplars, whose role it was to ensure that their men did not drift toward wildness on the frontier. According to Stott, "During the period of greatest trans-Mississippi emigration, 1840–1890, the Prairie Madonna image encouraged men and women of western European descent to move west as families by reassuring them that they could maintain the separate spheres of gender identity and preserve American culture as they knew it."[53] At this time, women of the West were often presented as the victims of violence, never as the perpetrators. However, the Prairie Madonnas began disappearing as the century wore to a close, to be replaced by tougher "pioneer women." The transformation, which reached its apotheosis in the 1920s, resulted in such statues as August Leimbach's *The Madonna of the Trail* (1928), which was commissioned by the Daughters of the American Revolution, and which featured a large, mature woman holding a baby in one arm, with a boy clutching her skirts and a rifle tucked under the other arm. Despite the title, which suggested earlier depictions, there was nothing gentle or submissive about this madonna. The popularity of the image can be seen in oil baron Ernest W. Marland's 1926 commission for a statue titled *Pioneer Woman*. Marland commissioned twelve sculptures, which toured the United States and were voted on by viewers. The winning entry was cast in a nineteen-foot monument for Marland's hometown, Ponca City, Oklahoma. Of the twelve sculptures, five featured women carrying rifles (a sixth carried a hatchet), and every one of the women carried a baby as well.

The armed pioneer woman provided an image of Anglo-Saxon strength in contrast with the weak women of late nineteenth-century America, who many feared were on the verge of committing "race suicide" through their sickly delicacy. A popular text published in 1878, William W. Fowler's *Woman on the American Frontier: A Valuable and Authentic History of the Heroism, Privations, Captivities, Trials, and Noble Lives and Deaths of the "Pioneer Mothers of the Republic,"* offers a good example of the popularization of the image of the frontierswoman. In it, Fowler celebrates pioneer women for sharing with their husbands "the instincts, the gifts, and motive power of the most energetic race the world has ever seen—the Anglo-Saxon."[54] These women, according to Fowler, provide a reproachful contrast: "quite unlike her delicate sisters of modern days," they were "hardened by exercise in the open air" (160). In his narrative, Fowler describes how "women with muskets at their side lulled their babies to sleep" (81). No matter how maternal these women might have been, they were tough, as evidenced by Mrs. Noble, who in 1644 killed a moose to feed her children, or the Kentucky woman who in 1792 bit a musket ball into pieces in order to shoot more Indians, or Miss Hannah Fox, an early Rhode Island settler, who was forced to saw off her own hand with a dull knife in order to escape freezing to death while wedged under a tree (73). No matter how many Indians they killed, Fowler's pioneer heroines never left their feminine side behind: "In these women of the Revolution were blended at once the heroine and the 'Ministering Angel'" (130). But, no matter how angelic they may have been

August Leimbach made twelve reproductions of this popular statue, titled *The Madonna of the Trail*. Note the rifle tucked under the mother's arm and the toddler leaning against the gun as he clutches his mother's skirts. Photo courtesy of Brian Gadbery.

to their families, these women led lives surrounded by violence and were clearly capable of dealing death when need be.

The pioneer women described by Fowler, though strong and pure, still seemed like impossibly rugged figures: "The life of the pioneer woman, from the earliest times, was, and now is, to a large extent, a military one. She was forced to learn a soldier's habits and a soldier's virtues . . . averting danger with all of a woman's fertility of resource, and meeting it with all the courage of a man" (179). In other words, she was a far cry from the most famous armed woman of the Wild West show, a sweet, cute, pliable figure in whose hands the gun seemed not so much an instrument of death as a playful implement.

While Fowler linked the strength and success of pioneer women to their Anglo-Saxon heritage, a series of popular accounts published in the late nineteenth century laid the blame for female misbehavior on the frontier to racial deficiencies. The mixed racial backgrounds, compromised sexual status, and violence of armed female characters in dime novels were often thematically interrelated. The names of the characters clearly indicated their nature: "Hurricane Nell," "Rowdy Kate," "Bowie Knife Bessie," "Wild Edna," and "Phantom Moll."[55] These figures, as Teresa Jordan has pointed out, "venture into the rough and tumble frontier to seek vengeance for lost maidenhood or murdered parents."[56] In Ned Buntline's *Bob Woolf, the Border Ruffian; or, the Girl Dead-Shot*, a knowledgeable innkeeper says of Hurricane Nell, "Her whole life is dedicated to the one terrible object, *revenge*. She roams through the wilderness in various disguises, and every few weeks some one finds a dead outlaw, wi' her death mark upon him. . . . She comes and goes at will. No one dares to cross her path. She is a modest and pleasant companion, to those she fancies, but to her enemies she is an actual terror. Why, sir, once I seen her shoot a feller, in yonder, just for forcibly kissin' an Indian girl, 'ginst her will."[57] Hurricane Nell, as a victim of sexual violence herself, is clearly sensitive on this point.

The racial background of such characters is often ambiguous. In "Captain Crack-Shot, the Girl Brigand," the title character, the adopted daughter of "Mexican Mag," is described by an old scout as "a hummer! A reg'lar ourang-outang daredevil, wi' no more regard for law an' persons than the wildest cat thet ever held a jubilee in ther Arcadian forests o' yore!"[58] In this description, there is little to distinguish between Mexicans, wildcats, and "ourang-outangs."

Although the dime-novel characters have tainted pasts, they are not necessarily criminal. Fourteen-year-old Wild Jeannette, the Maid of the Gold

Hills, is wild and disheveled: "Her features and complexion were of a Spanish type, and yet, had she been seen upon the streets of a great city as she looked in that mountain pass, she would have been taken for a little gypsy. Her garments, though made of some coarse fabric, and after the style of a half-civilized Indian girl, were clean and tidy. Her little brown feet and round, shapely ankles were bare."[59] Jeannette is able to kill bears and shoot robbers in the face. She has been raised by a taxidermist, who took her "from the sin and wickedness of a mining camp, years before, where her mother, a beautiful, gifted, but broken-hearted woman, had yielded up her life, begging of the kind-hearted naturalist to see that her little Jeannette was cared for." Jeannette may not be wicked herself, but she is far from civilized.

Fathers in these stories sometimes collaborate with their daughters in acts of terrible violence. In Ned Buntline's "Merciless Ben the Hair-Lifter: A Story of the Far South-West," Ben's daughter, Anna, joins him in killing Indians: "With a whisper to his girl to begin on the right, he would take the left, the Hair-Lifter fired, and at the flash of his gun Anna's Winchester spoke out with its sharp voice of death."[60] Anna's mother is nowhere in sight: the girl characters of dime novels are generally free from the civilizing influence of a white woman.

The linkages that dime-novel authors made between the sexual misdeeds, violence, and mixed racial backgrounds of their heroines were echoed in popular descriptions of the most famous living (or recently deceased) frontierswomen of the time. The notorious armed robber and gang leader Belle Starr, with whom Wild West show woman Annie Oakley was often favorably compared, provides a case in point. From the moment that Belle Starr's death became known to the public in 1889, discussions of "the bandit queen," as she was quickly dubbed in the popular press, focused on her ethnic identity. Outlaw Cole Younger asserted in his 1903 autobiography that "Belle Starr was not a Cherokee."[61] Captain Kit Dalton, who, in the subtitle of his 1914 tell-all memoir, *Under the Black Flag*, identified himself as *A Confederate Soldier: A Guerrilla Captain under the Fearless Leader Quantrell, and a Border Outlaw for Seventeen Years*, wrote that "Belle Starr was the unfortunate combination of a Cherokee squaw and a *pale face* lady of the upper tendum—a savage of the bloodiest type; a lady of tender emotions; a finished graduate of Carlisle University and a typical daughter of the plains." To Dalton, Starr's "savage" blood was clearly to blame for her criminal behavior, which was chronic and dramatic.[62] A popular 1898 account of Western life described Starr as a "champion and leader of robbers; herself a

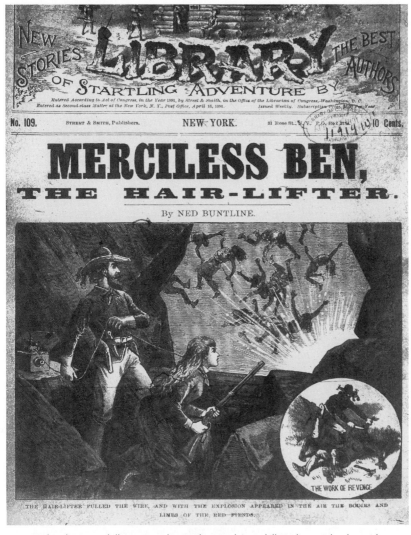

NEW STORIES LIBRARY OF STARTLING ADVENTURE BY THE BEST AUTHORS

Entered According to Act of Congress, in the Year 1901, by Street & Smith, in the Office of the Librarian of Congress, Washington, D. C.
Entered as Second-class Matter at the New York, N. Y., Post Office, April 16, 1891.   Issued Weekly.   Subscription $2.50 per Year.

No. 109.   STREET & SMITH, Publishers.   NEW YORK.   31 Rose St., N. Y. P.O. Box 2734   10 Cents.

MERCILESS BEN,
THE HAIR-LIFTER.
By NED BUNTLINE.

THE HAIR-LIFTER PULLED THE WIRE, AND WITH THE EXPLOSION APPEARED IN THE AIR THE BODIES AND LIMBS OF THE RED—FIENDS.

THE WORK OF REVENGE

In this dime-novel illustration, the neatly attired Anna kills Indians right alongside her father. Ned Buntline, "Merciless Ben the Hair-Lifter: A Story of the Far South-West," *Street and Smith's New York Weekly*, March 6, 1882.

sure shot and a murderess. . . . During her career she is supposed to have directed, from the background, many of the most daring acts of the Spaniard and numerous other desperate gangs."[63] Having been raised in a wealthy Missouri family, she sometimes insisted that men perform the small courtesies for her due any lady—such as picking up her hat when it fell off her head. However, she made her request "with telling oaths" and while holding a pistol on the ill-mannered offenders."[64] Belle Starr, in this portrayal, could only extract at gunpoint the courtesies due a respectable lady.

While untamed, violent Western women were negatively represented in the popular press, at least one such woman fought back, taking advantage of the widespread interest in frontier life and working hard to craft her own image. She did this despite being condemned by many of her contemporaries for what a later biographer called "her dissolute behavior, including drunken sprees and alcoholism, her liaisons with numerous male companions called 'husbands' whom she regularly deserted, her occasional prostitution, and her generally disruptive activities."[65]

In fact, Calamity Jane forged a somewhat successful career representing herself as an icon of armed western womanhood. In the summer of 1876, Martha Jane Cannary, also known as Calamity Jane, rode into Deadwood, South Dakota, to become (in legend, at least) the lover of Wild Bill Hickok and a rider for the pony express, delivering the U.S. mail between Deadwood and Custer. Featured in dime novels[66] and in Wild West shows, she peddled her autobiography, *Life and Adventures of Calamity Jane, by Herself* (1896), while traveling from town to town. In her autobiography, she represented herself as tough and free from social constraints. Cannary writes that by the time she was thirteen, when her family emigrated from Missouri to Montana, "the greater portion of my time was spent in hunting along with the men and hunters of the party, in fact I was at all times with the men when there was excitement and adventures to be had. By the time we reached Virginia City I was considered a remarkable good shot and a fearless rider for a girl my age."[67] The rest of the short work details her adventures cross-dressing as a scout for General Custer ("It was a bit awkward at first but I soon got to be perfectly at home in men's clothes" [125]), her achievements on the worst routes ("It was considered the most dangerous route in the Hills, but as my reputation as a rider and quick shot was well known, I was molested very little" [125]), and her holding captive, with the help of a meat cleaver, the killer of Wild Bill Hickok. These lurid autobiographical details enhanced the image of the armed woman prevalent in dime novels, but they seemed to cast doubt on more wholesome representations of armed women. The wildness of the frontier could not always be contained by women—in fact, Belle Starr and Calamity Jane clearly preferred to embrace the wildness rather than stamp it out.

Against the backdrop of these often tough, masculine, not-quite-white western women, the female sharpshooters of the Wild West shows emerged. As Gail Bederman has observed, the discourse about civilization

Martha Jane Cannary, also known as Calamity Jane, refused to conform to conventional notions of femininity. Courtesy Colorado Historical Society (BPF F 5812)

Calamity Jane wears a conservative dress and uses her pistols to protect a wounded man in this illustration from a dime novel. Reckless Ralph, "The Queen of the Plains; or, Calamity Jane," *Street & Smith*, no. 130, September 30, 1891.

that began to develop in the late nineteenth century stressed the difference, in advanced civilizations, between men and women: "Savage (that is, non-white) men and women were believed to be almost identical, but men and women of the civilized races had evolved pronounced sexual differences."[68] The cowgirls and female sharpshooters of the Wild West shows appeared to be far less hard bitten than their pioneer foremothers. Moreover, the most successful stars left their audiences in no doubt that they were white, civilized women and that their behavior could not be confused with that of either men or savages.

Although the show performers were sometimes made into characters in dime novels,[69] they generally represented themselves—and were represented in the press—as completely wholesome. Thus, they managed to thoroughly sanitize the image the Western armed woman. Though they may have looked like the heroines of lurid fiction, with their buckskins and fringes, the West they inhabited was a much cleaner, simpler place than that of the dime novels. Unlike Hurricane Nell and her cohorts, they never had to defend Indian girls against rape by settlers. In fact, there was rarely more than a hint that the weapons they so expertly handled could be used for violent means.

The show performers also divorced the image of the armed woman from that of the pioneer mother, Fowler's "women with muskets at their side [who] lulled their babies to sleep." Although the most successful female sharpshooters packaged themselves as thoroughly domestic, they tended to be childless. In the publicity materials of one famous sharpshooter, guns were even presented as a substitute for babies. May Manning Lillie, a Smith-educated Philadelphia debutante and Quaker, initially disliked the Kansas ranch life to which her husband, Pawnee Bill, introduced her following their 1886 wedding. But when her first child died at only six weeks of age, and she "learned that [she] could never bear another child," she "took an interest with [her] husband in western affairs." Thereafter, as a gushing newspaper profile put it, "her recitals and soirees became target matches with the rifle and six-shooter."[70] Within months of her tragedy, when Pawnee Bill's Great Wild West Show opened for the first time in 1887, she debuted as a sharpshooter.[71] Soon, she was being billed as "the greatest Lady Horseback Rifle-shot of the World" in the show's promotional material.[72] May Lillie became quite famous, but she suffered an injury during her husband's shooting act in 1899 that resulted in the amputation of two fingers. Her career as a markswoman ended there.

The racial slippage that occurred in some early Wild West advertising soon disappeared. For example, May Lillie's parents were horrified, in 1888, to see their daughter's picture in the show paper and to find May described there as an Indian girl.[73] The advertisement did not reappear. As time went on, the racial identities of the Wild West show women became clearer, and none was more explicitly white than the iconic Annie Oakley of Buffalo Bill's Wild West. A comparison of Oakley and her less remembered (and more racially ambiguous) rival, Lillian Smith, provides a perfect opportunity to explore the peculiar relationship between women, guns, and race, made manifest through performance. Oakley presented herself as a model of Anglo-American womanhood by sewing her own costumes and expressing her opposition to female suffrage. On the other hand, when Smith, who was dark skinned and plump, eventually left Buffalo Bill's show, she repackaged herself for a competing show as a Native American, the Sioux princess Wenona. Oakley's whiteness and ladylike behavior clearly set her apart from the less savory examples of armed women that were floating around popular culture.

Annie Oakley and Lillian Smith became famous at a time when exhibition shooting was a wildly popular sport, and it was probably the first sport that was open to women on equal terms with men.[74] Champion shooters were plentiful in the 1870s and 1880s, and along with men like Captain Adam H. Bogardus, who initially became prominent in 1869, were women like Mrs. John Ruth, who made a name for herself in 1880 with exhibition shooting in Deerfoot Park in New York City. Mrs. Ruth broke glass balls while holding her six-pound pistol "sideways and upside down and then stood with her back to the target, took aim in a small mirror, and shot a ball swinging back and forth on a string."[75] The program for Cummins' Wild West Indian Congress of 1903 lists "Miss Hartzell, Champion Rifle Shot of the World."[76]

What distinguished Annie Oakley was that she presented herself as a Victorian lady who also happened to be an expert markswoman. Oakley was born Phoebe Ann Moses to a poor Ohio farm family in 1860; as a child, she helped support her family through shooting game and selling it to a grocery store. Her marriage to Frank Butler, a sharpshooter whom she beat in a Cincinnati contest, spurred her development as a markswoman. She and Frank, her manager, traveled with the Sells Brothers Circus as a husband-and-wife act, but she did not become internationally famous until she began performing for Buffalo Bill's Wild West in 1885, stepping in as a replacement for Captain Adam H. Bogardus.

The combination of Annie Oakley, who made shooting seem a palatable, wholesome sport, and deemphasized the violent possibilities of guns, and William F. Cody, who made the bloody drama of Western conquest into family entertainment, was an apt one. In 1883, Cody opened his first Wild West show.[77] Nearly from the beginning, the shows were extremely popular: in 1885 over a million people attended Buffalo Bill's shows. The early shows featured reenactments of historical events, such as an Indian attack on the Deadwood stagecoach, and exhibitions of western skills, such as rop-

Annie Oakley appeared girlish and demure in her publicity shots. Here, her femininity seems uncompromised by the firearms with which she surrounds herself. Buffalo Bill Historical Center, Cody, Wyoming; Vincent Mercaldo Collection; P.71.351.3.

Annie Oakley believed that every woman should know how to use a gun.
She personally taught 15,000 women to shoot. Buffalo Bill Historical Center,
Cody, Wyoming; Gift of Guthrie L. and Euradean Moses Dowler, the great-niece
of Annie Oakley; P.69.1954.

ing and riding wild bison and riding wild Texas steers. Within two years of the opening of Cody's extravaganza, over fifty rival shows had imitated its features. Perhaps the most famous performer in Buffalo Bill's Wild West was Oakley, who, by turning the shooting into a harmless sport, desensitized audiences to the violence inherent in "taming" the West.[78] Oakley relieved audience anxiety about firearms, but she also epitomized the "civilization" that the Wild West shows and world's fairs promoted. As historian Robert W. Rydell has pointed out, to "alleviate the intense and widespread anxiety that pervaded the United States, the directors of the expositions offered millions of fairgoers an opportunity to reaffirm their collective national identity in an updated synthesis of progress and white supremacy."[79]

Oakley signaled her commitment to maintaining ladylike behavior at every turn. She never wore pants onstage, always wore her hair long, and rode sidesaddle; she publicly stated that riding astride was "a horrid idea."[80] She made most of her own costumes and spent hours sitting in her tent between shows, embroidering. Oakley neither smoked, drank, gambled, nor cursed. She told newspapers that "there is nothing so detestable as a bloomer costume. Do not think that I like women to go in for sport so that they neglect their homes. I don't like bloomers or bloomer women."[81] She was outraged when people saw her as a "new woman." Her act was clean cut and wholesome; she often included her manager-husband, to whom she remained married for the rest of her life, and their dog in performances. Oakley was instrumental not only in attracting women to the Wild West show but also in making shooting appear something that even a lady could comfortably do. Oakley's trademark skip and pout, her use of her dog and her husband in her act, and even her childlessness helped her present herself as a dutiful daughter with a spunky side. To add to the impression of her being girlish, her marriage to Frank Butler was framed as a match between a teenager and a much older man (although in her autobiography she claimed that she had been fifteen when they met and sixteen when they married; in fact, she was about twenty-two to her husband's thirty-something when they married).[82]

Oakley's act embraced a version of pioneer life that was highly genteel. Unlike Fowler's version of the frontier, Oakley's was not a wilderness where women killed wolves in tooth-and-nail combat, sawed off their own hands to free themselves from traps, or engaged in any of the other activities that marked the truly hardy pioneer woman. Oakley's act separated her, as well, from the good-hearted but uncontrollable women of dime novels—she was no "Rowdy Kate" or "Wild Edna." Although frontier life was generally acknowledged to be rough, and frontier men were widely regarded as rugged in proportion, women were supposed to remain ladylike, and it was this aspect of western settlement that Oakley stressed. Even the women who traveled and settled along the Overland Trail, whose exploits were dramatized in Buffalo Bill's Wild West, were expected to maintain their feminine qualities. As historian John Mack Faragher has written, the difference in the "projected and perceived views of the emigrants" on gender expectations "was the difference between masculine self-indulgence on the one hand and feminine self-denial on the other. Swearing, drinking, and the good times of hunting, fishing and card-playing were all marks of an indulgent type. Patience, propriety, morality, and godliness—seemingly the virtues of women—were a counterpoint to male worldliness."[83] Women rode side-saddle on the trail, for those who mounted a regular saddle found themselves the object of ridicule. Few women on the frontier adopted the dress reform of a bloomer costume, even faced with the complete impracticality of floor-length dresses. Oakley's talent was to make female pioneer life look fun and easy, and she made shooting seem like a game, rather than a violent act.

However, Oakley felt threatened to the point of quitting the Wild West show by the appearance of the woman who was her chief shooting rival. Lillian Smith, whom Buffalo Bill dubbed "the Champion Rifle Shot of the World," often received equal billing with Oakley and captured an equal amount of attention from reviewers. Smith joined the show in 1884, and two years later an article in the St. Louis Globe Democrat introduced her as the "famous California huntress," who went by the title "The California Girl." The reviewer gushed: "Miss Lillian Smith, fifteen years old, who is with the Buffalo Bill Wild West, has a most remarkable record for a child of her years. It reads like a romance, and many of her feats with the rifle are marvelous."[84] (A New York Times article in 1884 put her age at twelve; in fact, she was born on February 3, 1871).[85] Smith's feats included using a pair of lever-action Winchester rifles to hit a plate thirty times in fifteen seconds and breaking ten glass balls on strings swinging from a pole, then shooting the strings from the pole.[86]

According to the Wild West show program, Smith had begun shooting at age seven, "when she expressed herself as dissatisfied with 'dolls,' and wanted a 'little rifle.'" Her early rejection of traditional femininity stood in direct contrast to Oakley's embrace of pure womanhood; according to Oakley's official biography, she had taken to using a gun to help support her family, not from any lack of interest in girlish things. Smith seemed to take particular pleasure in competing directly with men; as noted in the program, at a turkey shoot in 1883 in Benito County, California, "Lillian reportedly killed so many turkeys that the managers arranged with her 'to drop out and give the boys a chance at the turkeys, too.'"[87] An 1886 review in the *Republican* commented that "this is the sort of girl to best illustrate the women's rights business."[88] Oakley, however, publicly declared her opposition to women's suffrage.

Some publications attempted to fit Smith into a more ladylike mold. *Brick Pomeroy's Democrat*, which often published unchanged, as journalism, the public relations materials issued by the Wild West show, described Smith as being "as modest and beautiful as she is accomplished with her single-barreled repeating rifle."[89] This rhetoric echoed journalism about female shooters from Martha Maxwell to Annie Oakley. In the article's illustration, Smith wears a lace collar, and her hair is swept up in curls under a feathered hat. However, Oakley had a major advantage over Smith when it came to public relations. Smith was defined as Indian by the racial laws of her time; the 1880 California census records showed an I, for Indian, rather than a W, for white, beside Smith's name in the personal-description column.[90]

Moreover, not everyone agreed that Smith was "as modest and beautiful" as *Brick Pomeroy's Democrat* made her out to be. Two of Annie Oakley's recent biographers, Shirl Kasper and Glenda Riley, point up the vulgarity of Smith's behavior. Kasper approvingly says that Oakley "didn't brag boldly like Lillian Smith."[91] She mentions rumors that Smith cheated (although both biographers acknowledge Smith's great skill with a rifle). Riley writes that the "stout and vocal Lillian Smith" was criticized by Annie Oakley for her "shoddy work, poor grammar, and what Oakley later called her 'ample figure.'" As Riley notes, Smith "boasted of her skills, dressed in a less-than-modest fashion, and fraternized with the men in the Wild West troupe."[92] Riley cites Oakley's rivalry with Smith as the reason Oakley and her husband left Buffalo Bill's show following the London visit in 1887. Smith had gained press coverage for demonstrating the mechanism of her Winchester repeating rifle to the Prince of Wales and to Queen Victoria; in fact, the press lavished much more attention on Smith than on Oakley throughout the visit.[93]

Lillian Smith did not last with the show, perhaps because of the romantic complications in which she became entangled. An 1889 letter home from C. L. Daily, one of the cowboys with the show, reported that "Jim Kid, my tent mate, has been having a great time lately. He received a letter a few days ago saying that his wife (Lillian Smith) had gone off with another cow-boy, Bill Cook, by name, half white and half Indian. He was with the show last year and was a great friend of Kid's. When Jim got the letter, he almost went crazy . . . He thinks an awful sight of Smith."[94] Smith left the show that year, the same year that Oakley rejoined the show.[95] She went on to marry three more times; one of her husbands was Eagle Shirt, a Sioux performer with the Millers' 101 Ranch Wild West shows.

Smith resurfaced in Pawnee Bill's Historic Wild West and Great Far East and Cummins' Indian Congress and Wildest West as "Winsome Wenona, the Wonder Woman Shot of the World." In the photograph accompanying Pawnee Bill's publicity for Wenona, the former Smith, dressed in a feath-ered buckskin costume, has very dark skin and straight hair in braids.[96] When Wenona died, her *Billboard* obituary parroted the information pro-vided in her Pawnee Bill show biography.[97] But the accounts of Smith's life varied considerably over the years. The publicity for Pawnee Bill depicted her as "a Sioux Indian girl and the daughter of one of the most prominent chiefs of that nation. . . . Her dress is at all times that of the Siouxs [sic] and their language she prefers to that of ours."[98] A later version of her life described her as the child of a Delaware lighthouse keeper who relocated to California for the sake of Lillian's shooting career; another account de-scribed her as the daughter of Crazy Snake, a Sioux chief; and yet another account claimed that she was the daughter of a woman who had been taken prisoner by the Sioux after their attack on a westward emigrant train.[99]

Annie Oakley toured with Pawnee Bill's show in 1888 but did not over-lap with Smith. In contrast to Smith, who ran off with a "half-breed" while with Buffalo Bill's show, and who finally embraced an Indian identity, Oak-ley was horrified by the idea of interracial romance. She was appalled when Pawnee Bill advertised the marriage of the Kaw Indian chief Wah-Ki-Kaw and the white woman Annie Harris. "An Indian had the nerve to become en-gaged to a non-descript," she wrote in her autobiography; "so the wedding was advertised."[100] When Oakley posed in Indian costume for a postcard, she took care that her skin remained white and that her outfit looked as though it belonged at a costume ball. It is true that she was "adopted" by the Sioux chief Sitting Bull, who dubbed her "Little Miss Sure Shot." However, though the Wild West press literature made much of this adoption, Sitting Bull's gesture was based on his first brief meeting with her—and Oakley herself treated the whole affair as an amusing joke.[101] While Annie Oakley firmly situated herself within the ranks of the cowboys, Smith drifted from whiteness into an Indian identity and from there out of history.

Descriptions of Smith's behavior suggest that she was unwilling to embrace the model of Victorian womanhood on which Oakley built her career. An article in Oakley's scrapbook from the *Sacramento Record Union* commented unfavorably on Smith's language. The specimens it quoted from Lillian's days as a preteen sharpshooter included such things as "Swab off the target, pap, and let me bang de eye," and "Swing de apple dere, young fellers, an' let me bust his skin."[102] Unlike Oakley, who always wore carefully hand-sewn outfits, Smith appeared at shooting matches attired in such getups as a white summer dress "incongruously accompanied by a yellow silk Mexican sash and a plug hat," as one newspaper article had it.[103] Perhaps slipping out of the strictures of genteel Anglo-Saxon femininity and into an Indian identity enabled Lillian Smith greater freedom, not just as a dark-skinned person but also as an unconventional woman.

There are many reasons for Oakley's survival and Smith's oblivion. Oakley was a consummate publicist and spent a great deal of time polishing her image and networking with celebrities. The rumors about Smith's cheating, if well founded, could have certainly threatened her image. Michael Wallis, a historian of the 101 Ranch, where Smith ended her days, asserts that many of Smith's and Oakley's contemporaries thought that Smith was the superior shooter by far.[104] Yet it is also possible that Oakley, with her prim and proper image and her wholesome appeal, could more effectively sell the idea of women and guns to a mass audience than could the dark-skinned, less genteel, and vocal Smith. No matter how many women were competing as sharpshooters in the late nineteenth century, the fact remained that American gun culture was a masculine domain. Only a real lady, like Oakley, could make guns safe for women while ensuring that the armed woman would uphold white supremacy.

LITTLE BIG GAME HUNTER

The influence of Annie Oakley extended beyond the Wild West shows to a new appreciation of shooting by women. Oakley herself taught 15,000 women to shoot.[105] Perhaps more important, she provided a model for other women who wanted to engage in armed adventures without encountering public disapproval. One woman, Osa (Leighty) Johnson, who first came to public attention in the 1920s, seems almost a spiritual descendant of Oakley. In 1910, she was a sixteen-year-old girl living in Chanute, Kansas, when world adventurer Martin Johnson came through town to show his "cannibal reel" of his trip through the Solomon Islands with Jack London. Osa married Martin within a few weeks, and she joined him for his trips to Africa and elsewhere. The Johnsons became the foremost adventure filmmakers of the 1920s and 1930s, and after Martin's death in a plane crash, Osa published a best-selling memoir of their time together, *I Married Adventure: The Lives and Adventures of Martin and Osa Johnson*.[106] In it, she details her life as Martin's helpmate, companion, and fellow shooter of wild game; she killed animals as they charged her camera-wielding husband.

Although Osa grew up hunting rabbits with her father, her career as an armed woman, for whom shooting was both public and emblematic, began when Martin took her to visit Jack and Charmian London. "I've never felt as proud," she tells her readers, "nor have I ever seen Martin as proud as when Jack gave me his best gun."[107] Although Osa traveled and worked with Martin for twenty-six years as half of their filmmaking team, she presents herself as happiest in the role of helpmate. Writing of her first ocean crossing, she tells us of how the captain was impressed by her immunity from seasickness: "Everything brightened, and especially when it became apparent that the captain now regarded me as a right and good companion for Martin. Nothing more than this could I ask of either heaven or earth, and cannibals and snakes became mere trifles to take in my stride. At least, so I thought" (111). Although she and her husband spend years among Africans and Pacific Islanders, exposure by no means leads to cultural sensitivity on her part: "It was incredible to me that anywhere in the world there could be wilder, more vicious-looking people" (112). Indeed, she often barely regards those she encounters as human: "We saw peering at us men whose black faces were so seamed and hideous, it was hard to believe they were men at all" (115).

At first, she keeps an automatic to protect herself against the indigenous peoples she encounters. On one expedition, she writes, there were "four white men, twenty-six trustworthy natives and myself, all armed with repeating rifles and automatic pistols" (138). As always, she stresses her white womanhood in the context of the white male and Solomon Islander population. In recalling their time in Borneo, she contrasts her fussy, if armed, femininity with Martin's masculine sense of purpose: "A man of unerring singleness of purpose, he used his energies for the things that really counted. While I fussed about the house—quite as if we were settling down for at least a year—cleaning it, reorganizing it, routing the deadly scorpions out of the corners, teaching the cook some of the dishes which I knew were good for Martin, and between times prowling around the garden with my .22 and polishing off the somewhat too numerous snakes, Martin was going quietly about arranging our first trip into the interior and learning Malay" (164). Here, shooting becomes as feminized as cleaning and arranging for the preparation of nutritious meals. Even when Osa's presence in the field is challenged, the challenge is issued to her husband, and it is he who responds:

> "She ought to be at home with her mother or in school," [the president of the British North Borneo Company] said impatiently, fixing me with a scowling, contemplative look. "Women weren't made for such hardships . . . you would take a woman, young and soft, your *wife*, sir, into such dangers! Why, you must be a madman!"
>
> Martin smiled. "I know that's how Osa looks, Sir West, soft and weak, but when you consider that she's the only woman who ever dared to cross Malatia down in the Solomons, and that she's even been where white men haven't dared to go among the savages of the Hebrides, then you'll realize that there's more to her than you'd first imagine." (165)

It goes without saying that both men are defining womanhood as white womanhood; what is more interesting is that Osa makes such a point of defining her adventures only as the actions of an extremely dutiful wife. Thus, rather than challenging conventional gender roles, she gladly accepts them, standing by her man under any and all circumstances. To improve her "none too certain aim" (168), she uses crocodiles for target practice while Martin takes pictures. When they get ready to embark on a Kenyan trip, they decide that in order to save the expense of hiring a white man to do the job, Osa will be the designated hunter. Martin's father, along on the trip, explains Martin's reluctance to take on this manly role: "'Funny thing,' father Johnson put in thoughtfully. 'Martin never was one for killing' . . . He scratched his head. 'And I guess I'm partly to blame for encouraging him to feel that way'" (205).

As it turns out, Osa sees her shooting as more than her wifely duty. She considers it a part of her responsibility as a white woman, as she explains when she tells us about the ideology of the great white hunter: "A native head-man or gun bearer is only as great as his white *bwana* (master) and . . . if a white hunter fails to live up to a certain standard, then his servant in turn becomes the laughing stock of his fellows. An African servant, Blaine had informed us, is faithful, humble and admiring, and asks but two things of his master: one, that he never run away; two, that he be a good shot" (214). Since Martin does not care for shooting, Osa has to uphold his racial duties and secure the respect of their servants.

At first, her feelings for the animals sometimes get in the way of her work as a hunter. After killing an antelope, she is unnerved:

> The soft eyes of the lovely creature were wide open and they seemed to look straight at me with reproach for taking his life. I turned away and burst into tears.
>
> "I wish I hadn't killed him!" I sobbed in Martin's neck, "he's so harmless—and so beautiful!" (219).

Indeed, when she is alone, she opts not to kill a gazelle, though she needs to feed her husband. But without "black boys now demanding meat" (223), she is free of her racial obligations. Nevertheless, she is soon using her gun for other purposes. As Martin films, Osa shoots a herd of charging buffaloes whom he has instructed their "boys" to herd toward the camera. Her killing a leopard is cause for celebration: "Our boys sang and danced with joy. The *bwana* and *bibi* (mistress) were becoming real hunters" (233).

Appearances could be deceiving. Pascal and Eleanor Imperato, the Johnsons' biographers, note that "Osa was routinely sent out with rifle in hand to provoke rhino, elephant, and even lion as Martin cranked the camera." However, they also point out that, though she was a skilled sharpshooter, there was always backup, usually in the form of Martin's assistant, a young American sharpshooter who was mentioned only in passing by either of the Johnsons in their public writings; he provided cover for both of them with a rifle—but off-camera. Osa's image as the armed, cute, diminutive white woman was too marketable for the Johnsons to dilute.[108] Reviews of the Johnsons' work tended to focus on Osa. Thus the *New York World* said of their 1923 film *Trailing African Wild Animals*, which climaxes with Osa's saving Martin from a charging elephant by killing it with her Winchester rifle: "Her distinctly feminine personality forms a striking contrast with the barbaric and quite evidently dangerous surroundings. . . . The young lady not only takes a very active part in the proceedings, and proves herself possessed of courage and no little skill with the rifle."[109] Martin wrote about this incident in a letter home: "I'll wager there is not another woman on earth who would have had the nerve to turn the crank [of the camera] in the face of what seemed like certain death, and then to have grabbed up a gun and have the presence of mind to shoot! There are mighty few men who would have done the same. I know I would have deserted the camera before she did and I would have run like hell."[110]

However, the Johnsons' films, as well as Osa's books, made sure to leave the impression that Osa was no threat to Martin's masculinity. In the Johnsons' most famous movie, *Simba* (1928), careful editing leads one to think that it is Osa, rather than her assistant, who brings down a charging lion with a couple of well-aimed shots. After local tribesmen laud her as a heroine, Osa is shown in camp rolling out piecrust with a bottle.[111] Thus, she is depicted as both a crack shot and a dab hand at cooking. Martin's father, appalled by the gender roles among the Africans they see, voices his opinion: "I thought it was only Indians made their women do all the work, like I saw when I was a young man back in the States. Why, these fellows are lazier than they were."[112] Yet Osa is able to maintain her white femininity only by redefining shooting as women's work.

Taking care to differentiate herself in appearance and behavior from the Africans, Osa makes it "an invariable rule to keep my hair well brushed and arranged, and to give as much attention to manicures and beauty treatments as though we were in the heart of New York rather than in the depths of so-called darkest Africa." She feels that she "owe[s] it to Martin to look my best no matter what the circumstances."[113] She can thereby remain visibly "civilized."

Osa is blissfully unself-conscious of her racism and of her glaring insensitivity. On a night when "a marrow-chilling drizzle" has forced her to have three extra blankets heaped on her husband and five on herself inside their tent, she proceeds "to worry about the black boys lying outdoors on the bare ground": "With no more cloth among the entire seventy-five than would make a pair of trousers, they simply built a fire and lay beside it, miserable and shaking." However, her concern only goes so far. As she reflects further, she realizes that the "boys" themselves are responsible for their condition: "I was both sorry for them and annoyed. If they hadn't been so lazy, they would have put up some grass shelters for themselves. The more I thought about this the more annoyed I became. They'd probably be down with pneumonia in the morning, but they'd get no sympathy from me" (243). When her husband orders that the porters be whipped because they seem to be malingering (their feet are bloody and they are dying of thirst), Osa sees the whippings as the porters' own fault and for their own good: "[Martin] was shocked to find their lips swollen with thirst and to learn that they had not filled their canteens. The order which Jerramani had passed on to the head-man of the Merus had been airily dismissed as a vagary of the white 'mbwana" (256).

In the calculus of the safari, black life is never as important as white money. This is evident when Osa reflects at the outset of a safari with two hundred black men: "We had been told, and also knew from experience, that before the end of the long and harsh trip a certain percentage of this number was almost sure to die. Picked carefully, these men always appeared to be of equal strength and fitness when we started out, but fevers, illnesses, accidents or wounds of one sort or another almost invariably took a toll. And even graver, if possible, than this responsibility was the one we owed to the Museum of Natural History, to George Eastman and to all the others who had invested confidence and money in our undertaking" (275). Finally, it turns out that even the skills that the porters have spent their lifetimes learning can be improved on by whites, as is illustrated when three Boy Scouts come to spend time with the Johnsons on safari: "The porters were quite awed by the boys; not merely because they were white, but because there was no native feat of skill at which the youngsters did not prove more proficient" (317). Osa's sense of racial superiority seems to have no bounds.

After her husband's death in a 1937 plane crash, Osa remained a celebrity. She produced a hugely successful line of plush animal toys called Osa Johnson's Pets, and a Burpee sweet pea variety was named after her. Her autobiography, a number-one national best-seller in 1940, sold half a million copies within its first year of publication. As Kenneth Cameron has written, the Johnsons "erased the Explorer's class; determinedly Midwestern plain 'Mr. And Mrs.,' they did without British-accented voice-overs or associations of aristocracy."[114] More than that, however, Osa Johnson completed the task that Annie Oakley had begun in the 1880s: she gained acclaim as an armed woman who could reinforce, rather than threaten, established racial and gender hierarchies. Johnson, like Oakley before her, was able to desensitize audiences to the violence involved in "taming" the wilderness. Just as Oakley had made western expansion seem a fun adventure, so Johnson, with her carefully staged self-representations as a thoroughly domesticated, far-from-feminist armed woman, made imperialist adventuring in Africa seem reassuringly familiar. The photographs of Johnson's whipping up ostrich egg omelets for breakfast and making wild plum pie for dessert suggested that American expansionism was just an extension of the pioneer spirit celebrated in popular fiction fifty years previously.

Annie Oakley was certainly no slouch when it came to crafting her own image, but Osa Johnson proved to be a master of several media, including books and films, in conjuring up the charm of armed white womanhood. Whereas Oakley had impressive, measurable skill with a gun, Johnson relied on the magic of film editing to present herself as an accomplished hunter. Osa Johnson effectively took the armed white woman into a new era, using technology to celebrate American expansionism rather than to nostalgically re-create pioneer times, to unabashedly assert white supremacy, and to erase any fears among her audience that arming women could unsettle power relations between the sexes.

Osa Johnson's success might best be measured by comparing her to the earlier celebrity hunter Martha Maxwell. Commentators on Maxwell's exhibit at the Centennial Exposition of 1876 speculated endlessly about the state of Maxwell's marriage, about the degree of her racial purity and the extent to which she, as a western woman, was really civilized. Fifty years later, Johnson was able to portray herself in a way that could only reassure cultural conservatives. Moreover, Johnson used media to distance herself from the violent aspects of weaponry. While Maxwell's cute tableaux of dead squirrels and ducks may have won over some spectators, her taxidermy collections were visceral reminders of her skill with a gun and of the death she was capable of causing. Spectators at her exhibit were close enough to smell and touch the animals she had killed. Johnson's audiences, on the other hand, were treated to a cinematic spectacle that turned killing into bloodless adventure.

Yet Osa Johnson, though she may have represented the culmination of an ideology linking the armed white woman with American ideals, represented only part of the story of her time. Films of her domesticating the wilderness existed simultaneously with images and narratives of armed female gangsters, who seemed to embody all of the uncontainable violence and sexuality that cultural critics associated with women's liberation. Although female criminals initially seemed an urban phenomenon, by the 1930s they were wreaking havoc across the rural Midwest, and they sometimes nostalgically invoked the Wild West in ways that Annie Oakley could never have imagined.

MAID MARIANS AND BAD MOTHERS

FROM THE GUNGIRLS OF THE 1920S TO

THE GANGSTERS OF THE 1930S

The complex topography of women and guns shifted during World War I, as women entered the labor force in unprecedented numbers, taking the jobs that men left to join the war and working to support the war effort.[1] Feminist journalist Mabel Potter Daggett, among many others, noted the great rise in women's employment. As she wrote, "There is no task to which women have not turned to-day to carry on civilization," including work in munitions factories: "A woman made the shells with which [the soldier's] gun is loaded."[2] The increased economic power and greater visibility of working-class women during and after the war, as well as the suffrage that Woodrow Wilson presented as women's due for their war work, led to new social anxieties on the part of traditionalists. These anxieties focused in part on women whose sexual capacities and violent tendencies seemed emblematic of what could go wrong when conventional gender roles were upset. Armed women, including both gangsters' molls and bank robbers in their own right, like the notorious Brooklyn gungirls, were the objects of widespread curiosity in the 1920s. However, the unprecedented social crisis caused by the Depression fostered the development of celebrity female bandits, which led some conservative observers to place the blame for America's problems at the feet of armed criminal women.

During the 1930s, a period when many feared that the Depression, widely viewed as a crisis of capitalism, had caused a "crisis of gender," the female gangster stood at the crossroads of public debate about women's social roles and about women's capacities for violence. Frequently, and luridly, depicted in detective magazines and tabloid newspapers, female criminals like Kathryn Kelly (wife of "Machine Gun" Kelly), Bonnie Parker (the female half of Bonnie and Clyde), and Ma Barker (of the Karpis-Barker Gang) were the object of the FBI's ire and the public's fascination. As media creations and as manipulators of their own images, armed criminal women were many things to many people. As the subject of countless illustrations in popular magazines like *Spicy Detective*, the armed woman was sexy and dangerous; to J. Edgar Hoover, she was the cause of crime in America, either through bad motherhood or through unnatural domination of her man. She was a mythopoetic bandit in the style of Maid Marian and celebrated in such songs as Bonnie Parker's "The Ballad of Bonnie and Clyde." She was an American primitive, a symbol of new womanhood, and an exemplar of great romance. She was even, if one were to believe Bonnie Parker's mother, respectable and domestically inclined.

Moreover, the "Americanization" of crime and criminals forced a shift in the eugenics-driven debates about the problem of crime. During the 1920s and early 1930s, criminals were widely perceived as "ethnic." The same eugenics principles that had led political and social thinkers around the turn of the century to encourage upper-class white women to hunt and engage in trapshooting prompted in the 1920s worries about weaponry in the hands of racial undesirables. As David E. Ruth has noted, "Most eugenicists fretted about Nordic 'race suicide' and pointed to crime as another reason to close the gates to immigrants."[3] Yet by the early 1930s, public attention shifted from the urban, ethnic gangster to a rural, all-American type of criminality. It is my argument that the racial fears focused on ethnic gangsters were now displaced onto female gangsters: gender, in effect, became racialized, and Hoover and others on the right saw criminality as deeply intertwined with the breakdown in gender roles.

J. Edgar Hoover struggled to transform the way the public thought about the female criminal. Rather than let her be fodder for entertainment—as the scantily clad staple of detective magazines and the subject of breathless articles in the tabloids—he wanted to make her into a symbol of what was wrong with America. Hoover and his allies insisted on the Americanness of the criminal as if to emphasize that the threat was no longer from outside (dangerous immigrants) but from within (women who had broken free of traditional structures). At a time when fears about the deleterious effects of immigration had given way to anxiety over the American character, rural female criminals were at the center of discussions about what ailed the heartland and about what was wrong with American womanhood itself. By tracing the rise of the female criminal in popular culture, from being the subject of tabloid articles and cheap fiction in the 1920s to being the focus of concerns about social decay in the 1930s, one can see how she became a pretext for anxieties about women's increasing power. And by looking at the careers of some of the most famous female criminals of the day, most notably Bonnie Parker, one can learn how these women were able to skillfully manage their own public images, presenting themselves not as eugenic disasters but as star-crossed lovers or even would-be mothers.

IF ROSIE CAN'T HEAR IT WITH FLOWERS, SHE'S GOT TO HEAR IT WITH RODS

The female criminal of the 1920s fascinated the public because she symbolized the slipperiness of class and racial identity and because she was a representative of an underworld that received heavy media coverage. It has become a commonplace to say that the 1920s were a period of sexual liberation. According to historians John D'Emilio and Estelle Freedman, "One reason the twenties have loomed so large as a critical turning point is that patterns of behavior formerly associated with other groups in the population had, by then, spread to the white middle class."[4] White middle-class women had opportunities to engage in sexual behavior previously identified with other classes and other racial groups; the burgeoning of urban culture and mass culture meant that they might well be mingling socially with representatives of these other groups. As Geoffrey Perrett has pointed out, although Americans believed that the twenties had ushered in what a 1927 *Harper's* article called "Our Permanent Crime Wave," "there was virtually nothing in the relevant data to show that crime in the 1920s was more prevalent than a decade before, or a generation before. If anything, they showed a slight decrease overall."[5] Yet the theater of gang warfare, which included lavish funerals for mobsters and dramatic shootouts in public places, turned crime into spectacle.

The armed female criminal in popular fiction of the 1920s and very early 1930s is sexual, ethnic, destructive to men, and generally destined for a bad end. For example, Polack Annie, the protagonist of Jack Lait's novel *Gangster Girl* (1930), is lethal: she "had bumped off the two toughest gorillas in her native town, Chicago, and because of [her] deadly red hair and tilted nose and adolescently ripe form more than a dozen gangsters had been chopped down with machine-gun bullets."[6] She is a classic gangster's moll, if perhaps a bit more active as a criminal than most. Urban gangs in movies of the early thirties (*Scarface, Public Enemy, Little Caesar*) and fiction are portrayed as ethnic, and the women of the gangs figure as temptresses leading men to perdition. For eugenicists worried about the delete-rious effects of immigrants on the moral fiber of America, characters like Polack Annie embodied the dangers facing the nation.

Although the female criminal may have been white ethnic (generally eastern or southern European) and lower class, she was often portrayed in popular literature as having social ambitions or pretensions. In "The Lady from Castle-Bar," for instance, which appeared in the December 1929 issue of *Gangster Stories*, Rosalie Caldrone, the "devilish, vivacious offspring of the union of an Irish beggar of life and a Spanish siren," balks at letting the police call her by the more familiar name "Rosie" because "I'm a lady, see."[7] Her heritage clearly marks her for a bad end; "It's the blood strain," explains the police sergeant to his colleague, following her early arrest for shoplifting. As the narrator tells us, "If the Irish in Rosie Caldrone made her the best moll in town, then the Spanish that surged madly through her veins made her the best sweetheart of the bunch." Sexually rapacious and bloodthirsty, she comes across in her desire to be a lady as grimly comi-cal, though readers of 1929/30 may have found their laughter to have an anxious edge. Rosie was, after all, a prime example of the wrong sort at-tempting to move up the class ladder. As one of her cohorts, "Killer Luigi," remarks of her, "If Rosie can't hear it with flowers, she's got to hear it with rods" (363). Caught between sex and gunplay, the ethnic gun moll had no other register.

The ethnic female criminal was an exemplar of popular social theories that, as Bram Dijkstra notes, tied uncontrolled female sexuality to racial degeneracy and social unrest. In this regard, Dijkstra cites *The Rising Tide of Color against White World-Supremacy* (1920), by prominent race theorist Lothrop Stoddard, which added the threat of Communism to the mix: "Bol-shevism is, in fact, as anti-racial as it is anti-social. To the Bolshevik mind, with its furious hatred of constructive ability and its fanatical determination to enforce levelling, proletarian equality, the very existence of superior bio-logical values is a crime."[8] Thus, the sexual woman not only made evolved men lower themselves into a primitive world of arousal, enabling misce-genation; "she also," according to Dijkstra, "symbolized the political threat of the economically exploited classes whence she most often emanated."[9] However, the armed ethnic female criminal, violent and sexual as she may have been, was clearly outside mainstream society. The Polack Annies and Rosie Caldrones of fiction were lurid characters—but they mainly confined their activities to the underworld.

Because the ethnic temptresses were easy to identify, they seemed containable. More threatening were the armed women who managed to slip in and out of respectable society, like the only slightly wilder cousins of the seemingly respectable young women who frequented nightclubs, drank, and smoked cigarettes. The gun moll was in a sense the ultimate flapper—a thrill-seeker bored with traditional roles and employments, a creature of the city. And if the gun moll, as a passive consumer of violent excitement, was dangerous, her more active counterpart, the gungirl, appeared to be not just a flapper but possibly a feminist.

Tabloid newspapers and detective magazines both shaped and profited from public fascination with gangsters and gang women, whose lives of sex and violence were presented to readers for maximum titillation. Popular accounts often focused on the female gangster as a hanger-on in search of cheap thrills. As Walter Noble Burns wrote in his history of urban crime, *The One-Way Ride: The Red Trail of Chicago Gangland from Prohibition to Jake Lingle* (1931), "If the lot of gangland women seems hard and woefully sad, they are far from viewing their situation in any such tragic light. Gangland has its fascinations. The women who breathe in its tense atmosphere enjoy the thrill of danger and its raw drama and would not exchange it for the dull routine of more peaceful environments. They are like women of the old frontier who preferred the perils of the wilderness to prosaic existence in towns and cities." However, unlike the stoic frontier heroines whose experiences were celebrated in "pioneer women" statues, in popular histories, and in Wild West shows, gangland women were not wielding weapons to build a nation. Rather, they were attracted to violence for its own sake. Strongly implied in Burns's and others' accounts was the notion that these women had no claim to an American identity.

From Burns's point of view in the early 1930s, it is clear that female gangsters have been seduced by the culture of glamour. In an era offering the possibility of new roles for women, gang women resemble "the fair ladies of the days of chivalry, who were happiest when their knights were driving spears into the hearts of foemen or splitting skulls with battle axes. Gangland is romance, and the drab, stereotyped world beyond its dangerous borders is fit only for slaves of the typewriter, school teachers, or some anemic feminine souls content to settle down with some white-collar clerk in dreary comfort and obscurity."[10] Rather than settling for the traditional jobs available to women, which Burns sarcastically characterizes as slavery, and as rendering women weak and bloodless, gang women seek greater opportunities. However, the women Burns describes are not actors; they merely draw their kicks from witnessing male violence. In his account, gangland women are passive consumers of sexualized violence, in much the same way that tabloid readers are.

Commentators of the time differentiated between gangsters' girlfriends and female gangsters (or gungirls), who were portrayed as much higher up in the echelons of gang women than those who were just sexually involved with gangsters. However, they saw both groups as connected to crime for specifically feminine reasons. The detective story author Arthur B. Reeve wrote in his 1931 volume, *The Golden Age of Crime*, "There is a wide difference between the gungirl who robs for pretty clothes, or maybe just a thrill, and the gun moll who has bound herself forever to the intractable destiny of the underworld."[11] While the independent female criminal may have superficial interests, she at least has some agency. By contrast, the criminal's girlfriend is passive, lovelorn, and dependent.

In this account, gangsters' lovers are suicidally drawn to the nexus of sex and violence. According to Reeve, gun molls basically sign their own death warrants as soon as they become romantically involved with criminals. "'Once in the racket' applies to the women as well as to the men of the underworld—'always in the racket.' Gangland draws no line at sex. A woman can 'know too much' the same as a man" (142). Yet women in the underworld, because of their basic feminine nature, run a greater risk than their men do. "When a prominent gunman 'throws down' his moll, she's very likely to have her death ticket written if she happens to know anything that might go bad for him. Women have a way of departing from the underworld in moments of jealousy" (143). Because a woman scorned would be inclined to inform on her ex-lover out of feminine vanity, she presents a threat to the gang. Indeed, "when a wanted gangster is captured it is nearly always through a woman" (153).

While the female criminal of the 1920s and early 1930s served as an irresistible symbol to a public fascinated by, if not concerned with, the loosening of women's sexual morals and what appeared to be a national crime wave, writers often blamed public interest for the production of female criminals. Reeve saw a manifest change in public perception and criminal performance: "The romantic glamour that the newspapers threw around the Brooklyn gungirls in the last decade served more than anything else to give impetus to the wave of female criminality which in 1930 reached the highest point in the history of the nation. . . . [Holdup woman] Celia Cooney would not receive the publicity today that made her so famous in 1921 and 1922. Hundreds of our modern maidens could outshine her in the way they handle their gats and maneuver hold-ups" (149). The sophisticated gungirls of the early Depression era were outperforming their role models.

Although Celia Cooney has been largely forgotten today, in her time she was a celebrity. Between the announcement of her first crime, on January 6, 1924, and her capture on April 22 of that year, New York newspapers had a field day, publishing dozens of articles about Cooney's escapades. In a series of articles in the *New York World*, Cooney's exploits were at first cast as an example of new womanhood gone wild, then of motherhood gone tragically wrong, and finally of deficient eugenic practices. This sequence of explanations for female criminality was one to which commentators would revert during the 1930s. In fact, J. Edgar Hoover's extensive writings on female bandits would employ the same themes, albeit in purpler prose.

The early articles in the *World* focused on Cooney's flapper status, and one long piece in particular explicitly linked the bandit's crimes to social concerns. "Is Dread Bob-Haired Bandit Female Dr. Jekyll–Mr. Hyde? Former Gangster Has Theory," blared the headline; the subheading read, "Strange Phase of Modern Feminism Keeps Whole of the Police Department Guessing." The author of the article asked, "Is the bob-haired bandit the first specimen of a new variety of criminal? Or is she an old variety acting in a new way?" Focusing on the "slim figure in the flapper winter uniform of sealskin (perhaps) coat, bob, and tight little hat," the writer drew attention to her status as a new woman of uncertain class status (was the sealskin real?), someone who was able to hold five "husky" clerks at bay "under the steady muzzle of her little gun." The article pointed up the discrepancy between the delicate stature of the "bob-haired nuisance" and her criminal ability: "She swears competently when she feels like it, is always the boss of the job and generally enters first and alone." The development of the bob-haired bandit, then, almost seemed like the inevitable outcome of flapperdom. She was assertive, fashionable, far from genteel, but terribly effective.

It was also possible that the bandit was an example of a fractured personality, a woman who performed her expected gender role by day, only to escape it by night: "Police theories to account for this peculiar development of modern feminism are many. One of them is that she is a female Dr. Jekyll and Mr. Hyde, a stenographer meekly taking orders by day and a bandit giving orders, pistol in hand, by night." Behavior of this type would make the bob-haired bandit a character in the familiar mode of cheap fic-

s Dread Bob-Haired Bandit
Female Dr. Jekyll-Mr. Hyde?
Former Gangster Has Theory

The GUN IS IN A POCKET of The DRESS CONCEALED by A RUFFLE, AROUND The WAISTLINE WHICH HANGS DOWN OVER The POCKET.

The GUN IS ALWAYS DRAWN with The RIGHT HAND from The LEFT SIDE

KETCH SHOWING HOW BOB-HAIRED BANDIT CARRIES HER WEAPON

Strange Phase of Modern Feminism Keeps Whole of the Police Department Guessing Hard.

Reformed Underworld Leader Believes She Is Graduate Gun-Toter for Male Thieves.

By MABEL ABBOTT

Is the bob-haired bandit the first specimen of a new variety of criminal?

Or is she an old variety acting in a new way?

Is there only one of her, or are there two, or more?

Why does she choose chain stores to rob and preferably those dealing in groceries, drugs, or tea and coffee?

A course in the psychology of bob-haired bandits would be welcomed with enthusiasm by a harassed police force, at a loss for precedents from which to make deductions as to where and when this 1924-model hold-up woman will appear, or how to catch her.

Child of 1924.

She made her debut literally with

In 1924, the public was fascinated by the motivations of the "bob-haired bandit,"
Celia Cooney. The sketch purports to show how she keeps her hidden weapon at the ready.
Mabel Abbott, "Is Dread Bob-Haired Bandit Female Dr. Jekyll—Mr. Hyde?"
New York World, April 13, 1924.

tion. Beyond this, however, the Jekyll-and-Hyde explanation highlighted the potential for subterfuge in every woman's behavior and the opaqueness of even the most innocuous woman's motivations.

The *World* consulted a former "member of underworld gangs" who saw the female criminal as poor but pathetic, unemployed and craving new clothes, unable to commit crime without the encouragement of a boyfriend (whom she probably met "in a cheap dance hall"). Although she toted a gun, she had no intention of using it: "She goes out to get enough to buy a new dress and keep her parents from scolding her."[12] This theory fit in with the profiles of other female criminals regularly covered by the *World*, who could be counted in the dozens. For instance, nineteen-year-old Irene Johnson's motivation for entering a life of crime was described in an April 15, 1924, article following her arrest as a "craving for fine clothes, which the meager wages earned by her as a cigaret maker could not satisfy."[13] Grasping and materialistic, sensual creatures like Johnson could easily fall prey to the temptations of urban culture, but they were clearly of a lower order than the newspaper's readers. Perhaps by belittling the female criminal's reasons for theft, the article could make her seem less threatening.

However, the former gangster quoted in the article on the bob-haired bandit had a more complex social theory about female criminals. They were nothing new, he pointed out: "We have always had girl bandits. . . . They are the same ones who used to be 'boob bandits' a while ago." Much of what this ex-gangster had to say was technical, concerning the way in which female criminals hid their pistols in the ruffles of their dresses, but his most interesting remarks had to do with the transformation from boob bandit to bob-haired bandit. According to him, a woman criminal begins as a soldier in a general's army, working for typically feminine rewards: "She has been promised a percentage, plus everything from new shoes to a new evening gown, swell times and automobile rides. She gets the promise, and that's about all. A number of girls have told me about being double-crossed in such cases." Eventually, "the girl who has been double-crossed is out for revenge. She wants to show that she can pull off a job to [*sic*]. She has graduated from being a girl bandit that has been 'boobed' time and again into a bob-haired bandit. Now, instead of standing lookout for a male companion, she has them stand lookout while she does the job. She is going to be sure that what she gets is HERS!"[14] Although she may have initially been gulled by promises of finery and may be motivated by vengeance, the bob-haired bandit comes to understand her own economic self-interest, and to gain agency in her quest for cash. It is unlikely she will commit crimes for the chance to ride in some gangster's car; rather, she will become the driver.

Yet once Celia Cooney, the bob-haired bandit, was captured, it turned out that she was not a hardened feminist but a grieving mother. Below the April 22, 1924, headline of the *New York World* announcing that "Bobbed Bandit Confesses Shooting Clerk in Hold-Up; on Way Here with Husband," the subheading seemed to tell its own narrative: "'Don't Blame Eddie,' Says Mrs. Cooney; 'I Led Him to It'—Death of Her Baby Takes Fight out of Her, but She's the Stronger."[15] Subsequent stories revealed that she and her husband, at his suggestion, had taken up robbery to support the baby they were then expecting and that Celia Cooney's "participation had resulted in the infant's death." She was "not of the flapper type" and "never" had been.[16] The story was rapidly rewritten—instead of a modern feminist, she was a bad mother, perhaps grieving (the "fight" taken out of her by her loss), but certainly responsible for the child's death.

In an editorial by Walter Lippmann written two weeks after her capture, Celia Cooney, seemingly the most daring Brooklyn gungirl, was ultimately represented not just as society's victim but also as a eugenic mistake. Lippmann pointed out that the "story had, as the press agents say, everything. It had a flapper and a bandit who baffled the police; it had sex and money, crime and mystery. And then yesterday we read in the probation officer's report the story of Cecilia Cooney's life. It was not in the least entertaining. For there in the place of the dashing bandit was a pitiable girl; instead of an amusing tale, a dark and mean tragedy; instead of a lovely adventure, a terrible accusation."[17] Lippmann detailed the tragic life of Celia Cooney: her birth as the youngest of eight to an alcoholic father, the commitment of her siblings to an institution, repeated abandonment by her mother, her work as a child laborer in a brush factory, her "associating at night with sailors picked up on the waterfront" when she was fifteen. For Lippmann, there were eugenics lessons in the story: "Fully warned by the behavior of her parents long before her birth, the law allowed her parents to reproduce their kind."[18] Lippmann's pseudoscientific explanation seemed to contain the threat posed by Cooney. She was not a "dashing bandit," but a "pitiable girl," not a strong woman bursting the bounds of social convention, but a pathetic loser. Her story was a matter of eugenics, not of feminism. However, Lippmann's analysis also hinted that Cooney's case was not anomalous, since an indulgent state permitted unfit parents to keep bringing potential criminals into the world.

Although most fictional and tabloid gunwomen of the 1920s were portrayed in lurid, unflattering terms, there still existed a minor literary tradition of upper-crust armed ladies, women with last names like "Race," hailing from hometowns like "Saxon Falls," whose criminal activities seemed almost to be a more glamorous extension of the strenuous living recommended by Theodore Roosevelt. While white ethnic women criminals were portrayed as dangerously sexual and pornographically interested in violence, as eugenic mistakes and bad mothers, another category of armed females, who existed in fiction, if not in fact, used their good genetic backgrounds to their advantage in pursuing glamorous lives of crime. Chaste, motivated by social concerns, and family-oriented, these women used the gun as a means to the end. Their guns helped them not only to right family wrongs and achieve social reform but also to marry well.

In detective magazines in the 1920s and well into the 1930s, the upper-class, WASP female criminal was exempted from being portrayed as a pathetic, violent nymphomaniac. For instance, Mary Lou Brewster of Saxon Falls, the protagonist of "Man-Killer," a novelette that appeared in *Greater Gangster Stories* of April 1933, explains to the boss whose gang she is trying to join that "I'm not looking for romance, thrills and adventure. I want money—big money—at the expense of Society. We Brewsters had plenty at one time, and we'd still have it if wasn't for Judge Sutton and his kind."[19] Although her boss—upon first meeting her—calls her a "man-killer," the only death she causes occurs toward the end of the story when she kills an arrogant baby-murdering gangster named Bragg under the approving eyes of the police; she thereupon marries her talented, morally upright gangster boss. In this story, Mary Lou's efforts ultimately appear to be a form of social do-gooding.

One fictional female gangster of the 1920s is portrayed as being a criminal mastermind in her own right. Yet she is also a dutiful daughter helping her father carry on the family business, which just happens to be crime. A series by Charles W. Tyler for *Detective Story Magazine*, which ran from 1918 to 1931, features Blue Jean Billy Race, a stick-up woman who spends most of her time robbing millionaires on their yachts. However, even this daring criminal ends up reforming and marrying the detective who pursues her.[20]

From the beginning of *Quality Bill's Girl*, a novel drawn from the series, it is clear that Blue Jean Billy is a virginal, dutiful daughter whose immersion in the criminal life has nothing to do with sexuality, urbanity, or racial weak-

Man-Killer

This detective novel heroine, Mary Lou Brewster of Saxon Falls, is well born and morally upright; the only man she kills is an arrogant, baby-murdering gangster. George J. Brenn's "Man-Killer" appeared in *Greater Gangster Stories*, April 1933.

ness. Blue Jean Billy is the motherless, well-educated daughter of a Yankee fisherman, the suggestively named Quality Bill Race, who becomes a criminal when he is arrested on suspicion of knowledge of a policeman's death at the hands of an outlaw fisherman: "During the old-fashioned third degree that followed, a zealous officer outdid himself just a little. Half through rage, half through accident, there was a slip, a wrenching fall—and Quality Bill Race, crook, was made."[21] Before, Blue Jean Billy assisted her father at sea; now, "in his life in the underworld the girl was still with him. She never deserted him. Again he taught her all he knew—not of the sea and the big, clean things, but of the muck and gutter wash of this life below the dead line" (19). His dying wish is that his daughter "make a lady uh yehself— some time—Jeanie—like yeh mother was. You're good—I've taught yeh th' crooked game—Gawd f'rgive me—but yeh ain' like them other women. Thank 'Im f'r that" (19).

Although her father speaks in dialect, as do all the other criminals, Blue Jean Billy's language is precise. She even corrects one of her wealthy victims, who asks her at gunpoint if "this is a holdup?" "Speaking in the vernacular of the place you choose to call the underworld; it is something a little softer than 'porch climbing'" (131). While she appears attractive in an evening gown, Blue Jean Billy is never described in sexual terms. The detective whom she eventually marries reflects on her robust healthiness: "Blue Jean Billy Race was inherently a woman of the sea. She was clean and brown and filled with a love of the wind and waters, of all big things out of doors under the blue heavens" (113). Her crimes are always against the rich of "Four Hundred Acre," whom she delights in robbing at gunpoint while they cavort on their yachts: "They were the enemies of the poor; the friends of the police" (26). Her criminal cohorts, the Shanghai Kid and Shaver Michael, chivalrously protect her as her father had requested them to do; they would not dream of approaching her sexually.

As her name suggests, Quality Bill Race's daughter is ethnically pure, in contrast to the other criminals whom she encounters, crooks with names like "Mulatto Baldy" Johnson, Engle J. Gottlieb, and Baron, the Wop ("who was not a wop at all") (42). Typical is White-line Bull Shattuck, who is "a cripple, both legs being off at the knees. His body was thickset, his head, it seemed, abnormally large. He reminded one more of a huge gorilla . . . His thick jowls, powerful neck and low forehead added to the impression he gave of being more animal than man" (155). Another criminal, Jiggs, "a sallow individual," speaks in "a shrill, squeaky falsetto tone" (157). While these criminals are maimed, animalistic, possessed of the sallow complexions of ethnic city dwellers, and of dubious sexuality, Billy Jean is a classic Yankee. Of Anglo-Saxon heritage, she is naturally attracted to the healthy, strenuous life. All the characters in the book recognize her higher standing (at one point, she successfully impersonates a Russian countess in order to fleece the rich at a gambling party): "She's always been a stuck-up thing— just like old Quality Bill—too good for the rest of 'em" (68), another crook reflects. The narrator tells us that "the carriage of the daring adventuress had been regal; her poise and natural grace a thing to be wondered at in one who chose the profession of a real yeggwoman" (53).

Given Blue Jean Billy's racial superiority and regal bearing, as well as the hopes her father expresses on his deathbed, it is only fitting that she end the novel by giving up her life of crime and marrying her equal. Robert Wood, the master detective who has been hired to apprehend her, is "just a plain, all-around he-man" (35). He never manages to catch her, but he is eventually trapped with her on a sinking ship. Although he is freed first, and is the one to free Blue Jean Billy, whom the reader sees for the first time "limp and helpless" (253), there is no indication that Blue Jean Billy is in any sense weakened or mastered by him. In fact, Wood, who has temporarily become a lobsterman in order to pursue his undercover mission, tells her that instead of arresting her he will declare the case annulled; then, having decided to take up lobstering as a career (working with her father's old fishing colleague, Portugee Joe), he proposes marriage, and she of course assents.

The novel is structured so that Blue Jean Billy, a dutiful daughter and natural aristocrat, will never be tainted by her association with the underworld life. In fact, the criminal life is only a means of maintaining closeness to her unjustly wronged, embittered father. It is a life she gladly gives up when she is able to encounter her double, the master detective, on equal terms and take up a life that, in Rooseveltian terms, is a perfect one for a woman: she will lead the strenuous life as a lobsterman's wife, but also be a lady.

The high-minded adventures of female characters like Blue Jean Billy and Mary Lou Brewster served to cast the exploits of low-life gun molls into greater relief. However, readers of the late 1920s and early 1930s had a hard time envisioning most female criminals, fictional or otherwise, as part of a romantic plot (as opposed to merely sexual one). In 1931, Popular Publications, one of the major publishers of pulp fiction, launched *Underworld Romances*. As its associate editor, Jean Mithoefer, recalled, the time seemed ripe for a magazine of this sort: "The publisher just thought, love stories were doing good and crime stories were doing good, let's combine them. But that magazine lasted just three issues, as I remember, because we couldn't get any good stories. The women love story writers wrote kind of silly gangsters, and we had some pretty tough crime writers who didn't know how to make their criminals act romantic. I don't know who the readers for that magazine might have been . . . maybe the wives of gangsters . . ."[22]

Underworld Romances may have failed for reasons as pragmatic as those Mithoefer outlines, but the early 1930s heralded a shift in public attention from the urban, ethnic gangster, who seemed to be almost a corporation man, to a new model of criminal—an all-American bandit, enmeshed in the myths of the old West. And the rural gunwoman, who was neither a flapper nor of foreign extraction, raised perplexing new questions about the nature of American women.

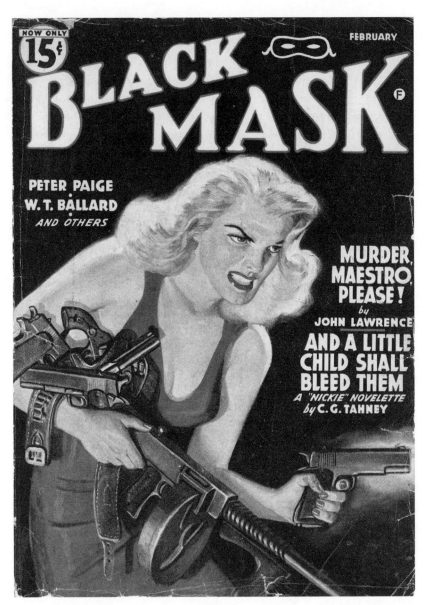

The women featured in pulp fiction of the 1930s and 1940s, as this *Black Mask* cover from February 1942 suggests, are sexy, dangerous, and heavily armed.

Although public fascination with crime did not necessarily diminish during the Depression years, its nature changed. A growing public hatred of bankers turned bank robbers into folk heroes. The poverty of the Depression years caused what was widely perceived at the time as a crisis in gender roles. In this context, female gangsters served as a fulcrum for public anxieties about and fascination with new womanhood.

To understand why armed female criminals were such celebrities, we must first look at their male counterparts and at the rise of the social bandit. Male bandits were often effective at casting themselves as part of a romantic western past, as inheritors of the daring exploits of such familiar icons as the James Gang and the Dalton Gang. However, the history of female banditry was complicated and not always easy for female criminals and their audiences to access. Thus, women bandits worked with but often modified the conventions of male banditry. Yet critical commentaries on these women focused almost exclusively on their gendered disorders and sought to disassociate them, in the public imagination, from any hint of heroic tradition.

On the day that Franklin Delano Roosevelt took office, in March 1933, every bank in the nation was closed. The poverty of the early Depression years was overwhelming. As Malcolm Cowley remembered, in the winter of 1931–32 in New York, "whole families there were receiving an average of $2.39 for relief; that was for food, rent, clothing, everything."[23] Cowley, then an editor for the New Republic, saw thousands of letters come into the magazine: "One day it would be a Chicago brakeman out of work for two years, sitting down in a public library to write his life history on a five-cent school pad and to ask us what would happen to millions like himself. . . . A bank clerk would tell us how he happened to be watching a demonstration of the unemployed when the police charged in with nightsticks. His skull was fractured—and worse than that, his bank had closed three weeks later and he was now unemployed himself" (4).

Widespread skepticism about capitalism encouraged the revival of the folk criminal—or, to use Eric Hobsbawm's term, the "social bandit," who rises out of peasant society to rob the rich. According to Hobsbawm, the social bandit served to "remind [Americans of the thirties] of a sometimes imaginary heroic past, and to provide a concrete locus for nostalgia, a symbol of ancient and lost virtue."[24] Both the readers who eagerly followed criminal exploits in tabloids and newsmagazines and the criminals themselves embraced the image of the social bandit. That image is prominent in the autobiographies of two famous criminals of the time, "Blackie" Audett and Alvin Karpis.[25]

Audett in particular was prone to describing himself as a modern-day Robin Hood, a criminal who is recognized by most common people as being on their side, or at the very least, not their enemy. Because his autobiography was created with the help of an amanuensis who saw him as a noble primitive, those qualities are strengthened for the reader. His ghostwriter, Gene Lowall, writes in the foreword to the book that Audett's "associates had been rebellious spirits who wrote an inglorious page in American history. He, too, had been a rebellious spirit—a spirit quite possibly derived from the fraction of proud Indian blood that flows in his veins—and as such he found in the Dillingers and the Baby Face Nelsons something kindred in his own nature."[26] Perhaps because Audett carries for his ghostwriter such symbolic freight, his autobiography has the feeling of a folk tale—it is rife with improbable coincidences and grandiose moments.

Audett is aided in his numerous prison escapes by kindly farmers who give him shelter and by helpful railway men who conceal his presence from authorities. As he comments,

> It's a funny thing, but people in general ain't, as a rule, too hostile to bank robbers. That is, they ain't if you never hurt nobody in the heists. If you was halfway a gentleman in the robbery, people kind of was on your side after it was over. . . . Times was mighty hard back there in the early '30's and people didn't care much whether the banks got robbed or not. Maybe some of them sort of hoped they would. You take some family that's just been kicked off their place by the bank and lost everything they worked all their lives for, well, they ain't going to be too hostile, maybe, if you want to hide out around their haystack. (139)

Given Audett's account of himself, it is not surprising that he is so well received wherever he goes. If he is not helping out an impoverished widow who is supported only by her flower-selling daughter (124), he is giving a farmer $5,000 to prevent the foreclosure of his farm (140), or robbing a bank so that he can send the entire proceeds of his crime to a home for crippled orphans (183).

While Audett's autobiography has a somewhat dreamy, mythic quality, Alvin Karpis's is suffused with a kind of dry irony. The only time he casts himself as a Robin Hood figure is when he tells the story of using some loot to buy a Victrola and fifty records for a family of starving Oklahoma farmers: "It was the only time I saw any smiles. They were really happy."[27] Yet he is absolutely aware of the fleeting nature of the pleasures he provides, and he recognizes his distance from the rural poor: "The family threw a big dance. They spread cornmeal across the rough floor . . . and the people danced all night long. They whooped it up like it was New Year's Eve. It was a night of forgetting for them, and in the morning they went back to their rotten everyday routine. It was enough to make me glad I was a criminal and not a starving Okie" (125). His awareness of himself as a cultural figure comes out most tellingly in an episode near the end of his criminal career, before he is caught and sentenced to life in prison.

> Despite the heat from the FBI, I was still keen to get started on another job. It wasn't necessarily the need for cash that was driving me into action. It was the desire to be busy. I was aching for an exciting heist.
> And I had exactly the right job in mind. I'd been mulling it over for weeks. I was going to take a mail train. I thought of the great bandits of the old West, the James Brothers, the Dalton Boys, and all the rest of them. They knocked over trains, and I was going to pull the same stunt. (209)

Despite their willingness to go along with him, the men he recruits for the job are "slightly cynical about the sound of it." One of them, an experienced burglar named Ben Grayson, asks, "Who the hell robs a train in this day and age?" (210). Karpis does not spell it out, but one guess might be inspired criminals who long ago saw *The Great Train Robbery* and who are now influenced by the idea that they themselves could be pop culture heroes and not just reenactors of past glories. Just as Wild West shows had provided audiences from the 1880s through the turn of the century with inspirational visions of pioneer history, so filmed westerns could offer banditry as an all-American activity. In the end, it is Grayson who most enters into the spirit of the thing. "Ben Grayson turned up on the morning of the job looking like a holdup man from out of the past. He had pasted on a fake mustache, one of those long drooping jobs that the old-time train robbers used to wear. He had also rubbed some rouge on his cheeks and on his chin, and he looked like a complete villain" (214).

Grayson's costume has an effect, though perhaps not the one he intends. As the scene unfolds, Karpis is concerned about the presence of repairmen perched up on telephone poles at the scene of the planned robbery:

If trouble broke out, they could call for help. I began to think that maybe I'd better sic Freddie on them.

Then one of the repairmen distracted me. He started to laugh. He was really broken up. He nudged the other repair guy, and the second man started to laugh too. I couldn't figure it out. Then I looked in the direction they were pointing. It was Grayson. He had just arrived on the platform and, in his eight-inch mustache, he looked as weird as hell. (215)

Even though the proceeds of the robbery are surprisingly small, Karpis is not too disappointed: "I'd accomplished what I'd set out to do—I'd held up a train in fine style just like the famous old Western bandits" (218).

While criminals reveled in their all-American antecedents, gleefully re-enacting stagecoach robberies from the old West, police writers were disturbed by the shift in crime from an urban, ethnic phenomenon to one that was identified with 100 percent Americanism. FBI director J. Edgar Hoover warned that "there has been too much sentimental gush over the mentally cleansing effects of the wide open spaces."[28] However, "a great part of our desperate criminal population spends much of its time in rural hideouts, where the principal occupation is either that of the nimrod or of piscatorial pursuit" (95–96). Not only was crime moving out of the cities and into the countryside; worse, those responsible for it were not immigrants but native-born Americans of Anglo-Saxon descent. In his 1936 book, *American Agent*, Melvin Purvis of the FBI wrote that "there had been a tendency among the casually informed to assume that most of our desperate criminals are recruited from the racial groups of south Europe. The fact is that most of the top-flight hoodlums of the Middle West were 100-percent-American boys with no foreign background whatsoever."[29] As J. Edgar Hoover warned in his 1938 book, *Persons in Hiding*, "It is all very well to blame foreign countries for crime, and to shrug away the menace of law infraction by saying that we can expect nothing else as long as we have slums or city congestion, but the facts do not wholly bear out these contentions."[30] Reeling off the names of the famous criminals of the Depression era—Barker, Wright, Delaney, McLaughlin, Gibson, and so on—Hoover notes that they are "monotonously of a type we have come to classify as 'American,' against the Latin or North of Europe 'foreigners.'" Of course, the Depression was an era in which not only the definition of Americanism expanded but also a wide variety of groups were eager to stress their Americanness and their American antecedents. As Communist Party leader Earl

Browder's most famous slogan went, "Communism is twentieth-century Americanism."[31]

Radical activists of all stripes, from the Communists to Huey Long, were proposing political solutions to the problem of economic inequality. Yet quite plausibly the reason Hoover chose to focus so strongly on the "all-American" public enemies, and especially the women among them, was that he recognized the mythological appeal of the social bandit: the symbolic weight he or she took on, and how easily he or she fit into the romanticized past for which many Americans yearned. Thus, Hoover's task was to wrest the gangster, especially the female gangster, out of the realm of nostalgic Americanism and into the realm of disease and dangerous sexuality.

FEMALE GANGSTERS AND THE CRISIS IN GENDER

While the most prominent female criminals of the Depression era may have been as famous as their late-nineteenth-century predecessors, they differed from them in some significant ways. The female outlaws and wild women of the 1880s—most notably Martha Jane Cannary, also known as Calamity Jane, and Belle Starr—were generally described as racially tainted, or at the very least racially ambiguous, and were contrasted with more ladylike, Anglo-Saxon western women, epitomized by Annie Oakley. However, the famous armed women of the 1930s collapsed these contrasting categories: they were both bad and white.

Just as Alvin Karpis evoked the James Gang and the Dalton brothers when reenacting their exploits, female gangsters of the 1930s could, if they chose, look back to a generation of western "bad women." However, the audacious behavior and wild living that enhanced the masculinity of male bandits was less celebrated in women. Moreover, as I have discussed in chapter 2, during the 1880s and 1890s, a negative image of the armed woman appeared: the threatening, sexually uncontained, racially ambiguous figure of the outlaw western woman, as embodied most notably by Calamity Jane and Belle Starr. Female outlaws of the 1930s had to do more than reenact the exploits of Belle Starr; they had to reinvent their roles.

For armed women who chose a life on the wild side, the gender politics of the 1930s, and the gender role shifts caused by the Depression, made their place in the culture far more problematic than that of their male counterparts. While male bank robbers and stick-up artists fit easily and happily into the roles of mythic bandits, female gangsters attracted attention as exemplars of the gender crisis that was said to ail America. And as native-born descendants of "pure" Anglo-Saxon ancestry, they seemed to indicate that the moral degeneration to which ethnic women had been prone in the twenties had now begun to affect the American character.

During the 1930s, economic conditions not only changed patterns of employment but also had major effects on marriage and birth rates. These new circumstances caused commentators to revisit and sometimes revise popular social theories that characterized women as racialized degenerates and feminism as an "abnormal" departure from the traditional social structure. The economic upheavals of the Depression, as many commentators have noted, caused shifts and stresses in gender relations. During this period of significant unemployment, what was considered standard women's work—such as teaching and other low-paid professions—still existed, even as a lot of men's work was shut down. By July 1932, as Malcolm Cowley recalled, "the marriage rate had fallen all over the country, and the divorce rate too; divorces cost money, but one kept hearing of more and more families in which the husband, no longer the breadwinner, had simply disappeared. Physicians reported that impotence, apparently caused by discouragement, was becoming a common symptom in men under forty. Though probably not for that reason, the birth rate was also falling; in the preceding year it had been 14 percent lower than in 1926, as if people were hesitating to bring life into an uncertain world."[32] More troubling to many commentators, though, was that it was not just workers who were bearing fewer children. During the 1930s, upper-class birth rates, which had been steadily declining, hit their lowest point ever.[33]

One result of the economic strains of the Depression was a growing public disapproval of women's moving beyond their roles as housewives. During the Depression, as Susan Ware writes, "working women, especially if they were married, faced strong public hostility to their very participation in the work force. . . . A 1936 Gallup poll asked if wives should work if their husbands had jobs, and 82 percent of all Americans said no."[34] Married women in paid employment were seen as cheating both their professions and their marriages because their dual responsibilities at home and in the workplace were overwhelming. Critics feared that married women who worked would produce fewer children.[35] Moreover, working women were seen as taking jobs that rightfully belonged to men. This public prejudice was reflected in federal regulations that prohibited more than one member of the same family from working for the civil service, as well as policies in school systems and a range of industries from banking to public utilities that restricted the rights of married women to work. One-quarter of the National Recovery Administration's codes mandated wages for women that were lower than those for men.[36]

Both academics and the popular press were fascinated by the "problem" of working women. Many analysts studying the issue found that when women were subordinate to men in their work, they were adhering to their essential nature. For instance, a three-part series that *Fortune* magazine ran in 1935 posed the question of why so many women were employed in business (or, to put it in *Fortune*'s deathless prose, "what kind of nation is this callipygian nation of silk knees, slender necks, narrow fingers, and ironic mouths which has established itself upon our boundaries?").[37] The answer, it seemed, was that women were suited to being office workers because "their conscious or subconscious intention someday to marry, and their conscious or subconscious willingness to be directed by men, render them amenable and obedient and relieve them of that ambition which makes it difficult for men to put their devotion into secretarial work" (55).

Paradoxically, even as women's essentially obedient nature made them suitable for secretarial work, it was the problems caused by the inroads of feminism that had changed the nature of marriage and reduced male dominance in the home, thereby driving men to employ female secretaries. The American man "resented the loss of his position. He regretted the old docility, the old obedience, the old devotion to his personal interests. And, finding himself unable to re-create the late, lost paradise in his home he set about re-creating it in his office." Thus, ironically, the problem of female employment had been caused by a backlash against feminism: "Woman's greatest industrial conquest has been made, as her great conquests have been made from time immemorial, through the male and not despite him" (55). While secretaries may be successful, "it is a triumph for their womanhood and not for their ambition" (86).

Into this anxious public conversation about women's changing roles stepped the director of the FBI, J. Edgar Hoover, who manipulated social anxieties about women's position in the culture and used the terms of the eugenics movement to situate women as central to the crime problem in America. In essence, Hoover attempted to solve the problem of gangsters' popularity, and the FBI's corresponding unpopularity, by focusing on female criminality as the root of America's problems. While it was hard for him to combat the public fascination with such larger-than-life bandits as John Dillinger and Pretty Boy Floyd, it seemed more feasible to lay the blame for moral degeneration, including even male criminality, at the feet of gangster women.

In 1934, the FBI faced a public relations crisis. It was widely criticized for killing, rather than arresting, John Dillinger, whom Hoover had dubbed "Public Enemy Number One." Movies featuring gangsters enjoyed an extraordinary degree of popularity. As former president Jimmy Carter recalled of seeing men in chain gangs during his boyhood in small-town Georgia: "We boys were fascinated with criminals and their punishment, and would observe the chained men from a distance, imagining them to be mysterious gangsters and discussing Pretty Boy Floyd, Baby Face Nelson, Al Capone, or John Dillinger, who were all very famous and whose exploits we followed closely. In our rubber-gun battles, we preferred to play the gangsters instead of the FBI agents or the local sheriff."[38] The FBI faced some real obstacles in its effort to win the approval of the public.

In fighting back against favorable public perceptions of gangsters, Hoover chose what must have seemed an easy target: female crooks. As Hoover said to a Justice Department official who criticized his outspoken attacks on the criminal justice system, "I'm going to tell the truth about these rats. I'm going to tell the truth about their dirty, filthy, diseased women."[39] The FBI launched an extensive public relations campaign to demonize criminals, particularly criminal women, including the relatively anonymous gun molls, or gangsters' consorts, as well as the two most famous female gangsters of the decade—Bonnie Parker, of Bonnie and Clyde, and Kate "Ma" Barker, of the Karpis-Barker Gang. A main element of this strategy to strip crime of its romance involved gendering crime, and criminals, as feminine and portraying the FBI as ultra-masculine.

Writers of admiring books about the FBI painted criminals as little better than animals, and criminal women as the most bestial of the lot. In his *Farewell, Mr. Gangster!* (1936), Herbert Corey makes the point bluntly in a chapter called "Romance in Crook-Hunting": "There is no romance in crime. So far as the records show the standards of life among criminals are those of pigs in a wallow." The women, he says, "rank little higher than sows."[40] Although Corey displays a great deal of misogyny, he does not see women as criminal masterminds: "Woman does not amount to much in crime. Her morals may be as bad as those of her man, but her mentality is weak" (193). At best, he views the female criminal as distracting: "Woman in crime is often weak, frequently noisy, sometimes violent but rarely helpful" (195). He is unrelenting in his efforts to strip female criminals of any moral advantage readers might presume them to have, and he stresses that their sexuality degrades them: "No attempt is being made to suggest that the criminal woman is of a higher type morally than her consort. She merely grades below him mentally and is his associate because she is on a par with him in physical matters" (200). Popular "scientific" theories about gender gave credence to such a view. As Madison Grant, the head of the New York Zoological Society, wrote in *The Passing of the Great Race* (1916), "Women in all human races, as the females among all mammals, tend to exhibit the older, more generalized and primitive traits of the past of the race."[41] Corey and some of his contemporaries went further, though, by describing female criminals in terms that were both contemptuous and pornographic.

Writers sympathetic to the FBI sometimes became positively frenzied in their attempts to disillusion the public about female criminals. In his popular book *Here's to Crime!* (1937), *American Magazine* reporter Courtney Ryley Cooper railed against the romanticization of the gun moll in the popular imagination: "To persons who do not understand how wholeheartedly the gun moll enters into a criminal life, her existence is usually conducive to the deepest sympathy. One looks at the background: lack of home, sordid surroundings, eagerness for sparkle and glamour, a love of adventure—whereupon the wells of compassion become exceedingly well filled."[42] According to Cooper, this sympathy would be misplaced. Gun molls are "heavily supplied with the sex urge" (197), for "this type of woman possesses primeval ideas concerning her relationship to the male" (199). In other words, she is promiscuous. The gun moll is a rotten mother: "It is in a gun moll's blood to look at the world through entirely different eyes from those of true motherhood" (208). The refusal to bear children had long been linked by race theorists to racial degeneracy. As Robert W. Chambers had written in his novel *The Crimson Tide: A Story of Bolshevism in New York* (1919), "The woman who shrinks from motherhood is as low a creature as a man of the professional pacifist, or poltroon, type, who shirks his duty as a soldier."[43] What exercises Cooper most of all is the idea of the gun moll as consumed by venereal disease: "The evidence that a woman on trial had gonorrhea or syphilis would do more to convict a gun moll—especially if she were pretty—than the oratory of a dozen district attorneys" (209). Indeed, "if I appear to be giving special emphasis to the fact that the average gangster and the average gangster's moll are rotten with gonorrhea and syphilis, this is done with thorough deliberation. It seems to be the only way in which the tinsel can be stripped from these filthy beings, the pedestal torn from beneath them" (211). Cooper sums up his research into gun molls by writing that "I have found them to be nothing but a selfish, law-hating, piglike crew of filthy sluts, and the sooner they are so regarded by the general public, the sooner will the professional criminal lose one of his most valuable allies" (220). These views may fairly be seen as reflecting J. Edgar Hoover's: Cooper, who contributed the foreword to Hoover's book *Persons in Hiding* (1938), was seen by the FBI leadership as sufficiently sympathetic to merit personal access to the bureau's director. In addition, the FBI fed him inside information on cases.[44]

Academic specialists supported this picture of female criminals as disease ridden, oversexed, and mentally defective. Noted criminologists Sheldon and Eleanor Glueck, in their study *Five Hundred Delinquent Women* (1934), wrote that the inmates of the Massachusetts Women's Reformatory whom they studied were "burdened by feeble-mindedness, psychopathic personality, and marked emotional instability. . . . The great majority were venereally diseased before they were twenty-one years old. . . . Illicit sexual indulgence was the chief form of their adolescent and early-adult misbehavior. All but two percent of our women had been sexually irregular prior to their commitment to the Reformatory."[45] The Gluecks stress that "the young wives neglected their family responsibilities" (301). In more than one instance, they disapprovingly cite a woman's failure as a housekeeper. "She made no effort to keep her miserable little home in any kind of trim" (56), they write of Minnie, "a descendant of a degenerate, run-down Yankee family, notoriously feeble-minded" (54). "She was found to have very little liking or ability for housework or sewing. She considered it too 'nerve-racking' and would not 'waste' her time making clothes for herself or her child, because 'you can buy them'" (172). The Gluecks also criticize the female criminals for their maternal failures: "That the unfortunate social heritage of these families will in large measure be handed down to subsequent generations may be inferred from the fact that in at least four-fifths of the cases the attitude of our women toward their children was one of indifference if not of actual hostility." The Gluecks conclude that "this swarm of defective, diseased, antisocial misfits, then, comprises the human material which a reformatory and a parole system are required by society to transform into wholesome, decent, law-abiding citizens!" (303).

Hoover took these academic conclusions one step further; he saw criminal women as more than just diseased mental defectives, poor mothers, and rotten housewives. In contrast to writers of the 1920s and early 1930s, who described gun molls as pathetic creatures, lured into the underworld by love, and unable to act on their own, Hoover depicted them as central to the enterprise of American crime: "They are more than consorts, they are mainsprings. Gangs could not exist without them" (154). For instance, according to Hoover, the kidnapper Machine Gun Kelly was himself terrorized by his wife, Kathryn Thorne Kelly, who despite being "attractive to look upon, of good carriage, and pleasing mannerisms," was "one of the most coldly deliberate criminals of my experience. Here was a woman who could conceive a kidnapping [of the millionaire Charles F. Urschel], and force it through to a conclusion largely through her domination of her husband, who, in spite of his terrorizing name, could only bow before her tirades—and do as she bade him. If ever there was a hen-pecked man, it was George (Machine-gun) Kelly" (143). Courtney Riley Cooper echoed this assessment. In his words, Kathryn Kelly was "the brains of the Urschel kidnapping and the nagging, cruel, domineering wife of henpecked Machine-gun Kelly."[46]

In Hoover's account, it was Kathryn, herself "addicted to firearms," who packaged the small-time hood George Kelly as a legendary criminal.[47] She began by buying him a machine gun and accompanying him out to the country for target practice:

> Kathryn garnered the empty cartridges, to be kept for such times as she could hand them to friends, remarking:—
>
> "Here's a souvenir I brought you. It's a cartridge fired by George's machine gun—Machine-gun Kelly, you know." (149)

Although Machine Gun was sent to prison and released, he was of insufficient criminal stature to suit his wife: "The prodding, the sneering, the nagging which went on in the Kelly family as a result can only be gauged by Kathryn's attitude during times which are matters of record." However, when her husband became so obnoxious that he was threatened with murder by two other criminals, "it was then that Kathryn Kelly really took over the directorship of his affairs. . . . There appear evidences that Kathryn embarked upon what might be called a popularity campaign in gangdom. . . . Always she praised her machine-gunning husband. His name began to appear more frequently in crime annals. So did Kathryn's" (151). No matter what she proposed, "the man who was supposedly one of America's worst criminals weakly assented to her demands" (159). In his recounting of the story, Hoover seems as irritated by Kathryn Kelly's success at packaging herself and her husband as he is by her "domineering" nature.

If Hoover paints Kathryn Kelly as a criminal mastermind, he reaches for a different set of images for some other gun molls. He has contempt for Alvin Karpis's "cheap, deluded, silly little moll, Dolores" (42), whom he characterizes as an oversexed girl, "a little cabaret pick-up of a gun moll" (43). Dolores Delaney, the mother of Karpis's child, claimed innocence of the gang's activities, and she becomes for Hoover a symbol of a particularly female form of evil. "This blissful type of ignorance, as displayed by the average gun moll, always has interested me strangely. The one quality which woman is supposed to possess is that of curiosity. Yet the gun moll seems always able to convince the world in general—especially those sentimental moo-cows of scant knowledge but loud voices who are forever interfering with businesslike law enforcement by their turn-the-other cheek theories of crime eradication—that she was born entirely without the quality which made Eve eat the apple" (54).

Because women are inherently curious, gun molls' claims of innocence are prima facie laughable. Moreover, those claims are tied to the molls' greed: "Why should a girl bother her head over unpleasant things like an accusation of murder against her paramour when it might interfere with her enjoyment of a new diamond ring, bought with a part of the blood money?" (59). In other words, both gun molls and the "sentimental moo-cows" who abet them contribute to criminality through their essentially female characteristics, which are curiosity and the sentimentality that contrasts with masculine "businesslike" law enforcement. Yet masculine sentimentality of a different sort also enables female criminality: "American chivalry is to blame for our gun moll" (54).

Hoover saved his greatest ire for two women he saw as criminal masterminds, whose lives and deeds were emblematic of the feminine degeneracy that caused crime and tainted all of American life. One of these women, Bonnie Parker, was a genuine celebrity, who worked hard at keeping herself and her consort in the public eye. However, the other one, Ma Barker, was not really a criminal, although she did travel with her criminal sons and their partners in the Karpis-Barker Gang. It was only after her death in a hail of FBI gunfire that Hoover was able to transform her into what he described as "the most vicious, dangerous and resourceful criminal brain of the last decade" (9). Kate Barker, who had never been arrested, had left no traces in the public record, and it was therefore easy for Hoover to make up anything he liked about her.

Hoover's treatment of Kate "Ma" Barker, who unlike Bonnie Parker was not involved in the creation of her own myth, provides the clearest illustration of his mythmaking bent. Hoover's work was reinforced by FBI agent Melvin Purvis, who in his best-selling memoir *American Agent* (1936), described Barker in dramatic terms: "Ma Barker, grim, gray-haired, well into her fifties, was a criminal herself and the mother of three criminals . . . Ma Barker could handle a machine gun as well as the next man when the occasion demanded, and indeed she subsequently died with that weapon in her hand. Between mother and sons there was a savage love and loyalty. When they went out on the bank robberies she planned, their first duty, once the job was completed, was to telephone their mother that both were safe and sound."[48] According to Purvis, Ma Barker "ruled like a queen. Her word was law; those who did not approve of the matriarchy had her boys to deal with" (152). Barker, as a perverse mother, upset the natural patriarchal order of things: thus, she was even more dangerous than a childless female criminal.

In *Persons in Hiding*, Hoover expanded on this description of Barker as a dangerous mother. He presented her as an "outstanding example" of what he considered was responsible for most criminal behavior, "the evils of parental overindulgence" (8). The "criminal careers" of the Barker boys "were directly traceable to their mother; to her they looked for guidance, for daring resourcefulness" (9). As an overly powerful mother, Barker was able to exert her evil influence in leading her overly devoted sons into wrongdoing.

Although Hoover blamed mothers for the waywardness of male gangsters, he suggested that women were themselves to blame for their own criminal behavior. For instance, Ma Barker's "childhood had been that of an ordinary Missouri farm girl—church, Sunday School, picnics, hayrides, candy pulls and the little red schoolhouse. . . . Later on Kate Barker, looking down the path of criminality, was told by her flesh and blood that she must pursue that path alone" (10). Hoover described Barker as a gang leader whose tender care of her outlaws flowed from her perverted maternal instincts: "Here was a chief counsel who looked after criminals with the care of a mother for a sick child" (19). And it was the death of her son Herman in a shootout with the police that "turned [Barker] from an animal mother of the she-wolf type to a veritable beast of prey" (22).

In his descriptions of both Bonnie Parker and Ma Barker, Hoover—like other commentators of the mid-1930s—turned away from earlier theories of criminality that focused on urban immigrants and looked instead to Anglo-Saxon primitives as the source of crime. Using available stereotypes of poor southern whites in general and mountain people in particular, Hoover found a way to ensure that even the rural women of Anglo-Saxon heritage who committed these crimes would be seen by the public as backward, violent, and uncivilized. As Altina L. Waller has written of the most famous instance of Appalachian violence, the feud between the Hatfields and McCoys that took place between 1878 and 1880, "The feud was a convenient way of emphasizing the point that mountaineers were savages in need of modernization, both economic and cultural."[49] Thus, Hoover was effectively able to portray both Parker and Barker, but particularly the latter, as the antithesis of the "modern" FBI.

In fact, in the public relations battle between Alvin Karpis and Hoover that followed Barker's death, the two men based their analyses of her on her ties to the Southern mountain region, an area first viewed by sociologists, and then seen by the public, as the birthplace of primitive Anglo-American identity. In answer to Hoover's portrayal of Barker as a violent, barely literate primitive, Karpis offered a portrait of Barker as an amusing hillbilly. These characterizations were really just variations on a theme. As Kathleen M. Blee and Dwight B. Billings have documented, the stereotype of the comic hillbilly, which was firmly in place by the turn of the twentieth century, and was subsequently elaborated on by writers and filmmakers throughout the century, had as its flip side that of the violent Appalachian, prone to feuding. Appalachian women were often depicted as "treacherous, deceptive, and sly."[50] This is illustrated in what a turn-of-the-century writer for *Frank Leslie's Popular Monthly* had to say about a mountain girl whom he asked a question: "A change came over the child's face, and she backed away in distrust; the guile of the serpent crept up and flamed in her fox-like eyes, and she answered quickly, and with a furtive glance around, 'I don't know!' . . . Duplicity and cunning were bred in her bone, and had been fostered year by year as she grew."[51] The girl—animalistic, deceptive, criminal —comes across as a young version of the Ma Barker described by Hoover.

Alvin Karpis paints a very different picture. In his autobiography, he flatly rejects Hoover's premise: "The most ridiculous story in the annals of crime is that Ma Barker was the mastermind behind the Karpis-Barker Gang."[52] Karpis's account is in many ways the more plausible of the two. As he points out, Kate Barker was never photographed or fingerprinted by the police, which would seem to be nearly an impossibility for a career criminal. For Hoover, on the other hand, this fact is evidence of her expert criminality: "If her sons could not learn the lessons of safety which she strove to teach them, she, at least, could give a demonstration of their effectiveness. In all her life, she was not once arrested. . . . Barely able to read and write, she nevertheless knew every trick in the encyclopedia of criminality."[53] However, Karpis reaches for the same stereotypes in showing why Barker could not possibly be an evil mastermind. In both cases, her guilt or innocence hinges on her identity as a woman of the Ozarks.

While Hoover presents Ma Barker as vicious and cunning, perhaps because of her southern mountain background, Karpis construes her background in a different way, viewing her as "just an old-fashioned homebody from the Ozarks. . . . She was a simple woman."[54] If Hoover's Ma Barker is "not a 'hillbilly,' but the daughter of parents predominantly Scotch-Irish" (10), Karpis's version is the comic hillbilly: "Ma was superstitious, gullible, simple, cantankerous and, well, generally law-abiding. She wasn't suited for a role in the Karpis-Barker Gang" (82). In fact, it is precisely her background that makes her ignorant: "She was, after all, a woman from the Ozarks and had no sophistication and no background that would make her want to know more about how we earned our money. She never read newspapers or looked at magazines and, as [her son] Freddie was always pointing out, the only radio stations she tuned into were the hillbilly stations, the ones that didn't bother with news" (82). In his descriptions of her, Karpis frequently stresses this aspect: "She sounded like a real little Ozark hillbilly" (83).[55]

Although Karpis, who lived with her and her sons for years and took the role of a son to her, wanted Ma Barker to enjoy sophisticated things, "she liked," he says, "simple pleasures more than expensive treats. Bingo, for instance—Ma was nuts about bingo, and I took her to many games. Bingo bored me, but I didn't mind showing Ma a good time" (85). Rustic in her interests, Ma is also the antithesis, in appearance, of the sophisticated gun moll: "The strange things she did to her hair didn't make her more glamorous. . . . The night I took her to the 1933 Chicago World's Fair, she performed a real job on herself. . . . We visited all the exhibits that appealed to her, like the 'Ripley's Believe It or Not' show and the Motordome, and she stuffed herself with cotton candy all night. Well, after a few hours, what with the curls and the dirt and the dust and her windblown clothes and her face covered with dried cotton candy, Ma looked like an exhibit out of the Ripley show herself" (91).

Consider, by contrast, Hoover's description: "The eyes of Arizona Clark Barker [her full formal name] always fascinated me. They were queerly direct, penetrating, hot with some strangely smoldering flame, yet withal as hypnotically cold as the muzzle of a gun."[56] Karpis's evidence of her innocence, thus, is the flip side of Hoover's version of her guilt: a white primitive, she is so out of touch with the main currents of American society that she cannot be taken seriously as a criminal. Her simple nature is proof of her innocence: "With her personality, brains, and style, it was impossible for Ma Barker ever to become the mastermind of the Karpis-Barker gang."[57] Similarly, gang member Harvey Bailey remarked years later that "the old woman couldn't plan breakfast. When we'd sit down to plan a bank job, she'd go in the other room and listen to Amos and Andy or hillbilly music on the radio. She just went along with Freddy because she had no choice. Freddy loved his mother and wouldn't leave her to fend for herself."[58]

However, there was one way, both Hoover and Karpis agree, that Ma Barker did perform an incredibly useful role for the gang: "When we traveled together," Karpis writes, "we moved as a mother and three sons. Who could look more innocent?" This ruse fooled not only landlords and other civilians but also the police, who harbored their own stereotypes about criminals: "They could never believe that fellows who were kind to their mother could ever be members of a dangerous gang of criminals. They were wrong, of course. As wrong as the people who started the legend that Ma Barker was the brains of the gang" (91). For Karpis, Ma Barker's relationship with the gang was proof of her humanity and evidence against Hoover's reductive theories of female criminality.

Although Barker was useful to the gang during her life, she acted an even more helpful part for Hoover after her death. As Bryan Burrough points out, following the deadly 1935 shootout in which Ma Barker was killed by the FBI along with her son Fred, Hoover had the delicate task of "explaining to the nation's press just why his men had killed a grandmother with no criminal record."[59] Yet precisely because Barker was neither youthful nor glamorous, and had been completely uninterested in shaping her own public image, Hoover had an easy time selling reporters on his social theories. A multipart feature distributed weeks after her death by the King Features Syndicate presented her as "Ma Barker: Deadly Spider Woman" and breathlessly described how "the withered fingers of spidery crafty Ma Barker, like satanic tentacles, controlled the skeins on which dangled the fate of desperadoes whose activities hit the headlines on an average of once a week."[60] It would be hard to find a worse image of motherhood than this. Thus, Hoover took a public relations debacle that could have been worse than the FBI's killing of John Dillinger the previous year and turned it into the centerpiece for his gender-based theory of crime and punishment.

POSING FOR PHOTOS, AUTHORING BALLADS:
HOW BONNIE PARKER CREATED HERSELF

Of his meeting with Bonnie and Clyde, Alvin Karpis writes: "As for the couple, they looked like sharecroppers. He had a young face, a short fellow with light brown hair. She was a tiny thing, not more than one hundred pounds soaking wet, I imagined, and she had awfully squinty eyes. Both of their faces wore blank expressions, like many of the people you saw sitting on front porches in the rural parts of Texas and Oklahoma."[61] Yet if they looked like sharecroppers, they wrote and posed in a style familiar and appealing to tabloid readers. In doing so they managed to create a new kind of popular heroine.

Gangsters seemed to be everywhere in the early thirties. The adventures of Pretty Boy Floyd, Machine Gun Kelly, and the Karpis-Barker Gang were closely documented in the pages of newspapers and used as the plots for popular movies. Yet, even in this climate, Bonnie Parker and Clyde Barrow stood out as icons. For one thing, they were extremely active as criminals. Between 1932 and 1934, they went on a crime spree through Texas, Louisiana, Missouri, Kansas, Iowa, Arkansas, New Mexico, and Oklahoma, committing twelve murders and scores of robberies and engaging in nearly a dozen incidents of hostage-taking. They were also extremely daring: they smuggled weapons into the Texas prison system to free their confederates and became famous for their abilities as escape artists. They drove their stolen cars through the Texas countryside at speeds of up to seventy miles an hour, evading police traps, while other gang members, including members of both their families, were caught. Public fascination about them was fed not only by their frenzied pace but also by how they were portrayed in the press (sometimes in conflicting ways). The western locations of their crimes conjured up the exploits of some of the most famous bandits of the 1890s. Yet Bonnie and Clyde were not just nostalgic throwbacks: the cars they drove at high speeds gave them a modern freedom. While they presented themselves as romantic lovers, they also wanted to be seen as contemporary versions of Robin Hood and Maid Marian, who could claim virtue in fighting back against the predatory rich.

The rich variety of possible interpretations helped generate an enormous amount of publicity on the radio, in newspapers, and in crime magazines. Bonnie and Clyde worked hard to shape their publicity. They contributed to their own legend through photographs they took of one another, poems written by Bonnie Parker, and stories they sent to detective magazines; they even played up a letter Clyde Barrow ostensibly sent to the Ford Motor Company, extolling the Ford as the car he always stole when he had the opportunity.[62] One of the least flattering images of them—as the "snake-eyed killer" and "cigar-smoking gun moll"—had its origins in gag photos the two took of each other while enacting their own private fantasies of gangsterdom. When police seized one of their crime cars, in 1933, they found, in addition to blood and eleven license plates from different states, the latest detective magazines featuring stories about the pair.[63]

Bonnie Parker was horrified when police discovered and developed the gag photos that she and Clyde Barrow had taken of one another. Courtesy of AP.

Bonnie Parker helped burnish her own image. As historian Claire Bond Potter has written, "Romance and the production of a criminal self were inextricably entwined for those who followed Bonnie's career."[64] Before meeting Bonnie, Clyde was just another two-bit crook. Their romantic partnership elevated their criminal status. The discovery of two rolls of exposed film in an apartment used by the couple gave rise to new publicity, for the gang members were shown in gag photos wielding guns they had stolen from police officers, and there was an image of Bonnie brandishing two pistols and clenching a cigar between her teeth. First printed by the *Joplin World*, the picture of Bonnie then appeared in newspapers all over the country.

Gangsters worked in an uneasy relationship with crime writers, who brought them publicity but also distorted their stories. In Edward Anderson's novel *Thieves Like Us* (1937), one bank robber, T-Dub, explains to another how "I tried to make a hole in this prison in this state one time and it went haywire and this squirt comes to me and wants me to tell him all about it so he can write a big story for the magazine. . . . Everyone knew all about it anyway and this squirt said if I would tell him the straight of it he would get it printed and split the money with me."[65] The reporter turns a botched escape attempt into a cold-blooded calculation on the part of T-Dub: "You should have seen the way it came out in that magazine. I was the big shot, see. And I sent them two boys over that got killed first because I figured the guards would use up all their ammunition and then me and the other boy still down at the bottom of the ladder would have a clear way. Anybody knows that the chair boys get the first break and that's why they went over first. Hell, I didn't go on up because the damn ladder had broke. One of them joint ladders you know. Then that squirt putting it in the magazine like that" (69). Needless to say, T-Dub never gets his money; the squirt of a writer, completely ignorant of prison rituals and outlaw etiquette, is happy to exploit his informant, write to audience expectations of cold-blooded killers, promote his own career, and move on.

The story of Bonnie and Clyde is in large part the story of competing narratives about them as individuals and as representatives of the rural poor, especially the poor white family. The famous picture of the cigar-smoking, gun-toting Bonnie Parker makes for a sharp contrast with the dignified photo of the two lovers from the same roll of film, which was published in the memoir written jointly by (or "as told to") Bonnie's mother and Clyde's sister, titled *Fugitives: The Story of Clyde Barrow and Bonnie Parker* (1934).

Produced quickly to counteract the negative images of Bonnie and Clyde, the memoir insists on its subjects' dignity and even respectability, treading a third path between the depraved images of the pair trumpeted by the FBI and the bandit images produced by the pair themselves. Emma Parker and Nell Barrow Cowan set the tone for their memoir in the foreword: "Clyde and Bonnie had a love which bound them together in life and went with them to their graves. We believe that no two people ever loved more devotedly, more sincerely, and more lastingly than Clyde Barrow and Bonnie Parker. This love was all they had to set them apart from others of their kind; and it was not enough."[66] In a world in which the cards are stacked against them, a world of poverty and low expectations, "devotion" and "sincerity" as opposed to, say, passion, make the couple's love respectable.

Cowan writes of her younger brother's early dreams: "By the time Clyde was six, he knew just what he was going to be: A hero like William S. Hart, who was the big screen menace at that time . . . When we played, Clyde was the leader. He was Jesse James, or Cole Younger, or Buffalo Bill, or William S. Hart. He toted guns and shot from the hip with deadly aim, and cowards and redskins always bit the dust in the most approved fashion" (6–7). However, even as she notes her brother's immersion in mass-market fantasy images of criminality, Cowan insists on his respectability: "The most respectable and educated people were his friends, and the nicest girls fell in love with him" (17).

Bonnie's mother reveals that "her ruling passion all her life was babies. Clyde told me a month or so before he and Bonnie were killed, that she was always wanting to just 'borrow' some woman's baby for a few days. . . . 'Hold-ups were things Bonnie did get to really care for,' Clyde said. 'But the kidnapping racket was one where she'd have thrived, if all the people snatched had been one year old, or younger'" (54). At least in her mother's view, Bonnie embraced, rather than rejected, traditional gender roles, and she was aghast at the representations of her as masculinized. Emma Parker is eager to refute the newspaper and detective-magazine stories that alleged that "Bonnie was seen often with Clyde in night clubs and speakeasies, Bonnie always smoking a big black cigar and paying all the bills" (57).

Bonnie and Clyde were shot down by lawmen in an ambush on May 23, 1934, in rural northwestern Louisiana. They died almost literally in one another's arms; their "death car," which was exhibited at public events for years thereafter, and their bodies were targeted by souvenir hunters.[67] Clyde's funeral attracted thirty thousand spectators, and Bonnie's was mobbed as well. The largest wreath at Bonnie's was sent by an organization of Dallas newspaper boys, perhaps in thanks for the half million newspapers the account of the final ambush had helped them to sell.

As a media creature, and as a figure in the dream life of Americans longing for an imagined simpler past, Bonnie Parker, like other famous gangsters of the era, worked hard to shape her own image. Unlike Ma Barker, who was silent and who did not take an active role in the criminal life, Bonnie Parker fashioned herself as a heroine in a mold that had previously only been available to men. The image of Bonnie Parker made it possible for women thirty-five years later to envision themselves as all-American swashbuckling bandits. Hoover may have won the battle, in the sense that his agents killed or imprisoned the most famous female criminals of the era, but he lost the war for the place these women inhabited in the public imagination. Try as he might to lay the blame for American social decay at the feet of female gangsters, Hoover failed. It must have driven him crazy, some thirty-five years later, to be battling female radicals who not only embraced the left-wing politics he hated but also took their inspiration from the outlaw women he worked so hard to deglamorize.

4

RADICAL WOMEN
OF THE 1960s AND
1970s

In 1970, shortly before Weatherwoman Susan Stern was arrested as one of the Seattle Seven, on charges of inciting to riot, she and a female friend painted a mural on the wall of their collective house while they were tripping on acid: ". . . an eight-foot-tall nude woman with flowing green-blond hair, and a burning American flag coming out of her cunt! One graceful arm was raised in a fist; the other held a shotgun. Her breast was crisscrossed with a bandoleer. A caption beneath her said LONG LICKS OF LUST!"[1]

Was this blonde woman posed as Miss America, with a bandolier replacing her sash, a rifle her bouquet, and a raised fist her wave to the adoring crowd? Or was this a radicalized statue of liberty, carrying a gun as torch? Her height suggested overwhelming power, and her hair was green as well as blonde—she was both dream and nightmare. Was this aggressively sexual, violent woman threatening to consume a nation in flames? Or was she giving birth to a new nation? This vision of both nationhood and the destruction of nationhood (the burning flag), of maternity and a possibly terrifying sexuality (the vagina dentata), psychedelically inspired and painted as home décor, offered Stern's housemates her vision of the revolutionary American woman, circa 1973.

For many activists of color, her vision of a blonde Miss America, however revolutionary, was obsolete. The 1960s and 1970s produced more than the first generation of articulate, armed white female revolutionaries, women whose activism encompassed not only the goal of ending the war in Vietnam but also radical changes in gender roles, as signaled by Weatherman's imperative to "smash monogamy." The late 1960s also heralded the arrival of a cadre of black women leftists who used the gun to turn the eugenics arguments of the early twentieth century on their head—women who used weaponry in a struggle to combat what they viewed as a campaign of black genocide by the u.s. government and who gave birth, sometimes in prison, as part of a political program. This group included Black Power activists like Elaine Brown, the only national female leader of the Black Panther Party (BPP), and Assata Shakur, also known as JoAnne Chesimard, the Black Liberation Army activist who was sentenced to a long prison term for her role in an armed robbery, became pregnant and gave birth while in prison, and eventually made a jail break for Cuba. However, this focus on the politics of birth was not limited to black women: Weatherwoman Bernardine Dohrn, the "macho mama" who used women's violence as political theater, celebrated the killing of white babies as a eugenics program.

These women all embraced guns as a means of political and personal liberation, yet their motivations and ideologies cannot be lumped together. In this chapter I trace the ways that radical women of the 1960s and 1970s used the gun as a means of both placing themselves within and redefining an American tradition. For many black radicals the gun came to be both a badge of citizenship and a symbol for the dismantling of an oppressive state. For a number of white activists the gun was a central icon in their sometimes nostalgic reenactment of an outlaw tradition fueled by the popular success of the movie *Bonnie and Clyde*. I conclude by looking at the story of Patty Hearst, whose trial and the widespread media attention it attracted became a public forum on the cultural meanings of women's revolutionary violence. Thus, Stern's mural, with its blend of sexuality, violence, and Americanism, was only one vision of the armed revolutionary woman of the era. Through staging armed robberies, initiating violent confrontations with fellow radicals, and training with weapons to diminish the threat of male supremacy, a range of radical women explored the relationship between women's rights, racial survival, and the gun.

The armed woman seemed to be everywhere in sixties and seventies America: violent, sexual, and politically radical. There were now heated debates, both within and outside the left, over what it meant for American women to take up arms. As fugitive Jane Alpert wrote, "If to the straight world I appeared a nice young girl drawn tragically into crime, to the movement I was a fearless Amazon."[2] In feminist journals, theorists argued whether violence was necessary or counter to women's nature. Meanwhile, a rash of articles appeared in the mass media conflating feminism, violence, criminality, and politics. In this conflation, the case of Patty Hearst became a cultural flash point: was she a victim, a criminal, a revolutionary—or all three? Hearst's case, more than any other, demonstrated the difficulties that observers of the time had in distinguishing between realities and cultural fantasies about the armed woman.

By wielding guns, revolutionary women of the 1960s and 1970s claimed full American citizenship. And yet they sought to change, and in some cases worked actively to dismantle, the nation. Unlike the women soldiers of the Civil War, the female radicals of the Vietnam era did not try to work within the system as soldiers to challenge prevailing cultural assumptions about gender and about the form that women's patriotism could take. Rather, they fought in underground groups to bring about radical change: to end the war, to bring full civil rights to a wide spectrum of the disenfranchised, to shake the country to its foundations. At a time of crisis, when millions were questioning what direction the country should take, armed revolutionary women brought to the forefront provocative questions about gender, violence, and the meaning of Americanism. As Stern's mural suggested, some of these armed women were trying to redeem America, while others were trying to eradicate it.

Although I use sources ranging from underground comix and newspapers to sociological texts to frame my discussion, a great deal of this chapter is based on readings of autobiographies written by radical women during the seventies and decades later. Given the charged nature of the debate over violence in the 1960s and 1970s, these autobiographies must be read with caution and a keen awareness of the author's position in relation to both her presumed audience and the historical events in which she was involved. Autobiographies are wonderful sources, but they are carefully crafted literary works more than documentary accounts.[3] Women who wrote memoirs while they were still active in radical politics, such as Susan Stern of Weatherman, whose autobiography appeared in 1977, surely had a different perspective from those writing long after they left the revolutionary movement. Elaine Brown, who published her memoir *A Taste of Power* in 1992, years after she broke with the BPP, explored the ambivalence of her position in ways that women who published autobiographies while they were still active in radical politics did not. Activists like Assata Shakur celebrate the period as a time when political change seemed possible, whereas Brown and other writers looking backward tend to stress the destructive and hedonistic nature of their youthful radicalism.

The tone of these memoirs depends greatly on whether they were written for a mainstream audience as well as for a radical culture. Assata Shakur, who wrote her memoir, *Assata*, from exile in Cuba following her escape from prison, published her book with a small press and used the language and syntax dictated by her political beliefs (she refers to "amerika," for instance). By contrast, Angela Davis's *With My Mind on Freedom: An Autobi-*

ography had enough appeal for mainstream audiences to be selected by the Book-of-the-Month Club.

Davis published her memoir shortly after her acquittal on charges of kidnapping, conspiracy, and murder.[4] Uninterested in her own iconicity and unwilling to proclaim that the personal is political, Davis does not dwell in her autobiography on what fascinated the public about female revolutionaries, which was their combination of femininity and violence. Yet there was another Angela Davis, one who was favorably quoted by poet M. F. Beal in her defense of the Symbionese Liberation Army, *Safe House*: "For the black female, the solution is not to become less aggressive, not to lay down the gun, but to learn how to set the sights correctly, aim accurately, squeeze rather than jerk and not to be overcome by the damage. We have to learn how to rejoice when pigs' blood is spilled."[5] It would be easy to use this discrepancy as evidence that Davis was just the dangerous radical she was accused of being. However, her experience, and that of many other radical women of the time, must be seen within the context of movement violence, weapons fetishism, and the massive police repression faced by radicals, particularly black activists.

The autobiography written in the most charged circumstances of all must surely be Patty Hearst's, given her widespread notoriety and the cultural (and legal) debate over her role within the Symbionese Liberation Army. Hearst, more than any other writer discussed here, faced an enormous rhetorical challenge: she had to reframe her SLA experience for a largely unsympathetic readership. She needed to present herself not as a violent revolutionary but as a traumatized victim. Yet all of the women whose autobiographies I discuss wrote within a context of public curiosity and ideologically fraught arguments over the violent capabilities of women.

WHY NOW?

Before Susan Stern and her generation of revolutionary female activists burst on the scene, the armed woman seemed to have been almost fully domesticated. Within the world of the National Rifle Association and of gun manufacturers' ads, armed women, in their roles as mothers, wives, and daughters, appeared in large numbers between the end of the 1930s and the beginning of the 1960s. Competitive shooter Alice Bull became the first woman elected to the NRA Board of Directors in 1949. During the same period, a new spate of advertisements in gun magazines extolled target shooting as a sport for the entire family. In these ads, women often

Although women received weapons training during World War II, the armed services
downplayed that fact. Courtesy of Wisconsin Historical Society, 34548.

were shown in a support role, cheering on their sons, daughters, and husbands. Yet even when women were represented as shooters in ads, magazine articles, television shows, and comics, they were generally wholesome and domestic, a far cry from the female gangsters of the prewar decade. In fact, the deployment of women in the armed services during World War II, rather than resulting in a multiplicity of new images of armed women, led to some fairly tame representations of female shooters.

As Leisa D. Meyer argues, the establishment of the Women's Army Auxiliary Corps in 1942 "crystallized public fears that the mobilization of women for war would undermine the established sex/gender system, and both men's and women's places within it."[6] The greatest potential threat was the image of the armed female soldier. Thus, the armed services defined all women in the military as noncombatants, a stipulation established with the creation of the corps; the law enacted by Congress "prohibited the employment of women as combatants within the Army and was supported by succeeding Army regulations that prohibited the use of weapons or arms of any kind by members of the women's corps." This stipulation was not entirely honored: women who were assigned to an experimental anti-aircraft unit in Washington, D.C., for example, were given training in the use of guns and automatic weapons.[7] However, in popular culture, WACs were not generally associated with weaponry. A series of cartoons by Corporal Vic Herman, collected in the volume *Winnie the WAC: A Cartoon Visit with Our Gals in the Army* (1945), features a featherbrained girl who is more likely to arrive for mopping duty in an evening gown ("But I thought you said it was to be a G.I. party!") or to scream for the "Corporal of the Guard" when encountering a mouse than she is to engage in any heroics on the battlefield.[8] In fact, Winnie shows up for duty in full Native American headdress, her outfit completed by a mini skirt and a bra, telling her disapproving boss, "But I'm on the warpath!" The only time we actually see her wielding a gun is when she is standing in a tank, threatening a male soldier: "Well, do we have that date tonight or don't we?" Max Barsis's collection of cartoons, *They're All Yours, Uncle Sam!* (1943), features a pair of equally clueless twins, one a WAVE (the navy equivalent of a WAC) and the other a WAC, both prone to ogling officers and more concerned about absent boyfriends and unbecoming uniforms than about soldierly matters.[9]

Within the readership of NRA members, women in the armed forces were celebrated for their shooting feats, but in such a way that their primary status as wives, rather than as markswomen, was never in doubt. An article that appeared in the December 1945 issue of the NRA magazine *American Rifleman*, titled "More Women!," celebrated the rise in recreational shooting among women, noting that "service women in the three services that have permitted women to shoot have had the best opportunity to learn to shoot. WAVES, SPARS, and Women Marines have grasped this opportunity enthusiastically." (A SPAR was a member of the women's reserves of the U.S. Coast Guard.) For Eleanor Dunn, the author of this article, military experience offered women not only a chance to be patriotic but also an opportunity to strengthen their marriages: "If it's true that a community of interests makes for happy marriage, these women will have added one new common interest in their lives with shooting husbands. Lieutenant (jg) Lota Williams, of the SPARS, having qualified Expert with the carbine, will listen with intelligent understanding to her Navy husband's talk of guns." Women's shooting, she wrote, should be encouraged: "Why not teach 'the little woman' to shoot with you? You'll get out shooting more often if she can go along—and, besides, she'll provide a good lunch!"[10] In this case, the armed woman is literally responsible for domesticating the sport of shoot-

"Well, do we have that date tonight or don't we?"

In popular culture, WACS were usually depicted as sex-starved. Here, Winnie the WAC uses
weapons only to get a man. Cpl. Vic Herman, *Winnie the WAC: A Cartoon Visit with
Our Gals in the Army* (Philadelphia: David McKay, 1945).

ing: there is little difference between her shooting and her meal preparation.

Just as women in the armed forces were represented in official armed
forces literature and popular culture as being far from warlike, so the extremely popular female superhero Wonder Woman, who debuted in a

comic strip in the December 1941–January 1942 issue of *All-Star Comics*, was portrayed as an amazon who was not aggressive. Her creator, William Moulton Marston, explained: "Wonder Woman is a psychological propaganda for the new type of woman who should, I believe, rule the world. . . . What woman lacks is the dominance or self-assertive power to put over and enforce her love desires. I have given Wonder Woman this dominant force but have kept her loving, tender, maternal and feminine in every other way."[11] The formula was successful, and Wonder Woman became the star of her own comic book within months of her initial appearance. Although Wonder Woman did engage in violent action from time to time, the official line from her creator was that she was pacific in every way. She was far more likely to deflect bullets with her special bracelet than to wield firearms herself. Even the popular television show *Annie Oakley* (1952–56), starring Gail Davis, was made for children: although the character of Oakley was armed, she was completely nonthreatening.

All of these cartoon female soldiers and amazons were white, as was, of course, the character of Annie Oakley.[12] The notion of an armed African American heroine had to have been almost inconceivable given the long history of gun laws and popular stereotypes linking nonwhite gun ownership with criminality or insurrection. The armed woman of the period was invariably portrayed as unthreatening. Wonder Woman, the television character Annie Oakley, and the WACS invariably used guns in support of the state. By contrast, the generation of armed women, both real and fictional, that followed used guns with the goal of dismantling what they saw as an unjust regime.

CONTEXT: STATE VIOLENCE AND VIOLENCE AGAINST THE STATE

An interviewer for the organization Women against Prison asked imprisoned Black Liberation Army activist Assata Shakur to comment on the issue of women's violence: "There's been a lot of articles recently in the media blaming the Women's Movement for what they call 'the increasing violence of women.' To illustrate their point, they use you, the women of the S.L.A., the women who attempted to assassinate Ford, etc. What do you think of that?" Shakur responded, ". . . To blame the Women's Movement for creating a violent monster is insane. The violent monster is the American government."[13]

The extensive violence against radical activists of this period, much of it state sponsored, and the activists' response to this violence provide a great deal of the context for the development of armed revolutionary movements of the 1960s and 1970s. In general, the embrace of armed self-defense and the escalating violence of the American left began as a direct response to the violence, both governmental and extragovernmental, aimed first at civil rights activists and then at other leftists. Specifically, many women activists, as well as observers of all political viewpoints, linked their taking up of arms against the state to their gender identity. The female armed revolutionaries of the period explicitly connected their use of arms to their sexuality and maternity, and they saw engaging in violence as a path to liberation. An examination of these women makes us ask: how did they see the relationship between gender and violence? Why did they see violence as an emancipatory strategy?

Violence as a revolutionary strategy did not develop, at least in a public way, until the late sixties, in large part because the theater of victimized innocence proved to be a powerful spectacle. The nonviolence advocated by Martin Luther King was a big part of what made the civil rights movement acceptable to white America: the brutality of segregationist tactics against nonviolent marchers crystallized the moral drama of the movement. During the Birmingham civil rights marches of 1963, public opinion turned in favor of the civil rights movement when television audiences saw the spectacle of police commissioner Bull Connor's setting police dogs on and aiming fire hoses at the thousands of children who were marching through city streets. As CBS commentator Eric Sevareid noted on the evening news, "A snarling police dog set upon a human being is recorded in the permanent photoelectric file of every human being's brain."[14] According to Taylor Branch, the fire hoses "made limbs jerk weightlessly and tumbled whole bodies like scraps of refuse in a high wind."[15] When the bodies being tumbled were those of children as young as six, the image had to be indelible in the minds of viewers: here, unequivocally, was black innocence at the mercy of white violence. As Lance Hill notes, armed self-defense groups had existed throughout the civil rights movement, but they had "avoided open confrontation with authority and purposefully eschewed publicity—in part because they feared retaliation and in part because they wanted to maintain the illusion of non-violence in the movement."[16] Yet years of unceasing bombings, shootings, and beatings by hard-core segregationists administered against civil rights activists and against blacks, simply as a means of terrorizing the entire black community, caused many activists to question their public creed of nonviolence. Given this context, Stokely Carmichael's historic 1966 demand for "Black power!" and the subsequent de-

This 1961 picture of civil rights activists Robert F. Williams and Mabel Williams belied
the nonviolent image that movement leaders sought to project. From the collection of
John H. Williams. Courtesy of Mabel Williams.

velopment of the Black Panther Party for Self-Defense seemed inevitable.
As William L. Van Deburg writes, among black activists "the doctrine of
nonviolence became stigmatized as little more than a moral exercise."[17]

While the embrace of the gun by black civil rights activists occurred
within a context of racial violence, the violence of black nationalist groups,
as well as of certain factions of the antiwar movement, was spurred by the
escalation of the war in Vietnam and, more directly, by the efforts of the
FBI. The FBI's notorious COINTELPRO domestic spying and harassment programs, dating back to the Eisenhower era, were expanded in 1968 to target
black nationalists, so as to "expose, disrupt, misdirect, discredit, or otherwise neutralize" their activities, as an FBI memo put it.[18] The harassment
programs, which had earlier been used to slander Communist Party members in the 1950s, and to try to induce Martin Luther King Jr. to commit suicide in the early 1960s, were now directed at the Black Panthers and other
leftist groups.[19] The work of the FBI often went far beyond sending poi-

son pen letters. In 1969 the FBI collaborated with Chicago police to shoot sleeping Panther leader Fred Hampton in bed, kill Panther Mark Clark, and wound six other Panthers in an exchange that involved between eighty-three and ninety-nine police shots—and only one from a Panther gun.[20]

While the FBI collaborated in direct acts of violence, it also devoted a lot of effort to increasing violence within left-wing movements. As the San Diego field office informed the FBI headquarters in late November 1969, "Beatings, shootings and a high degree of unrest continues [sic] to prevail in the ghetto area of Southeast San Diego. Although no specific counter-intelligence program can be credited with contributing to this overall situation, it is felt that a substantial amount of the unrest is directly attributable to this program."[21] A Senate Select Committee investigating government intelligence operations in 1976 concluded that in its operations against the BPP the FBI "engaged in lawless tactics and responded to deep-seated social problems by fomenting violence and unrest."[22]

Sometimes FBI agents provocateurs directly incited violence. One of the best known of these provocateurs, Thomas Tongyai, known as Tommy the Traveler, was paid by both the FBI and local police to travel around western New York colleges for over two years, "urging students to kill police, make bombs and blow up buildings. . . . Tongyai constantly talked violence, carried a grenade in his car, showed students how to use an M-1 rifle and offered advice on how to carry out bombings."[23]

While the violence of male activists was certainly newsworthy, women's violence within the movement seemed more shocking to the media. Were these armed female revolutionaries "women's libbers" gone wild? Were they sexually liberated girls lost in orgiastic violence that resulted from their reputed promiscuity? Were the armed mothers of the revolution an update of the "pioneer mothers" whose images were so popular around the turn of the century?

BLACK POWER AND THE RIGHT TO BEAR ARMS

In *Black Macho and the Myth of the Superwoman*, Michele Wallace writes of the "Black Movement [as] nothing more nor less than the black man's struggle to attain his presumably lost 'manhood.'"[24] "To most of us Black Power meant woolly heads, big black fists and stern black faces, gargantuan omnipotent black male organs, big black rifles and foot-long combat boots, tight pants over young muscular asses, dashikis, and broad brown chests; black men looting and rioting in the streets, taking over the country by brute force, arrogant lawlessness and an unquestionable sexual authority granted them as the victims of four hundred years of racism and abuse. The media emphasized this image" (60). For the Black Panthers, the most successful and visible proponents of Black Power, gun ownership—those "big black rifles" that Wallace describes—was a key element of successful black manhood. Yet according to a 1969 survey conducted by Bobby Seale, two-thirds of the BPP membership was female.[25] How did the call to promote "collective manhood" resonate with the women in the Panthers, and in the Black Power movement more generally?[26]

To most outside observers, it was not masculinity or ideology but fire-power that was the most prominent feature of the Panthers. It was the Panthers' demand for inclusion in America's violent gun culture that seemed most newsworthy to the mainstream media. Newspaper stories gave scanty coverage to the Panthers' free breakfast programs, schools, free plumbing programs, free health clinics, and free transportation to correctional institutions for prisoners' families. In fact, Panthers were not simply wielding guns. They were also demanding and obtaining school traffic lights, protesting rent evictions, and informing welfare recipients of their legal rights.[27] Because this culture was explicitly male, and because the "big black rifle" seemed an extension of the "gargantuan omnipotent black male organs" described by Wallace, the women who embraced the Panther program, and became gun-carrying Panther leaders, sometimes struggled to redefine black revolutionary identity and the linkage between sexuality and revolutionary violence.

While the symbolism of the Panthers may have rendered weaponry as phallic, both male and female party members carried guns, for the Panthers were founded on a platform that explicitly tied gun ownership to political rights and freedoms. In sending an armed delegation of thirty Panthers (twenty-four men and six women) to the California state house in Sacramento in 1967 to protest a proposed gun-control law, BPP leader Huey Newton emphasized for television cameras and state legislators that "the Black Panther Party for Self-Defense believes that the time has come for Black people to arm themselves against this terror [the proposed law] before it is too late."[28] *The Black Panther* newspaper was unequivocal: "Revolutionary strategy for Black people in America begins with the defensive movement of picking up the Gun, as the condition for ending the pigs' reign of terror by the Gun."[29]

The Panthers claimed gun ownership for African Americans both as a key to racial survival and as a necessary element of American identity. They challenged the traditions, in many places hardened into law, that limited gun ownership to white men.[30] The eugenicists of the early twentieth century had explicitly promoted gun ownership for whites as a key element in the "survival of the race," but the Panthers upended these eugenics arguments by linking gun ownership to black survival.

There was nothing new about black armed self-defense. As John Mitchell Jr., editor of the black weekly the *Richmond Planet*, wrote in 1886, "The best remedy for a lyncher or a cursed mid-night rider is a 16-shot Winchester in the hands of a dead-shot Negro who has nerve enough to pull the trigger."[31] More recently, many civil rights activists had armed themselves, albeit without advertising that they had done so. It is true that the most memorable and widely disseminated images of the civil rights movement in Birmingham were the attacks by the white supremacist state against nonviolent black protesters. Yet, according to Dan Carter, following the 1963 bombing of the Sixteenth Street Baptist Church, which left four young black girls dead, the FBI, "well aware that hundreds of blacks had armed themselves to form a loose-knit defense force, refused to drive the assistant attorney general of the United States to King's command center at a private home in a black neighborhood. . . . The experience of being driven through an American city by black self-defense forces armed to the teeth seemed to unnerve the phlegmatic [assistant attorney general Burke] Marshall."[32]

By comparison, the Black Panthers, far from concealing their weapons, displayed them theatrically. As historian William L. Van Deburg writes, the Panthers

were armed to the teeth, employing their arsenal both as a self-defense mechanism and as an aid in recruiting 'the brothers on the block' to the organization. . . . Panther chapters conducted classes in the use of firearms, engaged in close order drill, and studied literature on guerrilla warfare techniques. Recognizing that they wore the Panther reputation for armed militance whenever they donned their uniform and strapped on a gun, recruits made certain that they knew how to defend themselves against all comers. . . . Upon leaving the training session, a typical Panther delegation might have in their possession several shotguns, a couple of M-1 rifles, and all manner of handguns. If challenged by the police, they coolly would recite the applicable legal codes to the officer as an interested crowd of prospective members assembled, eyes bulging at the sight of bold, dignified young blacks facing down armed white authority figures.[33]

More than almost any other group, the Panthers foregrounded gun ownership as an element of American identity—and then demanded that this
identity be available to all. Although the pundits and reporters who focused
on this posture may not have framed the Panthers' demands in quite the
same terms, it is clear that it was the organization's position on guns that
proved most disturbing to them. As Assata Shakur wrote, "Nobody gets upset about white people having guns, but let a Black person have a gun and
something criminal is going on."[34] Indeed, all of the press coverage of the
Panthers' protest at the California state capitol ignored the white protesters
from the gun lobby who were there for the same reason. The Panthers drew
the attention of the police as well: they were arrested and held for several
days on charges of disturbing the peace.

Panther women brandished phallic weaponry and cultivated, especially
in the early days, an androgynous look: the Panther uniform of black pants,
shoes, and beret, powder blue shirt, often worn with a turtleneck, and black
leather jacket; like the men, the women favored a natural hairstyle. Guns
were strongly associated with manhood, as former Panther leader Elaine
Brown recalls, "I did not resist at all when Crook strapped the two bando-
liers of shotgun shells around my waist before taking me to the San Diego
rally. He also placed two shotguns on the rear floor of his 'hoopty,' his automobile, in which we would ride to the rally. Guns were the natural accessory
of the new black militants, who were determined to claim their manhood
'by any means necessary.'"[35]

IDEOLOGIES OF GENDER AND VIOLENCE
IN THE BLACK POWER MOVEMENT

While Black Panther ideology may have emphasized guns as phallic, the
women of the movement had the means to combine guns with their sexuality in ways unavailable to men. They did this through bearing children
for the revolution and by choosing whom to sleep with, and predicating
that choice on political calculation. In her memoir, *A Taste of Power*, Elaine
Brown recollects how an instructor, Ericka Huggins, directed new recruits
to put their sexuality on the line: "As women, our role was not very different from that of the men—except in certain particulars. Ericka told us
point-blank that as women we might have to have a sexual encounter with
"the enemy" at night and slit his throat in the morning—at which we all
groaned. . . . Our gender was but another weapon, another tool of the revolution. We also had the task of producing children, progeny of revolution

who would carry the flame when we fell, knowing that generations after us would prevail" (136–37).

Like the "pioneer mothers" valorized in turn-of-the-century monuments, Panther women could clutch a gun in one hand and hold a baby with the other arm. Yet while the pioneer mother was usually wielding her weapon to protect the homestead in her husband's absence, the Panther women and other Black Power activists who had babies for the revolution focused more on having the baby than on creating a middle-class nuclear family in which to raise the child. The child was an affirmation of revolutionary hopes for the future, a strike against the threat of black genocide. For some activists, like Assata Shakur, who were actively involved in armed struggle against the state, a child was a way of ensuring survival when the fate of the mother was uncertain at best.

But there were contradictions between the role of the liberated revolutionary—who was armed, androgynous in appearance, capable of having babies for the revolution—and the support role demanded of women by many of the male Panthers. Ultimately, these contradictions proved impossible to reconcile for some women in the movement. The voices of black feminists during this period, while raised in essays and manifestos, were not always heard (or endorsed) by women involved in the Black Power movement: Frances Beale, in her breakthrough 1970 essay, "Double Jeopardy: To Be Black and Female," argued that "those who are asserting their 'manhood' by telling black women to step back into a domestic, subservient role are assuming a counterrevolutionary position."[36] Pauli Murray declared black women to be suffering under "Jane Crow," by which she meant the double burden of sexism and racism faced by black women, and the virtual invisibility of women in discussions of black liberation. As she pointed out, civil rights leader James Farmer, in his run for Congress against Shirley Chisolm in 1968, called in his campaign literature for a "strong male image" and a "man's voice" in Washington.[37]

Yet many women within the Black Power movement dismissed women's liberation as the indulgence of white middle-class women. As Linda La Rue asked in "The Black Movement and Women's Liberation," "Is there any logical comparison between the oppression of the black woman on welfare who has difficulty feeding her children and the discontent of the suburban mother who has the luxury to protest the washing of the dishes on which her family's full meal was consumed?"[38] For many female Black Power activists, the gun was the great equalizer. Women's participation in revolutionary violence became the means of gaining freedom both from the op-

This poster by the Black Panther Party's minister of culture, Emory Douglas, updates the image of the pioneer mother. Courtesy of Wisconsin Historical Society, 37628.

pression of the dominant culture and from the internalized oppression that manifested itself in the sexism of many black men. Often black feminists invoked women's potential for armed struggle in calling for equality with black men. "Women have fought with men, and we have died with men, in every revolution," fumed Mary Ann Weathers in 1970. "We do not have to look at ourselves as someone's personal sex objects, maids, babysitters, domestics, and the like in exchange for a man's attention."[39]

Elaine Brown, who became the leader of the Black Panther Party during Huey Newton's period of exile in Cuba, encapsulated the contradictions for women Panthers. She opens her memoir with her statement of affirmation to the Central Committee:

"I have all the guns and all the money. I can withstand challenge from without and within. Am I right, comrade?"

Larry snapped back his answer to my rhetorical question: "Right on!" His muscular body tilted slightly as he adjusted the .45 automatic pistol under his jacket. . . .

I watched them carefully, noting that no one moved in response to my opening remarks. Here I was, a woman, proclaiming supreme power over the most militant organization in America. It felt natural to me.[40]

Yet what was "natural" for women—violence? Power? How was it possible to think in such terms in an organization in which women, as a rule, were supposed to bolster the masculinity of Panther men? As Brown discovers, a sizable element of the movement believes that women should occupy a support role because of their inherent nature. When, at a party, she and a friend rebel against being told to get in line behind the men for food, they are brought up short: "Bobbi and I smirked and stood our ground —until a bald-headed dashiki came over to us, folded his arms across his chest, and explained the 'rules' to us in a way we could understand. Sisters, he explained, did not challenge Brothers. Sisters, he said, stood behind their black men, supported their men, and respected them. In essence, he advised us that it was not only 'unsisterly' of us to want to eat with our Brothers, it was a sacrilege for which blood could be shed" (109).

In suggesting ways that women can use their gender for the revolution, Ericka Huggins seems to echo Stokely Carmichael's infamous comment that women's proper position in the movement is prone; other men within the movement voice the same ideas.[41] Brown is disgusted when she watches Bobby Seale put a young supporter through her paces:

"This here is Sister Marsha," Bobby said. "I want you to meet her. Although she's only a young sister, she's got a full-grown dedication to this party. That's why she's the only sister on a security squad. She's one of the toughest sisters in the party . . .

"Marsha, tell the Sister here what a Brother has to do to get some from you," Bobby commanded.

Marsha was a child, maybe fifteen years old. . . . She stood at attention. "First of all, a Brother's got to be righteous. He's got to be a Panther. He's got to be able to recite the ten-point platform and program, and be ready to off the pig and die for the People."

"Right on, Sister Marsha!" the Brothers shouted.

"Can't no motherfucker get no pussy from me unless he can get down with the party," she added without prompting. . . . "A Sister has to learn to shoot as well as cook, and be ready to back up the Brothers . . ."

"And what else?" Bobby urged.

"A Sister has to give up the pussy when the Brother is on his job and hold it back when he's not. 'Cause Sisters got pussy power."

"Oo-wee!" the Brothers laughed.[42]

Brown is furious: "The word 'Sister' was sounding like 'bitch' to me" (190). Female sexuality is treated as just another perk for male Panthers, and the young teenager Marsha seems, in the eyes of the male Panthers, to be nothing more than a kind of prostitute or camp follower in service of the revolution. As Brown, along with the other women present, serves dinner and cleans up after the male Panthers at the event, she has a revelation. "Like most black women of the time, we considered the notion of women's liberation to be a 'white girl's thing.' Unlike the new feminists, we were not going to take a position against men. . . . We had no intention, however, of allowing Panther men to assign us an inferior role in our revolution" (192). One way of asserting her power within the movement is through her use of violence, directed not only at those she sees as enemies of the movement, but also eventually at her comrades within the BPP.

Brown, as she rises through the ranks, rejects many traditional aspects of womanhood. She finds liberation not through feminist analysis but through a kind of existential violence. After she has beaten up a woman attorney, she muses that "it is impossible to summarize the biological response to an act of will in a life of submission. . . . What I had begun to experience was the sensation of personal freedom, like the tremor before orgasm. The Black Panther Party had awakened that thirst in me. And it had given me the power to satisfy it" (319). In fact, in her linkage of orgasm, violence, and personal freedom, Brown comes to sound like Norman Mailer's White Negro. However, when Mailer says that "it requires a primitive passion about human nature to believe that individual acts of violence are always to be preferred to the collective violence of the State," he is describing his primitivist view of black manhood.[43] Brown appropriates Mailer's masculinist vision and claims orgasmic violence for herself, as a woman. In

doing so, she experiences the power to inflict violence not only as personally liberating but also as a means of resurrection for black women. "It is a
sensuous thing to know that at one's will an enemy can be struck down, a
friend saved. The corruption in that affirmation coexists comfortably with
the sensuousness and the seriousness in it. For a black woman in America
to know that power is to experience being raised from the dead."[44] For her,
violence becomes a means of personal as well as political liberation.

However, the use of violence can only get Brown so far in a movement in
which her male comrades can still use accusations that she is unwomanly
to disempower her. When an opponent accuses her of being a "man-hating
lesbian," she reacts. "I had joined the majority of black women in America
in denouncing feminism. . . . Now, hearing the ugly intent of my opponent's
words, I trembled with a fury long buried. I recognized the true meaning
of his words. He was not talking about making love with women—he was
attacking me for *valuing* women. The feminists were right. The value of my
life had been obliterated as much by being female as by being black and
poor. Racism and sexism in America were equal partners in my oppression" (367). From this point of view, Eldridge Cleaver's advocacy of rape as a
revolutionary strategy cannot simply be interpreted as black revolutionary
violence against whites; it has to be seen as male violence aimed at women.

However, the anger Brown feels does not yet lead her to a completely
new analysis of her actions. Her rage prompts her to claim violence as a
weapon in the struggle: "It was with this attitude that I insisted on attending the disciplinary session I had ordered for a Brother who had blackened
the eye of the Sister with whom he was 'relating,' because she had not properly cooked his greens" (368). Asserting her authority, Brown stands by
while four men attack the offender: "Their punishment became unmerci-
ful. When he tried to protect his body by taking the fetal position, his head
became the object of their feet. The floor was rumbling, as though a pla-
toon of pneumatic drills were breaking through its foundation. Blood was
everywhere. Steve's face disappeared" (371). In violence, Brown finds freedom as a woman. Yet it is striking how this violence, central to the Black
Panther Party, which Brown both metes out and falls prey to herself, re-
capitulates older patterns that have little to do with black liberation. The
violent "lynching" of Steve and the ten lashes with a whip to which Brown
is subjected early on, when she fails to complete an issue of the Black Panther newspaper on time, have resonances of slavery times.

Yet along with Brown's feminist growth through violence comes her
deployment of another revolutionary weapon: motherhood. Her daughter

Ericka was conceived in an act of revolutionary affirmation, during a period that bred despair, a time when many within the BPP were dying in violent confrontations with police, and when Brown could visit the Los Angeles police station and see a banner that read PIGS 11–PANTHERS 0. As BPP Minister of Information Masai Hewitt tells her when they are on the verge of becoming lovers, "It's been six months, twelve shootings, and six funerals since we met. . . . I've known you were the right woman since then" (195). As Brown recalls, "We were in a dream, mixed with vodka and tears. We needed each other. We would die soon. It was a foregone conclusion. He laughed. We made love, all night, into the morning. Our lovemaking was not desperate. It was a drink of water, a passionate moment of gratitude for a moment of living" (195).

Throughout Brown's narrative, her relationship with her daughter, from conception on, becomes a hallmark of her struggle to balance the personal and the political. The birth of her daughter changes her: "She was more than revolutions or oppression or freedom or time or death. To give that being life, I would die. I did die, for my ego vanished at the moment of her birth. Ericka" (216). Yet it is difficult for her, given the demands of party work, to spend time with the baby: "I saw very little of my child, who was living in one of the houses in which we collectively cared for the children" (275). When Brown is party leader in Newton's absence, she moves into an apartment alone for the first time and finds herself unsettled by the presence of a "second bedroom, reserved for Ericka, my daughter, who, at seven years old, had never lived with her mother. There was a disturbing unfamiliarity in having her close. I had been a Black Panther all her life—not her mother, in any meaningful way" (435).

In the end, when Huey Newton has returned, and the party has started to disintegrate under the strain of drug use and ultramacho behavior, Brown has a nervous breakdown. She comes to find herself through her daughter: "Watching her now, I began to wonder what I represented to her. I began to think of what I really was, without the pseudonyms of revolutionary, black, or woman. I had made myself into this or that, according to the tune of the time. I was terrified by what I was—a nasty nothing" (443). Brown is overwhelmed with the terror of having lost herself in the movement. Only through her daughter, both self and other, can she begin to reclaim herself as separate from her political identity.

When the woman who runs the Panther school is given a beating severe enough to break her jaw and land her in the hospital because she has been guilty of "a verbal indiscretion," while a male Panther who has broken every rule of party discipline is given bail money, Brown sees the handwriting on the wall. "The women were feeling the change, I noted. The beating of Regina would be taken as a clear signal that the words 'Panther' and 'comrade' had taken on gender connotations, denoting an inferiority in the female half of us" (445). Brown, about to be disciplined by the Central Committee, flees in fear for her life, taking Ericka with her. "I was abandoning something, but I was saving something. It was the hope, that had been my hope, and my mother's hope, and her mother's hope, and the hope of each of my people—mothers, aunts, brothers, fathers, children. If my life had any meaning left, this hope in one black child would live" (450).

In the end, Brown leaves the BPP and the Bay Area with the seven-year-old daughter she has never known well. Finally, it seems, Brown's attempt to redefine the relationship between revolutionary violence and sexuality cannot succeed. Maternity becomes a means of escaping—if not resolving—the contradictions Brown finds within the BPP's commitment to liberatory violence. However, Brown's view of motherhood as a pure commitment to a hopeful future, and an escape from the trap of politically motivated violence, stands in stark contrast to that of another black revolutionary mother of the period.

ASSATA SHAKUR AND ARMED MOTHERHOOD

Although Elaine Brown could finally not resolve the contradictions of the roles she played, as both mother and violent radical, the guerrilla mother became something of a visual cliché during the early 1970s, appearing on posters and in the pages of leftist magazines. Like the turn-of-the-twentieth-century "pioneer mother," the image of the armed revolutionary mother had iconic power. This emerges clearly from what Gilda Zwerman has to say of her interviews with incarcerated women who participated in acts of left-wing violence during the 1970s and 1980s: "The attraction of armed struggle seems to lie in the construction of reality and identity that is embodied in the role of the female in this type of movement: the female guerrilla—a woman with a rifle slung over one confident shoulder and a baby cuddled in her protective arms. . . . The female guerrilla symbolizes the stereotypical extremes of gender identity. It permits the traditional character and dichotomy between masculinity and femininity to remain intact, while giving the women access—albeit temporary and highly supervised—to the male realm of power and aggression."[45]

The model of the revolutionary mother was perhaps most controversially embodied in the United States by Assata Shakur (JoAnne Chesimard), who used her autobiography to recontextualize the police and media image of her as a dangerous radical. In his 1973 book, *Target Blue: An Insider's View of the N.Y.P.D.*, New York City deputy police commissioner Robert Daley echoes J. Edgar Hoover's descriptions of Ma Barker when he characterizes Shakur as "the soul of the gang, the mother hen who kept them moving, kept them shooting."[46] Shakur was a Black Panther whom police accused of being responsible for a number of armed bank robberies in the New Jersey area and the killing of a cop and of a New Jersey state trooper. Although Shakur was acquitted of almost all of these charges and had other charges, such as the murder of a drug dealer, dismissed for lack of evidence, she was convicted of murdering the state trooper, by a jury that included, as Shakur noted in her autobiography, "two friends, one girlfriend, and two nephews of new jersey state troopers."[47] Eventually, Shakur was sprung from prison by members of the Black Liberation Army (BLA), a Cleaverite faction that had splintered off from the Black Panthers. She then fled to Cuba, where she wrote her memoir.

Shakur was seen in the mainstream press as the epitome of the dangerous armed black militant. As she comments in her memoir, "White people's fear of Black people with guns will never cease to amaze me. . . . When Black people seriously organize and take up arms to fight for our liberation, there will be a lot of white people who will drop dead from no other reason than their own fear and guilt."[48] In fact, the BLA's political strategy was in large part based on preemptive strikes against cops: sudden and extremely brutal assassinations of randomly chosen officers. Needless to say, the practice of assassinating police officers earned the BLA the complete hatred of just about everyone in the law enforcement community.[49] In a book that is highly critical of the BLA and other armed radical organizations, John Castellucci conveys a sense of the threat they posed: "The BLA went underground to kill cops. It formed cells that were impossible to penetrate. As an organization, it was small and short-lived. Within a few years, most of its members had been killed in shoot-outs or imprisoned. While it lasted, however, the BLA exerted an influence out of proportion to its lifespan or size."[50] A key element of BLA ideology was that it was legitimate for revolutionaries to rob banks and that blacks could regain control of their communities by killing cops, both black and white. The BLA claimed responsibility for the attempted murder of two patrolmen who had been assigned to guard the home of a prosecutor in the Panther 21 case, and it took credit for the murder of two other patrolmen at a Harlem housing project.[51] In the two years following the schism in the BPP, the u.s. government attributed the deaths of twenty cops to the BLA. As Akinyele Omowale Umoja writes, "American police were seen as the occupation army of the colonized Black nation and the primary agents of Black genocide. So the BLA believed it had to 'defend' Black people and the Black liberation movement in an offensive manner by using retaliatory violence against the agents of genocide in the Black community."[52]

In other words, unlike the BPP, the BLA was truly a black nationalist organization. Its members were not interested in wielding guns in order to gain access to American identity; they were aiming to defend themselves against American forces. While Reginald Major could write in his 1971 book, *A Panther Is a Black Cat*, that the Panthers were fighters "moving to bring greatness to the American Experience" by "completing the work begun by the revolution of 1776,"[53] Shakur was deciding against becoming a teacher because "I wasn't teaching no Black children to say the pledge of allegiance or think George Washington was great or any other such bullshit." As she says of her name change from JoAnne Chesimard to Assata Shakur, which followed her becoming a citizen of the Republic of New Afrika, a black separatist group: "I didn't feel like no JoAnne, or no Negro, or no amerikan. I felt like an African woman."[54] Shakur uses guns to define herself outside of an American identity. As she writes, "Black people have got to be suicidal if they don't own and know how to operate a gun" (222).

While Shakur firmly rejects her American identity, she just as firmly embraces the link between womanhood and revolutionary struggle. As she writes in her autobiography, in choosing a new name, she finds herself confronting assumptions that make her uncomfortable within the Afrocentric movement: "At the time, there were little pamphlets being put out listing names and their meanings, but i had a hard time finding one i liked. A lot of the names had to do with flowers or songs or birds or other things like that." These "feminine" associations do not suit Shakur's more serious purpose. "Others meant born on Thursday, faithful, loyal, or even things like tears, or one who giggles." Shakur has a hard time locating herself in these traditional female virtues of girlishness or loyalty. "The women's names were nothing like the men's names, which meant things like strong, warrior, man of iron, brave, etc. I wanted a name that had something to do with struggle, something to do with the liberation of our people." The components of the name she decides on, Assata Oglugbala Shakur, mean "She who struggles," "Love for the people," and "the thankful" (189). Although

Shakur rejects feminized names for herself, she embraces her female identity for what it enables her to do: bear a baby for the struggle.

The struggle in which Shakur is engaged, though, is one that stresses the need to dismantle the governmental system through acts of disruptive violence. Shakur writes that "a war between the races would help nobody and free nobody and should be avoided at all costs. But a one-sided race war with Black people as the targets and white people shooting the guns is worse. We will be criminally negligent, however, if we do not deal with racism and racist violence, and if we do not prepare to defend ourselves against it" (140). In her autobiography, however, she does not dwell on crimes she may have committed; this is arguably because, as Margo Perkins has noted, "political autobiography is in major part concerned with redefining criminality (by challenging a status quo that overwhelmingly favors the interest of a capitalist elite at the expense of all others)."[55] Nevertheless, Shakur does not shy away from the topic of armed revolution: "One day, in the not-too-distant future, any Black organization that is not based on bootlicking and tomming will be forced underground. And as fast as this country is moving to the fascist far right, Black revolutionary organizations should start preparing for the inevitability."[56] As she notes, "Although i felt that the major task of the underground should be organizing and building, i didn't feel that armed acts of resistance should be ruled out" (243). It is her arrest and imprisonment for armed acts of resistance that create the conditions for her act of revolutionary maternity.

Needless to say, the BLA's ideological dedication to assassinating cops meant that each time a group member was captured, he or she would be subject to a high degree of abuse by the police and the criminal justice system. Shakur was held, as her lawyer Lennox S. Hinds notes, in unprecedentedly bad conditions: "In the history of New Jersey, no woman pretrial detainee or prisoner has ever been treated as she was, continuously confined in a men's prison, under twenty-four hour surveillance of her most intimate functions, without intellectual sustenance, adequate medical attention, and exercise, and without the company of other women for all the years she was in custody."[57] An international panel of jurists representing the United Nations Commission on Human Rights concluded that she was subjected to treatment "totally unbefitting any prisoner."[58] The evidence against Shakur seemed flimsy to many, and her case became a cause célèbre on the left. Shakur's case was internationally known: a reporter from the Soviet press agency Tass showed up to cover the trial, and celebrities ranging from

Angela Davis to Ruby Dee and Ossie Davis, from Harry Belafonte to poet Audre Lorde, helped raise money to defray her legal costs.[59]

As Shakur was being described by cops as a "mother hen," she actually became a mother. Her decision to become pregnant while facing a possible life sentence, by a man who was also on trial for crimes that could net him a long prison term, challenged established notions of motherhood. Like Ericka Huggins, Shakur addressed the ways that women could use their bodies for the sake of the revolution. While awaiting charges on bank robbery charges, she and one of her codefendants, Kamau Sundiata (Fred Hilton), were banned from the courtroom for protesting the conditions of their trials and kept in a holding cell together. "Each day we grew closer until, one day, it was clear to both of us that our relationship was changing. . . . For a few days the question of sex was there. Then, one day we talked about it. Surely, it was possible. But, i thought, the consequences! Pregnancy was certainly a possibility. I was facing life in prison. Kamau would also be in prison for a long time. The child would have no mother and no father." She, personally, would be able to offer the child little beyond the fact of its birth.

However, Shakur's commitment to the ideals of revolution finally sweeps away her objections. "Kamau said, 'If you become pregnant and you have a child, the child will be taken care of. Our people will not let the child grow up like a weed.'" Shakur struggles over the issue: "Since i was a teenager i had always said that the world was too horrible to bring another human being into. And a Black child. We see our children frustrated at best. . . . I remembered all the discussions i had had. 'I'm a revolutionary,' i had said. 'I don't have time to sit at home and make no babies.'" Yet, finally, Shakur decides that "I am about life. . . . I'm gonna live as hard as i can and as full as i can until i die. . . . I'm gonna live and i'm gonna love Kamau, and if a child comes from that union, i'm gonna rejoice. Because our children are our futures and i believe in the future and in the strength and rightness of that struggle" (93). Having a child will be an affirmation of her belief in the revolution and in the strength of her community. Shakur is overjoyed to learn that she is indeed pregnant: "I spent the next few days in a daze. A joyous daze." At first, however, the prison doctors deny that she is pregnant; then they strongly recommend that she get an abortion. They also refuse her gynecological care. When the baby is born, Shakur is able to see her for only a few hours before they are separated. Her commitment to motherhood is rendered an abstraction by the physical circumstances in which she gives birth.

Given the conditions under which Shakur's autobiography was produced, it is not surprising that it contains significant lacunae. For instance, she never even mentions the highly publicized prison escape, for which she is most famous. On one page she is promising her grandmother that she will not get used to prison; on the next page she is in Havana. Yet the way she introduces her decision to escape is noteworthy: it is in the context of her four-year-old daughter's weekly visit to her. Kakuya is enraged:

"You're not my mother," she screams, the tears rolling down her face. "You're not my mother and I hate you." I feel like crying too. I know she is confused about who I am. She calls me Mommy Assata and she calls my mother Mommy.

I try to pick her up. She knocks my hand away. "You can get out of here, if you want to," she screams. "You just don't want to." . . . I go back to my cage and cry until i vomit. I decide that it is time to leave. (257–58)

And yet after her escape, five years go by before Shakur speaks to her family again. She ends her memoir with her daughter stepping off the plane in Havana to be reunited with her. Her focus is such, however, that she does not mention all of the things that her aunt and lawyer, Evelyn Williams, discusses in her own memoir: Kakuya's life growing up in New York, her enrollment in the Alvin Ailey dance school, her gifts as a pianist, and, finally, the decision of Assata and her family to have Kakuya join her permanently in Cuba.[60]

Shakur writes from a perspective that is very much within the Black Liberation Army. Her use of the lower-case "i" and of "amerika" and "kourt" serve notice that she is telling her story from a vantage point that is not at all critical of her political past and present. Her autobiography thus does not dwell at great length on the five years between when she escapes from prison and when she is next able to contact her daughter. By contrast, Elaine Brown's memoir is a nuanced mixture of pride in the many achievements of the BPP, self-exploration, and ambivalence about some of the less glorious facets of the party, including her history within it. The mother-daughter reunion with which Elaine Brown ends her memoir thus has a somewhat more complicated cast to it. There are certainly similarities between the two women's experiences. Unlike Shakur, whose personal decisions are largely made (or at least presented) as political decisions, Brown feels and expresses a great deal of ambivalence about what she sees as the conflicting roles of mother and revolutionary. Her final choice to leave the party is framed within the context of her relationship to her daughter.

The Black Liberation Army used the gun to try to destroy the power of the state, whereas the Panthers sought to use American laws and a version of Americanism that placed the gun at the center of national rights and citizenship. Yet for Brown, as well as for Shakur, the decision to become a mother—a decision dictated by the imperatives of armed revolution—finally made it impossible to live in the United States. Violence, whether from the state or from within the movement, seemed to render American revolutionary maternity untenable for these black radical women. However, for many white women on the left, the decision to give birth to white babies was counterrevolutionary in and of itself, for reasons having to do both with eugenics and with their ideals of personal liberation. These women saw themselves less as third world guerrilla mothers than as outlaws—and it was hard to imagine Bonnie Parker with a baby on her hip.

NEW BONNIES: WHITE WOMEN IN RADICAL MOVEMENTS

Weatherwoman Susan Stern, reflecting on her mural's reception, noted that "it was the first thing you saw when you entered the Sundance house. It dumfounded the Ithaca men, and infuriated all the radical women. No one could understand exactly what I had tried to represent. Perhaps in my acid frenzy I had painted what I wanted to be somewhere deep in my mind; tall and blond, nude and armed, consuming—or discharging—a burning America."[61]

The discomfort that Stern's housemates felt while viewing her mural reflected larger debates within the primarily white radical armed movements of the sixties and seventies. In courtroom speeches, manifestos, memoirs, and letters to newspaper editors, male and female radicals questioned prevailing assumptions about the relationship of women to the gun.

White armed radical women used violence to survive within the macho left, deploying "equalizers" (as well as other weapons) to gain power. Unlike the black revolutionary women discussed in this chapter, they did not necessarily see maternity as a revolutionary act: remember that the woman in Stern's mural was depicted giving birth to a burning American flag, not to a baby. A nation transformed and purified through violence would be their legacy. As part of their survival strategy, they forged alliances with those defined by the government as dangerously violent: prisoners. One of the great issues that united the Black Panthers and the white left was the issue of prison reform. In 1974, when Patty Hearst was kidnapped, the California prison system had the third-largest incarcerated population in the world, behind only the prisons of the Soviet Union and China. By the late 1960s, many convicts in California had become radicalized, and many leftists were engaged in prison reform work there. Given the horrific conditions under which many inmates in the California prison system lived, there were sound political reasons for radicals to support prison education programs. Thus, there was a lot of interaction between white leftists and radical prison groups like the Black Family, which became the Black Guerrilla Family after the death of its founder, inmate George Jackson, whose *Soledad Brother: The Prison Letters of George Jackson* (1970) and posthumous *Blood in My Eye* (1972) were key texts for a generation of radicals.

The 1930s admirers of Bonnie and Clyde may have seen the outlaws as folk bandits, but the leftist prison-reform advocates viewed the convicts with whom they worked as political prisoners. As Eric Cummins has written, the radical convicts provided a supermasculine model for middle-class revolutionaries. And the most prominent among them was Eldridge Cleaver, who publicized prison conditions with his 1968 autobiography, *Soul on Ice*. As Cummins writes, "*Soul on Ice* whipped tough cultural observations in with a froth of sexual lore, and the result was a violence-steeped Maileresque black sexual-political myth, always careful to invoke Ginsberg and Burroughs and Kerouac, achingly self-conscious that its mass-press readership would be predominantly white."[62] (Michele Wallace illuminates the Maileresque element: "Mailer came up with an interestingly accurate idea about a peculiar phenomenon—the intersection of the black man's and the white man's fantasies, that is to say their frustrations.")[63] Cleaver seemed to fit Mailer's description, in his essay "The White Negro," of the existential primitive: "In the worst of perversion, promiscuity, pimpery, drug addiction, rape, razor-slash, bottle-break, what-have-you, the Negro discovered and elaborated a morality of the bottom."[64] Yet for a generation of young radicals whose view of revolution was often untainted by a deep knowledge of history or understanding of class politics, Cleaver's message provided a hip, seemingly left-wing call to action.

However, the left's embrace of Cleaver, who had famously described the rape of white women as "an insurrectionary act,"[65] proved problematic for movement women: given the glorification of a man who advocated raping white women as a political act, how were they to situate themselves in regard to violent action and to the gun?

For many white women revolutionaries of the period, the gun became a way to challenge cultural constructions of gender predispositions. These women opted to be neither mother lions nor victims in their relationships

Faye Dunaway made for a glamorous Bonnie in the 1967 Arthur Penn movie
Bonnie and Clyde, which sparked a cultural love affair with the outlaws.

to violence. Instead they become, in Susan Stern's term, "macho mamas." These women made the gun a crucial aspect of their political image—and inserted themselves into the world of new left machismo.

The image of the armed woman was given a huge boost with the enormous influence and popularity of Arthur Penn's biopic *Bonnie and Clyde* (1967), which presented the outlaw couple in a new guise: as J. Hoberman puts it, "Good looks, swell clothes, actorly assurance, and charismatic cool set *Bonnie and Clyde* apart from their dowdy environment."[66] *Bonnie and Clyde*'s influence extended into the realm of fashion (*Women's Wear Daily* pronounced the "gun-barrel gray of Bonnie's pistol" to be the new color for spring),[67] and the film was embraced by the new left. As portrayed by Faye Dunaway, Bonnie is a nihilistic outlaw, losing out finally only to the greater firepower of the state. And while women's magazines celebrated Bonnie's fashion sense, the left embraced the notion of the revolutionary as a romantic desperado—a vision that endured for years in underground newspapers and comix. As late as 1976, the pioneering feminist underground publication *Wimmen's Comix* could feature a cover by Melinda Gebbie showing women whose sexuality is wrapped up in violence: emblazoned with the title OUTLAWS, the image shows a woman in stockings, high heels, bra, and little else, knife between her teeth, crouched over the corpse of a man, while to her left a woman in high heels and cocktail dress smokes nonchalantly, and to her right a woman, a star emblazoned on her tank top, holds a smoking assault weapon.[68]

Sometimes women defined the use of the gun as inherently feminist when it entailed destroying a system they defined as male in its violence. Radical Susan Saxe, in her statement as she pleaded guilty to charges of bank robbery, theft, and conspiracy on June 9, 1975, critiqued the

> deep and significant split [that] has developed in the women's movement. On the one hand are women like Jane Alpert who feel that the Amerikan system can peacefully accommodate their feminist demands and that women as women have no obligation to support or protect any peoples' struggle that is not explicitly feminist in ideology or even separatist in practice. These women feel that it is permissible, even desirable, to collaborate with the state in the name of feminism. . . . On the other hand are we women whose growth into feminism has made us even more determined not to give in, not to accommodate ourselves to Amerika. . . . My feminism doesn't make me regret the destruction of a single National Guard Armory; it only makes me wish to see every last vestige of patriarchal militarism permanently blotted from the face of the earth.[69]

Jane Alpert, who in a memoir had detailed her journey from living underground while fleeing bombing charges to surrendering herself to the police and serving time, was reviled by many armed feminists; the title of her 1981 memoir, *Growing Up Underground*, seemed to imply that her rejection of violence was part of a maturation process. Moreover, she suggested that women's embrace of violence was part of their reliance on the men in their lives: "I wondered if what was true for Pat and me was also true of women in the Black Panther Party and the Weather Underground. Did all of us feel interested in bombing buildings only when the men we slept with were urging us on?"[70]

Alpert's position and Saxe's rebuttal of it found many echoes within the women's movement, as factions struggled over how compatible violence was with womanhood—and with feminism. An article in the December 1975 issue of *Plexus*, a Bay Area women's paper, noted that "the creation and perpetuation of the image of feminists as streetfighters and terrorists is yet another media move; this one sadistically aimed at undermining and discrediting one of the most primally non-violent, life-giving movements in the history of the world."[71] However, many other feminists saw gun violence as an important weapon in the struggle against patriarchy and for freedom, and derided feminist objections to it. "Naturally," wrote the poet M. F. Beal in response to feminist calls for nonviolence. "What else, after centuries of conditioning making violence taboo for women under any circumstances? Time is running out, however, and women may soon be forced to make choices. To continue to submit to or ignore growing violence against their sex is both masochistic and anachronistic."[72] Rather, she continued, it was time to celebrate a "new breed of revolutionary feminist," who was "currently in karate or kung fu classes and learning marksmanship at the local rifle range" (84).

A feminist journal of the time, *Dragon*, published instructions on making pipe bombs and produced a special issue called "Women and Armed Struggle."[73] An article in that issue, reprinted from *Plexus*, urged the importance of armed struggle, since "the extent to which parts of the women's movement are advocating non-violence corresponds to the extent to which their middle-class privilege allows them to do so."[74]

There were, of course, some within the left who saw the women's movement as getting in the way of women's revolutionary consciousness. As one *Ramparts* reader complained in a January 1974 letter to the editor, "If women in this country knew more about care and maintenance of firearms than of their cervixes, possibly this country would not be headed down the [same] road as Chile's."[75] The cultural critic Todd Gitlin has pinpointed when women on the left were breaking away: "One of the bizarre features of 1969, 1970, and 1971 was this deep divide in experience: the time was agonizing for movement men, exhilarating for tens of thousands of movement women. . . . Women had been the cement of the male-run movement; their 'desertion' into their own circles completed the dissolution of the old boys' clan."[76] Although Gitlin is talking about women who formed health collectives, newspapers, and other organizations dedicated to feminist causes, there were also women who stayed—and became powerful—within the left-wing organizations most prone to violence.

Some women saw guns as necessary to prevent sexual violence—and thus as a means of gaining equal rights. *The Woman's Gun Pamphlet: A Primer on Handguns*, issued by the Women's Press Collective in 1975, was written, its authors said, because "we decided one of the best things we could do for the women's community and women's movement was to share

The Woman's Gun Pamphlet (1975) was full of feminist gun humor.

our collected knowledge in a feminist gun pamphlet"; the authors expressed the hope that "G.C.R. (Gun Consciousness Raising) groups will spring up all over."[77] Women needed to arm themselves, the authors wrote, because "for men to maintain a successful oppressive patriarchy, women must be defenseless. If we feel helpless then we will be afraid to escape from ties with men and male institutions" (2). The authors of the pamphlet attacked ideologies that defined gun ownership as male: "Most women are taught that guns are out of their realm of reality—like high-paying jobs and self-respect. And that is part of the male propaganda—that women be afraid of guns—because men are afraid of women and a woman with a gun in her hand is indeed a wonderful fright" (4). In urging their readers to enter a gun store "and go home with a gun of your own—*a gun of one's own!*" the pamphleteers directly tied gun ownership to Virginia Woolf's rallying cry for women's rights of nearly half a century earlier.

Their final argument, however, linked gun ownership with the need to defend oneself against an oppressive state. Critiquing a TV movie on gun violence that ended with a plea for citizens to turn in their guns to the nearest police station, the writers editorialized:

> What a chilling, ominous demand! After all the stories we've heard about *unarmed* women being raped by police, often after having called for help against another rapist. After seeing the films and reports of armed police and soldiers forcing *unarmed* Jews into concentration camps, and *unarmed* Japanese-Americans into American concentration camps. After reading of camps being prepared in the U.S. in recent years. Being aware of the deepening economic depression and of the increase in violent crimes against women. They want us to turn in our guns?!!!" (43).

This analysis tied violence against women to state violence and offered gun ownership as the only way for citizens, especially female citizens, to defend themselves. If it was important for men, who could be herded into concentration camps, it was even more so for women, for whom any encounter with the police could end in rape.

Gun fetishism was rampant in underground newspapers. *The Rat*, a New York paper whose logo was a rodent with an assault rifle, published poems celebrating violence, such as

> Violence as an expression of energy
> uncontrolled energy manifested by a repressive environment.
> Karma seeking to create an environment that is liberatory.[78]

The *Rat* also ran a photograph of a sniper in a tree that bore the caption "the revolution has come it's time to pick up your gun."[79] The *Argus* featured a photograph of an angelic blond child holding a semiautomatic.[80] In underground comix, gun violence reigned. In the second issue of Jay Kinney and Ned Sonntag's *Young Lust*, a group of hippies save a woman from gang rape by police by blasting in with guns and killing twenty cops. In the final frame, as two lovers kiss in the background, and a bearded man holds a giant pistol in the foreground, one lover quips, "As Chairman Mao says: 'Love comes out of the barrel of a gun!'"[81] The *Berkeley Tribe* had a cover featuring a hand holding a gun and firing it, with a caption reading, "Ooh that felt good!"[82] The August 15–21, 1969, issue had a cover that featured an armed young hippie couple, the woman holding a baby and a pistol, the man holding a rifle.[83] An article in the January 16–23, 1970, issue of the magazine urged readers to "get on down to your friendly neighborhood gun shop, and, as the Panthers say, 'Seize the Time.'"[84] These examples, like the popularity of *Bonnie and Clyde*, support the notion of a larger cultural shift in consciousness about guns in general, with women's use of weaponry as a natural outgrowth of this shift. While Bonnie and Clyde may have been popular in their time among readers of tabloids and children playing cops and robbers, they certainly were not adopted by anyone on the left as culture heroes. However, for the producers and readers of underground newspapers, weaponry was part of a cool, revolutionary lifestyle—and Bonnie and Clyde were hip outlaws.

Along with the theatrical photos of heavily armed hippies that appeared in the underground press were articles about gun use. During the same period, the underground paper *Seed* excerpted both *The Whole Earth Catalog* and *Firearms and Self-Defense* for its "Spring Equinox Survival Supplement."[85] As historian Laurence Leamer suggested in 1972, the primarily middle-class producers of the underground newspapers, in an effort to forge alliances with the working class, used guns pornographically in their publications—and ended up alienating their intended audience:

> Many of the papers . . . print pictures and diagrams of rifles, pistols and other weapons. In this there is a conscious attempt to break out of bourgeois youth culture and forge ties with the lower classes, but ironically, the picture and diagrams are telling evidence that such underground papers are as middle-class as ever. Guns are very much a part of lower middle class and working-class American culture. A boy grows up with them. He respects them. He knows how to use them. And if he reads a radical paper, he certainly finds pictures or diagrams of guns superfluous or downright foolish. It is only those scions of the middle class, schooled in a tradition that considers guns illicit and somehow almost sensual, who need such elementary instruction.[86]

The middle-class revolutionaries used and posed with guns as part of a fantasy of racial and class transgression and participation in outlaw culture. It is important to remember that this was a relatively new posture and interest among the American left. It is striking that during the 1930s, the period of great political crisis that most recently preceded the 1960s and 1970s, the left was remarkably free of weapons fetishism.[87]

Once underground readers bought their guns, they were welcome to enroll in classes on "firearms and self-defense" at the International Liberation School, held on the University of California–Berkeley campus.[88] (The International Liberation School, a brainchild of Eldridge Cleaver, published such manuals as *Firearms and Self-Defense: A Handbook for Radicals, Revo-*

lutionaries and Easy Riders.)[89] Articles in the *Berkeley Tribe* offered tips on the best semiautomatic rifles to buy[90] and on how to shoot without flinching.[91] The author of a *Tribe* column called "Street Daughter" styled herself "Annie Oakely" [*sic*].[92] *Black Politics* reprinted articles from *American Rifleman*, as well as offering how-to articles titled "Weapons for Self-Defense," "How to Acquire the Rifle," "Teach Yourself to Shoot," and "Handguns."[93] For many women the use of guns was a way to gain power equal to their male comrades—and for the first time to be able to embrace a role as daring and transgressive as that of the outlaw.

MACHO MAMAS OF WEATHERMAN

Armed women held a prominent place in the best-known group of white violent revolutionaries, Weatherman, which had its genesis as an offshoot of the Students for a Democratic Society. Committed to "bringing the war home" from Vietnam to the streets of the United States, the members of Weatherman rejected conventional Marxist analysis in favor of a far more extreme, adventurist doctrine, for which they were roundly condemned by most leftists of the period. Spurred to acts of violence by their despair over the escalating conflict in Vietnam and as a means of helping oppressed people of color in the United States, Weatherman embraced theorist Régis Debray's theory of exemplary violence, according to which a small band of revolutionaries can engage in acts of violence and skip the tedious process of mass mobilization.[94] As former Weatherman leader Jeff Jones put it, he and his comrades learned from Debray that "a small group of very politically advanced, ideologically committed people can carry out revolutionary actions that will serve as an inspiration for other people."[95] This strategy ran counter to more traditional forms of organizing. Ron Jacobs notes that "most leftists saw [the nationwide General Electric strike in November 1969] as a chance to create new alliances and expand the movement beyond its student base. Weatherman, however, showed up at picket lines and demonstrations called to support the strike with signs and literature labeling the General Electric workers as pigs. A participant in the strike in the Boston area told of a Weather sign stating something along the lines of 'Ho Ho Chi Minh, the NLF [National Liberation Front] are going to kill GE workers.'"[96] Weatherman, at least during this period, saw workers, soldiers, and almost anyone but youth and prisoners as pigs, and this limited the group's appeal. Its essence was violent confrontation: fighting in the streets. The giant cardboard machine gun that hung suspended from the ceiling at the Weatherman war council in 1969 was a perfect expression of this. Because of its ideological commitment to and extreme focus on violence, as well as the prominent place that women occupied in the organization, Weatherman provides one of the clearest distillations of the relationship between (some) radical white women and the gun during the late sixties and into the seventies.

Weatherman featured some of the most prominent female leaders among radical groups at the time. As Cathy Wilkerson, a founding member, recalled in an interview, Weatherman "was trying to reach white youth on the basis of their most reactionary macho instinct, intellectuals playing at working-class toughs."[97] The "macho mamas" of the group participated fully in this enterprise,[98] and some law enforcement officials saw the women as the guiding force behind the violence. As ex-undercover FBI agent Cril Payne comments in his memoir, *Deep Cover: An FBI Agent Infiltrates the Radical Underground,*

> Women [were] more dedicated and potentially more dangerous than men as urban terrorists. Women who were passionately committed to their political beliefs took unbelievable risks to gain acceptance. For the most part, these risks involved brazenly illegal acts that their male counterparts would never even consider undertaking. I was never sure whether the difference resulted from women's seeking to justify their relatively new status as equals, but I am certain of one thing: female activists were the moving force behind the fundamental changes that occurred during those years of protest.[99]

Despite their machismo, the women of the movement did not simply imitate male behavior in their revolutionary endeavors. Weatherwomen often saw their sexuality, especially their capacity for pregnancy, as an uncomfortable yet integral part of their image as armed revolutionaries. This belief was shared by others, such as lawyers defending them in court cases.

One of the best-known firsthand accounts of life in Weatherman is Susan Stern's 1975 memoir, *With the Weathermen*, which from its first pages challenges received ideas about female autobiography in its treatment of the conventional markers of female experience. The dissolution of Stern's marriage to her college boyfriend and fellow radical, Robby, is dealt with casually in the first pages of the book.[100] The memoir begins with Stern's arrival in Seattle, where she and her husband have gone to make a fresh start following a difficult first year of marriage. By the third page of the book, he has moved out for a trial separation, though he reappears as a character throughout the eight years discussed in the book. Stern reads Betty Friedan and is transformed: "With a gallop, the Women's Liberation Movement was born. And yours truly was one of its first babies."[101] Yet her liberation was at odds with the feminism of many other movement women.

Stern was one of many women on the left who had begun challenging male supremacy within the movement. Robin Morgan, in her 1969 article, "Goodbye to All That," which appeared in the underground paper *Rat*, fired what Abe Peck has called "the shot heard round the Left."[102] "Women are the real Left," wrote Morgan. "We are rising, powerful in our unclean bodies, bright glowing mad in our inferior brains. . . . We are rising with a fury older and potentially greater than any force in history, and this time we will be free or no one will survive." In her celebration of female rage, Morgan sounded many of Stern's themes. Yet the two women's perspectives differed in some crucial ways on this issue, for Morgan singled out the "macho mamas" of Weatherman for pointed criticism: "'Left Out!' —not Right On—to the Weather Sisters who, and they know better—they know, reject their own radical feminism for that last desperate grab at male approval that we all know so well, for claiming that the *machismo* style and the gratuitous violence is their own style by 'free choice' and for believing that this is the way for a woman to make her revolution."[103]

Stern's autobiography provided an opportunity for those on the left and on the right to discuss the issue of women's revolutionary violence in general and the Weatherwomen's approach to violence in particular. Susan Brownmiller, a feminist leader best known for her groundbreaking book *Against Our Will: Men, Women, and Rape*, offered in the *New York Times Book Review* a devastating critique of Stern: "She was the 'macho mama,' aiming to be best and baddest among the women and earth-mother mascot to the men."[104] Brownmiller's criticism of Stern as a "macho mama" echoed other feminist critiques of Weatherman's emphasis on violence and its insistence that members "smash monogamy," breaking up long-standing personal relationships, as the precondition for revolutionary action. Perhaps most of all, feminists found problematic Weatherwomen's insistence that their engagement in violence was more important than their involvement in feminism.

The Weatherman essay "Honky Tonk Women," given out as part of a packet at the National War Council in 1969, described the transformative effect of involvement in Weatherman on women: "Completely transformed from passive wimps, afraid of blood or danger or guns, satisfied with the limitations set on us by hated slave relationships with one man, we became revolutionary women—whole people struggling in every way, at every level, to destroy the dying pig system that has tried to keep us and the rest of its leadership under its total control." For Weatherwomen, feminism came second to revolution: as the essay concluded, "We demand—not 'Bread and Roses' to make our lives a little better and shield us from struggle a little more—but bombs and rifles to join the war being fought now all over the globe to destroy the motherfuckers responsible for this pig world."[105] This dismissal of feminism did not sit well with women's collectives and feminist theorists. As the Bread and Roses collective pointed out, "Women in Weatherman are thus forced into a double bind. Not only are they told that their oppression, which they share with all other women, is less important or compelling than the oppression of blacks or Vietnamese, but their revolutionary commitment is measured by male chauvinist standards; they must struggle in terms defined by men. A woman becomes a heroine in Weather circles when she is a tougher, better fighter than the men, regardless of whether she's helping women's liberation."[106] It is little wonder, given the war of words between radical feminists and Weatherwomen, that Stern's memoir came in for criticism from feminists such as Brownmiller.

Yet Stern's memoir, with its emphasis on her sexuality and her violence, also became a target for more conservative observers: "Dragging a man to her mattress every night became as imperative as ending the war in Vietnam, as offing honky pigs," sniffed the reviewer for *Newsweek*.[107] The memoir provides a candid portrayal of how Stern supports herself much of the time through topless dancing or working in porno movies: "People may be horrified that a bonafide Women's Liberationist obtained money in this manner, but when it came to paying for the endless leaflets no one hassled me about where the money came from. The Movement came first. It didn't matter how I supported my habit. And, to be really honest, I never saw anything wrong with my topless dancing, or my body-painting experiences."[108] However, as the battle within the new left over feminism heats up, her work becomes controversial, and she at times encounters resistance, as from the people in the two Weatherman collectives in Seattle where she lives: "The people in both houses on Woodlawn were appalled that I would go-go dance. Not at a time when the Movement was in a crisis over Women's Liberation" (72). Yet it is her involvement in revolutionary politics that enables Stern to persist with earning money in ways that are at odds with the standard ideology of feminism: "Weatherman had swung a pendulum in me.

The vogue was to be tough and macho, and I was as overzealously aggressive and abandoned as a Weatherman as I had been timid and frightened prior to it" (72).

For Stern, her go-go dancing, her feminism, and her involvement in violent revolutionary politics are inextricably intertwined. Her perspective uncannily mirrors the fears of J. Edgar Hoover and the racial theorists of the early part of the twentieth century that women's sexuality would erupt in violence and disorder. An unsigned review of the memoir in WIN, a left-wing magazine funded by the Committee for Nonviolent Action, accused Stern, from the Weatherman perspective, of playing into the hands of the enemy: "It is no accident that The New York Times Book Review, Newsweek, and People magazine have given this book a lot of coverage—because it fits right into their strategy of counter insurgency: to attack us from within, to trivialize the sources of struggle, to undermine the integrity of our lives."[109]

Stern's book may have made many people, both on the right and on the left, uncomfortable because it expressed attitudes with frightening implications. For Stern, violence became a means of female bonding. As she puts it, she inhaled the air of violence as if it were a sweet perfume. Her experience was common to many of the women she met in her affinity group as she prepared for a violent street demonstration: "We wanted to fight. The women had waited for a chance to assert leadership all summer; the Ave riots provided the opportunity."[110] Weatherman saw the riots, which lasted for three days, as a great success. More important, in Stern's view, was their effect on the women of the group: "The major thing that came out of the Ave riots was a heavy corps of street-fighting women. The nights of rioting and fighting together had made bonds among the women that years of talking had not done. . . . Nothing but action, running in the streets, actually fighting with the pigs could have released such a pent-up force. We were tasting the macho strength that characterizes men, but we felt it keenly as women. Eyes glowing, we looked at each other warmly. Like a sweet perfume in the air we breathed in our first scent of sister-love" (79). Violence, thus, became transformative in a way that echoed traditional male initiation rites and that bore at least a hint of homoeroticism.

For many of the women with whom Stern associated, the move into revolutionary violence involved a redefinition of their gender identities. Like Panther women, they experimented with androgyny in their clothing and affect. Stern describes one of the members of her collective as an example of this: "With a tremendous effort she repressed her fears and timidity, and became a study of the tough, masculine woman that characterized so many

Weatherwomen. Wearing heavy men's boots, jeans, and an army jacket, her hair uncombed, no makeup, chain-smoking with trembling hands and drinking either tea or wine constantly, she learned the Weatherman line and stuck to it" (96).

The women did not simply imitate men; they used social expectations of their gender to take their targets by surprise. The novelty of women's violence worked to Weatherman's advantage when the women's caucus decided to stage its own action without telling the men in the group. They were successful in trashing an ROTC building in Seattle "because [the ROTC trainees] were caught completely off guard by the violence of our attack, and by the fact that women would fight a group of men" (122). Stern's view echoes that of Cril Payne, the FBI agent who wrote about his experiences spying on the radical underground.

Weatherman was notorious throughout the left for its seemingly mindless celebration of violence. The female leadership of the group at one point presented a frightening inversion of early twentieth-century eugenics arguments when it extolled the murder of white babies. This reached its nadir at the Flint, Michigan, War Council at which the group decided to go underground and commence its bombing campaign. As Stern recalls:

The theme of violence dominated the convention in other ways which disturbed me, because it seemed more the product of insanity and depravity than revolution. The major thing which horrified me was the interest in, admiration for and concentration on Charlie Manson and his Family. Almost everybody in the Bureau [the Weatherman leadership group] ran around saluting people with the fork sign [to symbolize the fork the Mansons left in the belly of one of their victims]. . . . There was a picture of Sharon Tate up on the wall, in tribute to Manson's murder of the star in her eighth month of pregnancy. (204)

At the council, Weatherman leader Bernardine Dohrn made a speech (which she later criticized) extolling the Manson Family murders. As Stern writes, "I didn't agree that all white babies should die; I had been a white baby once, and now I was trying to be a revolutionary. . . . I believe the Mansonite trip was born out of despair and frustration. It in no way corresponded to the quality of the rest of Weatherman politics" (204). Yet white infanticide became a rallying cry during the most extreme period of Weatherman: as Robin Morgan recalls, a Weatherwoman, on seeing her breastfeed her son, told her, "You have no right to have that pig [as in *white*] male baby." When Morgan, stunned, asked, "How can you say that? What should I do?" the Weatherwoman advised her to "put it in the garbage."[111] If women were struggling to break free of biological definitions of gender, what then did this mean for maternity? Was the very act of reproducing counterrevolutionary?

Although Weatherman at its lowest point celebrated white infanticide, those defending members of the group supported maternity when it was convenient. When Stern, on trial as one of the Seattle Seven for her role in the riots at the federal courthouse there, revealed to her lawyers that she was pregnant, they resisted her demand that she have an abortion. They wanted to present what they saw as a visual contradiction to the jury in hopes of getting her off:

> "But I don't want a baby," I pleaded with them.
>
> "It will look good to have you come in, glowing and pregnant, maybe with some knitting," Carl told me benignly. . . .
>
> "But I don't want a baby. I don't want it," I said desperately.
>
> Carl was the picture of patience. "Come on, now, Susan, you'd probably make a darn good little mother. You only have another five months to go."
>
> Nothing I said seemed to matter. Carl and Jeff insisted that if the jury was sequestered over Christmas vacation, it would be cookies for the defendants. In the end I agreed with them that it was too selfish of me to risk the men's lives, when I could always give the baby away if I didn't want it.[112]

Although she ultimately decided to go ahead with her abortion, her lawyers remained vehemently opposed to it. Stern's public persona was in question: she was on trial for being a violent woman, and how she performed over the course of the trial would make the difference between freedom and prison. After all, as she writes, the court "was a movie set" (285). For the jury, "we were part of the evidence. They regarded us with one arched eyebrow, as they might a pornographic movie" (288). As the sole female defendant, she herself felt the pressure in a different way: there was "no one but me to undertake the tremendous responsibility of being the female voice which would be carried to other women across the country" (257). Her being a woman entered into how she was treated by the lawyers: "If the trial was difficult for the men, it was harrowing for me. Tentatively accepted by my co-defendants as an Auntie Mame figure with an eccentric fascination for violence which they labeled Weatherman tendencies, the lawyers primarily viewed me as a major obstruction to their idea about running orderly trials. Michael Tigar's attitude toward me was that of a big strong hero who would take care of a frail, sickly, impulsive heroine. . . . Carl Maxey treated me like a lovable but unruly daughter. [Jeff] Steinborn was my lover throughout the ordeal, though we couldn't fuck" (293). And the judge was coy with her as well: "That was his manner with me throughout the trial—oh, that little sex kitten who got mixed up with those bad men" (294).

By foregrounding her sexuality in her court presentations, in her work as a go-go dancer to support the movement, and most of all in the mural she painted on her living room wall, Stern created an image of the revolutionary woman that blended crime and sexuality, violence and parturition. She presented this vision as the mother of a new America. Yet actual motherhood, for her, was a domesticating trap, a means of repackaging her, in her lawyers' eyes, as a reassuringly harmless figure. While it is easy to understand the reasons for the hostile reviews Stern received, it would be a great mistake to dismiss her memoir, which remains one of the most valuable insider sources on Weatherman, as well as a thorough exploration of the intersection between violence, radical politics, and sexuality.[113] For Stern, it would seem that her life as a Weatherwoman highlighted what anthropologist Michael Taussig calls "a certain sexual quality of the law and of breaking the law, the beauty and libidinality of transgression."[114] The 1975 publication of *With the Weathermen* not only occasioned the glee of mainstream reviewers eager to dismiss all radical protesters as dilettantes but also provoked the distress of many committed feminists and leftists, who saw Stern's self-portrayal as a caricature. However, the attention Stern's book received, while in many ways similar in tone, was not nearly as dramatic as the reaction to a contemporaneous event: the kidnapping, disappearance, and trial of Patty Hearst.

THE SYMBIONESE LIBERATION ARMY AND PATTY HEARST

In 1974, the image of Patty Hearst wielding a carbine during her first bank robbery ricocheted throughout American culture. Dangerous, radical, and sexy, this image appeared in Berkeley on posters proclaiming, "We love you Tania," which referred to the nom de guerre Hearst had taken when she joined in the escapades of her Symbionese Liberation Army captors. It illustrated articles exploring what had gone wrong with wealthy kids in America. Later it showed up at Hearst's trial, where it served to discredit her claims of victimhood. If the other women discussed in this chapter

Was Patty Hearst a victim or a crazed revolutionary? This *Time* magazine cover from April 29, 1974, contrasts a soulful, pensive Hearst with photographs of the revolutionary Tania and thus suggests multiple interpretations of Hearst's behavior.

TIME Magazine © 1974 Time Inc. Reprinted by permission.

struggled with the relationship between sex and violence, and the meaning of revolutionary maternity, Hearst was finally burdened by being, as the title of one popular book about her proclaimed, *Anyone's Daughter.*

At the time of Patty Hearst's arrest in 1975, five of the FBI's Ten Most Wanted were radical women. Although she never made the list, Patty Hearst was literally the poster child for women's violence on the left. Variously cast as victim, spoiled rich girl in search of sexual and political adventure, and prototypical seventies revolutionary, Patty Hearst was the subject of books and poems and was represented in movies, both mainstream and pornographic. The photograph of her cradling a carbine in front of an SLA banner became a best-selling poster.[115] It is striking that of all the radical women described here, it is Hearst, an ambiguous revolutionary allied with a political organization that seemed a funhouse version of the new left, who has survived in the popular imagination.[116]

The SLA was widely distrusted by members of the left—even in its very early stages, before its 1973 assassination of the respected black Oakland school superintendent Marcus Foster. It was important for members of the SLA that they have what they considered third world leadership, and this they found in the person of Donald DeFreeze, an African American escaped convict.[117] DeFreeze was politicized in the California prison system through the radical prison movement that had such a huge influence on the Bay Area leftist groups. By the early seventies, however, the prison movement was losing popular support, and few leftists would be willing to support the allegation made by Weather Underground spokeswoman Bernardine Dohrn that "the women and men in jails are POW's held by the United States."[118]

Many leftist critiques of the SLA focused on DeFreeze, who had been a "fundamentalist Jesus freak" just four years before emerging as field marshal of the SLA, and had also been a police informer.[119] As an article in the *Black Panther* pointed out, DeFreeze, despite an arrest record that included assault with a deadly weapon, burglary, parole violations, and attempted escape from the police, was given probation when he led police to his cache of weapons in 1967. The article strongly implied that DeFreeze was a state-sponsored provocateur, whose actions were designed to discredit the left, for "the release on probation of two Black men with police records [DeFreeze and an associate], apprehended in possession of more than 200 guns, including weapons, at this period in California could only have occurred with approval at the highest level for some benefit to police authorities."[120] Although the Weather Underground Organization claimed revolutionary "love" for the SLA, almost no other radical organizations either took the group's politics seriously or supported its seemingly random acts of violence.[121]

Yet the SLA came to appear to the media as an emblem of the radicalism of the period, especially following the kidnapping and seeming conversion of heiress Patty Hearst in 1974. Seized by the SLA from the Berkeley townhouse she shared with her fiancé, Stephen Weed, in February 1974, she was held captive by them, bound in a tiny closet, for six weeks. She reemerged in April, caught on videotape during a bank robbery. Wearing a beret and holding a machine gun, she proclaimed her new revolutionary identity as Tania. After most of the rest of the SLA was killed in a fiery shootout with the Los Angeles police, Hearst and the other two surviving members of the group went underground. Captured in September 1975, she raised a fist for the cameras and identified her occupation on jailhouse forms as "urban guerrilla." Five months later, she went on trial, defending herself as a victim of brainwashing. In late March 1976, she was convicted; she spent two years in prison before being given clemency by President Carter in February 1979.

In light of the SLA's sometimes cartoonish nature, it was predictable that the media did not generally take Hearst's politics seriously in its coverage of the case. But, then again, most mainstream accounts of revolutionary women tended to focus on their violence as criminality, rather than as political activism, and to blame feminism for its emergence. A subheading in the September 23, 1974, issue of *u.s. News & World Report* was pointed: "From car thieves to murderers, female outlaws are in the headlines—raising the question: are they influenced by 'women's lib'?"[122] The article featured pictures of 1930s outlaw Bonnie Parker, Weather Underground leader Bernardine Dohrn, Patty Hearst, and the Manson girls. In this conflation of an apolitical gangster, a fringe left leader, a kidnap victim who might also be a violent revolutionary, and teenage mass murderers, the article seemed to erase all distinctions but gender. The subheading invited one to think that women's violence, be it mass murder or bank robbery, could be a direct result of feminism. It would be difficult to find a definition of "women's lib" that could encompass the docile followers of a crazed killer: the inclusion of the Manson girls seemed to indicate that the article was pandering to the worst fears of its readers about the potential for female violence unleashed by the women's movement.

The communiqués issued by the SLA made it easy for the mainstream media to portray Hearst as a feminist run amok. According to Patty Hearst, the other members of the SLA considered DeFreeze a brave third world leader whose every whim must be obeyed.[123] But despite the SLA's seemingly slavish adherence to DeFreeze's word, members of the group saw it as a feminist organization. It was in fact a predominantly female group, whose members, in an October 21, 1975, communiqué, made "an effort to combat the attempts of the pig media to de-politicize the SLA and portray the women involved as empty headed, gun-carressing [sic] automatons." The statement went on to say that "women must participate in armed struggle and be fighters. Fighting armed is not 'macho.' Fighting for revolution with gun in hand is not just a man's game."[124] These words only reinforced the media portrayals of Hearst as a women's libber taking feminism to its seemingly logical conclusion of insane violence.

For very different reasons, it suited the purposes of both the mainstream media and revolutionary groups to exaggerate the violence of women within radical movements. There is a striking difference in tone between the female revolutionaries whom the sociologist Gilda Zwerman interviewed in prison, many of them serving life sentences and permanently separated from their children, and the image of the armed leftist woman that appeared in the 1970s in published autobiographies and in media accounts. While Zwerman's interviewees projected a public image of fearless amazons, "they remained uncomfortable with taking an active role in the violence."[125] Yet these women also felt that their own reluctance to engage in violence was a personal and political limitation to be overcome.

Academic texts, as well as the mass media, asked whether feminism caused violence and criminality. A popular sociology text of the period, *Sisters in Crime: The Rise of the New Female Criminal*, answered the question in the affirmative. Its author, Freda Adler, wrote that "on the surface there seems to be little connection between the 'masculinization' of female behavior and the civil-rights movement of the 1950s, but in perspective they appear to be twin aspects of an assault on the separate-but-equal philosophy which has maintained the white and male power structure."[126] According to Adler, "the coming" of the female criminal "was foretold in song and foreshadowed in unisexual styles of dress and hair and attitude long before it appeared on police blotters" (5). Like the moralists of the 1920s who warned of the social dangers posed by bobbed hair and flapper dresses, Adler connects clothing and criminal behavior. In her analysis, she moves swiftly between social movements and petty crime. In her first chapter, she sets up her argument by noting that "the *Zeitgeist* of liberation has been moving irresistibly across the land. A generation militantly young, black, and female has stirred to storm and controversy previously whispered plaint whose answer, as Bob Dylan so eloquently lyricized, 'is blowing in the wind'" (1).

However, she quickly backs off from any real social analysis by contending that "in another sense there are no social movements, only individuals reacting to the immediacy of their own felt experience" (2). Thus, the first example she gives of female criminality is of Marge, an apolitical middle-aged white woman who has turned from shoplifting to bank robbery. For Adler, there seems to be little difference between political violence and shoplifting or prostitution.

Considering that her premise is the connection between feminism and criminality, Adler's understanding of the social movement seems curiously limited. In delineating the changes in American feminism since the 1960s, she explains that "'women's lib' came to designate—perhaps for the majority of Americans—organized groups of women who were primarily shrill-voiced witches with slovenly, unloosed breasts. Not so today" (26). The new feminism, Adler explains, "includes the nuns who are asking for rights more closely aligned with the rights which priests enjoy, and the housewives who have come to expect their husbands to share more of the duties of the home . . . And, most relevant to our subject, it describes the women who have concluded that shoplifting and prostitution are not their style: embezzlement, robbery, and assault are more congenial to their image" (27). In Adler's breathless analysis there is little to distinguish the "American heiress kidnap-victim-turned-kidnaper, the thirteen-year-old girl who robbed a Greenwich village bank of over two thousand dollars; the skyrocketing increase in the rate at which women steal cars, burglarize stores, forge checks, embezzle funds, run away from their husbands, and engage in prostitution" (250). When there is no distinction between women engaging in politically motivated acts of terror, shoplifting, leaving bad marriages, or engaging in prostitution, a crime into which women are often coerced, then women's criminality becomes sensationalism and feminism is merely an ingredient in the sensation.

Outside observers of the case did not solely blame feminism for Hearst's crimes. For many commentators, the key to Patty Hearst's violence lay in her sexual awakening. Sounding like Hoover and the earlier eugenicists, several writers about the Hearst story linked her love of guns to her newly discovered love of sex. According to one of the earliest books about the SLA, *Exclusive! The Inside Story of Patricia Hearst and the SLA* (1974), written by Marilyn Baker, a public television reporter, the answer to Patty's conversion is obvious: it is sexual. Her first impression is that "Patty Hearst still seemed more paper doll than person. A pretty face seen in fuzzy focus in a high-school yearbook. A girl-child playing at conquests. A lover without orgasm."[127] When Baker listens to the communiqué that Patty Hearst issued following the death of her comrades, she states flatly, "So it had been love that had turned pretty Patty Hearst into a terrorist" (230).

Patty Hearst was symbolically a victim and an aggressor embodied in one woman. She was terrifying because her victimization made her an aggressor. The courtroom drama described by Susan Stern was amplified a thousandfold in Hearst's case. As the editors of the *Nation* wrote after her trial, "She was a kidnap victim. She was a gun-moll robber. She was a revolutionary. She was a poor little rich girl. Conventional, eccentric, exploited, exploiter, she was always a celebrity. . . . The question of who she was seemed to matter more than what she was, innocent or guilty." (She was, the editors concluded, "a pathetic adventuress spun from her family's clippings [coupons and newspaper morgue]. Her adventures have given radical chic an even worse name.")[128]

Hearst's autobiography is one of the great examples of a form one can only call a memoir of self-defense. It was published for an eager audience, one that was eager to condemn. Given her situation, the only way Hearst could exonerate herself from charges of criminality was to portray herself as a victim. As Shana Alexander wrote of her, "Though some saw her as a victim, most Americans then saw Patty as an ungrateful child, a sexual and political adventuress who probably had set up her own kidnapping. She swiftly became a female hate object, a modern witch."[129] In her autobiography, Hearst needed to persuade the American public that she was not, contrary to what she had confided to her childhood best friend in a jailhouse conversation shortly after her capture, "speaking from a revolutionary feminist perspective" (249). Moreover, she had to counteract an earlier autobiography she had dictated as Tania, in which she said, "If you believe the media you'd think I was totally weird—according to them, I never mean anything I say, and I'll do anything I'm told" (91).

Thus, she needed to focus on her extended captivity, blindfolded and bound in a tiny closet, raped repeatedly by her captors, hearing the "clicks and clacks of their rifle bolts and the ammunition clips being jammed into place."[130] She needed to focus on her abject reactions: "I wish I could say now that I stood up well under Cinque's interrogation, that I refused to reveal vital information, that I lied and fooled him. I told the SLA anything they wanted to hear. Terrorized, threatened constantly with death or being hung from the ceiling for being an uncooperative prisoner, I spilled my guts. . . . I was afraid and weepy, hardly the heroine" (52). In fact, at her trial, Robert Jay Lifton and other experts on the effects of extreme duress confirmed Hearst's account of her trauma, which was portrayed as similar to that of a prisoner of war (420). "I could not keep myself from crying, crying, crying," she wrote (69). According to Shana Alexander, whose book focused on the Hearst trial, almost all the reporters who attended it believed Hearst's story.[131] By the end of the trial, Hearst, who appeared zombielike to many observers, weighed eighty-seven pounds. But the general public still despised her.

William Saxbe, the U.S. attorney general, had denounced her after her videotaped bank robbery in which she first identified herself as Tania, as "nothing but a common criminal."[132] The government spent millions putting her on trial, and Hearst spent two years in prison before being granted executive clemency.

What finally undid Hearst in the eyes of the jurors was the discrepancy between her pathetic appearance during the trial and her image as Tania, urban guerrilla. As Shana Alexander described the problem,

> The tiny, dowdy, downcast creature at the defense table bore no resemblance to any of the famous newspaper photographs. . . . "I thought she'd be pretty, but she was just unattractive, not pleasant-looking at all,' said one male juror. ". . . There was no coloring at all in the face, and very hollow, depressed eyes." Because he still believed her truthful, he couldn't figure out why she looked so bad, and he ascribed it to the rigors of her captivity. . . . Then [Hearst's lawyer, F. Lee] Bailey had introduced the *Newsweek* cover, the "urban guerrilla" photograph, "and all of a sudden this picture comes around of a vibrant young woman who's *alive*, feeling, showing her emotions, attractive, lipstick on, a big smile." They seemed like two entirely different people, one of them animated, one a zombie. "At the time I couldn't figure out what the hell was going on. But I realize now that that's when my real serious doubts set in."[133]

Hearst, this juror seemed to suggest, came alive only through violence. Regardless of the violence to which she had been subjected—the captivity, the threats, the rapes—her appearance with a gun sexualized her in the eyes of the jurors and the public. Her lipstick, her big smile, her attractiveness as Tania suggested that the rapes to which she had been subjected and the phallic carbine she held in the bank robbery had made her both more dangerous and more womanly. In conversation with Shana Alexander, the psychiatrist hired by the prosecution in the Hearst case, Joel Fort, explained her closet rapes and her subsequent conversion to the cause: "It also seemed plausible to me that she got horny frequently. She's been sexually active since the age of fifteen, which I consider very healthy. I think if you'd had a period of deprivation and isolation for a few days or a few weeks, you'd want to have sex all the more—for pleasure, for companionship, and so forth" (489). Rape had revolutionized Hearst, and the gun had set her free. The contradictions that swirled around her rendered Hearst something of a Rorschach blot, a collection of signifiers without inherent meaning. These contradictions made it possible for jurors, and for the public, to project onto her popular culture dreams and myths about the armed woman. And her obvious victimization, finally, had no place in those fantasies. The fact that she appeared childlike, and had even shrunk to a child's size, during her trial, suggested that only violence, and sexualized violence at that, could make a woman out of her, and that in the absence of those elements, she could easily appear harmless.

Patty Hearst, thus, embodied a cultural nightmare about the violent potential inherent in all women and about the power of promiscuous sex to unleash that violence. J. Edgar Hoover, during the 1930s, had warned the public that violent women, if left unchecked, had the power to destroy the nation. Now much of the public, as well as the jurors in the Hearst case, seemed to agree. It was the stirring image of Patty Hearst as sexually vibrant while wielding her carbine—vibrant *because* of her gun—that undermined her case for good. The logistics of revolutionary life, including intramovement violence and the risk of imprisonment, made the role of the revolutionary mother lion very difficult for most women. Yet the childless "new Bonnies"—sexually liberated, resistant to maternity, and violent—ultimately sparked public rage. The image of the pistol-brandishing, sexually out-of-control new woman, undermining the white race through her refusal to bear children, seemed much scarier now that she was armed with ideology and was committed to, at the very least, radically transforming, if not outright destroying, America. Soon enough, the armed radical women of the seventies would come to seem safely vanquished—exiled, imprisoned, forced underground, or simply exhausted or disillusioned—but a new generation of right-wing women would then rise up, using the gun to re-create the nation.

ARMED WOMEN OF THE FAR RIGHT

RACE MOTHERS, WARRIORS, AND THE

SURPRISING CASE OF CAROLYN CHUTE

During the 1960s and 1970s armed women became left-wing revolutionary icons, but the 1980s ushered in a new political trend: armed female activists of the far right. By the 1990s, it was possible to open up a mainstream women's magazine like *Mademoiselle* and read an article titled "Women Who Love to Hate."[1] A 1992 cover story in the *Village Voice*, "Long Day's Journey into White," was illustrated with a photograph of a blonde skinhead, Liz "Valkyrie" Bullis, toting an assault weapon.[2] The online magazine *Salon* devoted an issue of its mothers' column to "Nazi family values."[3] In 1991, *Klanwatch Intelligence Report*, a journal aimed at people concerned about far-right violence, published an article titled "Cookbooks and Combat Boots," in which its author offered a snapshot of movement women: "The ideal Aryan woman must excel as warrior and nurturer. Like her mainstream model, the superwoman of the 1980s, who could 'bring home the bacon and fry it up in a pan,' she can build a bomb, handle automatic weapons yet still remain feminine and subservient to both her husband and the organization."[4] These articles posed a question intended to intrigue readers: how did women, who were supposed to be more peaceful and tolerant than men, become violent racist activists?[5]

Although photographic images of cheerful blonde girls wielding machine guns and sporting Nazi regalia are obviously striking and frightening, they are only one aspect of armed white womanhood on the far right. For my purposes in this book, it is more pertinent to consider how women operating within ultraconservative movements have used guns to define a new version of female American identity. How has the extreme right allowed these women to explore the relationship between femininity, violence, and the nation? According to Floyd Cochran, once the fifth-ranking member of the Aryan Nations, and now a prominent antiracist activist, "Women are entering the organized racist movement in record numbers."[6] Scholars of the movement estimate that women constitute nearly half of all new members in some racist groups.[7] Like the nineteenth-century men and women whose shooting on stage and in outdoor narratives was framed as part of a larger campaign to protect the white race, these modern activists conflate racist beliefs, a love of guns, and fixed (yet contradictory) gender roles.

It is difficult to speak of far-right women as a homogeneous group because they serve a number of roles within the movement. While some women fulfill very traditional roles as "race mothers," seeking to enhance white power by increasing the number of Aryan babies, others are armed skinheads, who engage in violent street fights. These women have varying relationships to guns. Just as a century earlier Annie Oakley domesticated the gun, using her femininity to change its image from a weapon to a sporting accessory, so today women on the far right are softening the image of guns (and of the groups they belong to). Guns allow some women the possibility for liberation within the movement, enabling them to be seen as equal partners in the battle, rather than merely as sexual accessories, for, as the sociologist Kathleen Blee has observed, "gender is unquestionably an important organizing principle for racist groups. Aryan masculinity is venerated as the bedrock of the white race, racist politics as the litmus test of masculine prowess. . . . The trappings of modern organized racism— from its militarized uniforms and command structure to its aggressive rhetoric and practices—project a sense of hypermasculinity, an exaggeration of masculine ideals."[8] Although the armed woman occupies a problematic position within the hypermasculine world of the far right, her visible presence is nevertheless seen as intensely desirable by male movement leaders —serving as a sexual object to attract potential male recruits and as a way of making organized racism seem less threatening to outsiders.[9]

In racist right chat groups on the Internet, the debate rages over whether women should be more than just breeders of white children. Rachel Pendergraft of the Grand Council of the Knights of the Ku Klux Klan (under the leadership of David Duke) makes the case for taking pride in maternity: "Some women may resent being reminded of their capabilities to be a mother. The feminist movement has encouraged women to feel ashamed of this wonderful gift. . . . However, whether we work inside the home, outside the home, or both, we can't escape the course nature has designed for us—motherhood. . . . We must not listen to the feminist myths, and we must reclaim our position as the daughters of the Republic—America's future is worth it."[10]

Yet there are other women on the racist right who challenge the expectation of female subservience, linking this "eternal servitude" to "being treated like a mud"—a racist term for nonwhites. In a far-right Internet forum, one correspondent weighs in: "Understand that no White woman worth her bloodlines will give her heart and body to any man so weak he would expect of her the behavior of a female wetback, who crossed the border yesterday in the manure truck. Stop whining about strong White women and look to them as partners in the Struggle, rather than just ovaries with tits who provide meals, sex, housecleaning, and child care for you."[11] Another correspondent, "Warrior Woman," taking part in the newsgroup alt.politics.white-power, contends that "the 'mothering' 'maternal' instinct genetically predisposes women to be liberalistic in their views. Women are much more likely to be sympathetic to the 'plight' of illegal immigrants, refugees, and non-White 'peoples.' . . . Thus, could it be said that the 'mothering' instinct which so many White males think is so wonderful and so 'beneficial' in women is actually working against the White rights movement?"[12]

Shocking, and journalistically appealing, as the reality of a gun-toting white supremacist mom may be, those who aspire to play that role generally fall on the very edge of the spectrum of American discourse. The American radical right today has a spectrum of its own: it blurs on one end into the various Ku Klux Klans, Aryan Nations, and other overtly racist parties; it shades in the middle into the militias and Patriot parties (of which Timothy McVeigh was the most notorious adherent); and at the other end of the spectrum are prominent public supporters of the movement, including Texas Congressman Steve Stockman, former Arizona governor Evan Meecham, and state legislators Larry Pratt of Virginia, Charles Duke of Colorado, and Don Rogers of California.[13] Although the right-wing militias have certainly shrunk in number and membership since 1994, when McVeigh bombed the Murrah Federal Building in Oklahoma City, their rhetoric continues to permeate American political discourse.

While there is overlap among racist groups, their views on American nationhood differ greatly, from the Aryan Nations mom who pulls her child out of public school because she was instructed to say the pledge of allegiance ("'One nation under God!' Christian exclaims. 'Heck, no!'"),[14] to the Ku Klux Klan, who often identify greatly with the South as a region, rather than with the nation as a whole.[15] However, the militia movement is grounded in an unorthodox interpretation of the u.s. Constitution—and particularly in a focus on the Second Amendment. The Militia of Montana (best known for its involvement, with the Montana Freemen, in a 1996 siege with law enforcement) publishes an Internet newsletter ("The Militia-man's Newsletter"), called *Taking Aim*, that has as its epigraph the Second Amendment and that deals almost entirely with gun rights.[16] For this reason, it makes most sense for my purposes to focus on armed women within the militia movement, for their participation is inextricably tied up with issues of American nationhood. (While skinhead women, by contrast, are often involved in extreme violence, they are more likely to beat people than to shoot them—and skinheads have little commitment to the idea of the American nation. Neo-Nazis are more interested in a pan-Aryan vision than in promoting the United States per se.) However, the rhetoric by and about women emanating from militias has much in common with that from other far-right groups. The preoccupations of militia women with issues of maternity, appropriate gender roles, and violence not only echo the preoccupations of women along the far-right spectrum but also mirror, in distorted form, the issues of left-wing revolutionaries of earlier decades.

Following the fall of the Berlin Wall in 1989, and the end of the cold war, armed female radicals used guns, and created a rhetoric surrounding guns, to forge a new vision of America, one in which rural families would use arms, if necessary, to ward off the incursions of an invasive government. As antimodernists, they harked back to an imagined bucolic past. Freed from the threat of communism, they worried instead about creeping globalization. Although these right-wing women paid lip service to preserving a patriarchal order, women were at the center of this vision.

In this chapter I will begin by examining the foundational event for the contemporary militia movement, the 1992 standoff at Ruby Ridge, Idaho, in which one armed woman died at the hands of government snipers; her heavily armed young daughters subsequently became icons for the militia movement. From there, I will move on to Carolyn Chute, perhaps the only literary writer in the United States who is also a militia leader—and whose recent fiction most fully articulates the primitivist nostalgia embedded in this vision of the nation. Chute moves effortlessly between her role as the author of literary fiction and her leadership of a political group founded on gun ownership, one who espouses beliefs common to far-right sects yet is hailed by liberal columnists as a working-class, anticorporate leader. Of all the women active in the militia scene during the 1990s and 2000s, Chute has best been able to package a pro-gun, antiglobalist, romantic vision of yeoman workers in a way that is accessible and appealing to a broad audience. Chute's work clearly articulates the role of the armed woman in her dream of a newly constituted American nation.

To understand the work of this most mainstream of militia women, we should briefly examine the rise of the militia movement in the United States. The militia movement has its roots in the early Ku Klux Klan and more recently in the Minutemen, a 1960s offshoot of the John Birch Society with a focus on armed guerrilla warfare against communism. As Kenneth Stern writes, "Some of the Minutemen's guns were supplied by the u.s. government. Under a program begun in 1903 to promote American marksmanship in case of war, firearms and ammunition were loaned to clubs affiliated with the National Rifle Association (NRA). Minutemen were encouraged to join the NRA, not only to get access to the hardware but also to fight against gun registration."[17] Thus, the Minutemen tapped into mainstream gun culture in their attempts to overthrow what they considered socialist institutions (their training manuals included such skills as making mines to blow up roads and bridges) as well as in their plans to assassinate those they considered "Communists and one-worlders," such as Senator William Fulbright.

The rhetoric of militias has in many ways become commonplace on the right, and nowhere more so than in the militias' link between gun ownership and citizenship. This linkage, which is a bedrock of militia ideologies, is of course endorsed by such organizations as the NRA. However, the militia movement as a whole did not crystallize until 1992, following the events at Ruby Ridge—a tragedy that solidified antigovernment sentiment across the conservative and far-right spectrum and that gave the nation its first sixteen-year-old, swastika-wearing, gun-toting heroine.

SARA WEAVER, RUBY RIDGE, AND MILITIA FAMILY VALUES

The contemporary militia movement came of age in the aftermath of the Ruby Ridge catastrophe. A year-and-a-half long government siege of the home of Randy and Vicki Weaver, Aryan Nations sympathizers, ended with the death of Vicki and their fourteen-year-old son, Sam, at the hands of FBI sharpshooters. Following this debacle, the Weavers' sixteen-year-old daughter, Sara, became enshrined as a heroine of the far right. The events at Ruby Ridge confirmed the beliefs of many on the extreme right, as well as mainstream conservatives, that government had gone too far in interfering with the lives of Americans. For eleven days in August and early September 1992, at a cost of a million dollars a day, agents of the FBI, the Bureau of Alcohol, Tobacco, and Firearms and the Special Operations Group, an elite u.s. marshals force, surrounded the Weavers' mountaintop cabin. Inside the cabin, Randy Weaver and his three daughters waited with the body of their son and brother Sam and the body of Vicki, who had been shot by sniper Len Horiuchi in the face while she held her infant daughter in her arms, lying under the kitchen table. At the roadblock at the base of the mountain, neighbors, skinheads, and neo-Nazis from fourteen states taunted the government agents and waved signs to show their support. After several days, the brown-shirted youth were joined by more moderate people, who said "their eyes had been opened by the case." Plenty of those present were women. They were not just groupies who surrounded the visiting skinheads but also Patriot movement women, who locked arms in a chain while they faced the roadblock and yelled at government agents that "never will you take another woman down!"[18]

In many ways the tragic events at Ruby Ridge revolved around the women of the family, despite the fact that it was Randy Weaver's refusal to come down off the mountain that instigated the standoff.[19] As Jess Walter reports, the government (as well as many of the Weavers' friends and acquaintances) saw Vicki as the real leader of the family.[20] An informant from inside the U.S. marshals office told writer James Aho that "it was a matriarchal thing."[21] Vicki had made the decision to move from Iowa, where the Weavers were from, to Idaho in order to home-school their children; Vicki's apocalyptic visions guided many family decisions; her ceaseless hard work preparing years' worth of survival food, making clothes, and growing vegetables kept the family going during Randy's long stretches of unemployment. Dave Hunt, the deputy U.S. marshal first charged with getting Randy down off the mountain to his court date, found out by interviewing people involved in the situation that "[Randy] was not in control, Vicki was. Randy wasn't even clear on the doctrine he followed."[22] Furthermore, inside the cabin, sixteen-year-old Sara and her ten-year-old sister, Rachel, refused to let their father end the standoff. As a thirteen-year-old, Sara had greeted visitors wearing a semiautomatic pistol holstered in her World War II gun belt; Sara and her younger siblings had taunted a neighbor family by wearing swastikas and marching with their guns in front of the family's house, shouting white power slogans. Sara seemed as committed to far-right ideology as her mother, and she seemed to offer Randy her mother's strength and leadership during the standoff.

Much of what has been written about Ruby Ridge since the standoff, particularly in conservative accounts, depicts Randy Weaver as a strong, central masculine figure. For instance, as the subtitle of Alan W. Bock's *Ambush at Ruby Ridge: How Government Agents Set Randy Weaver Up and Took*

His Family Down reveals, Bock sees Randy Weaver as the protagonist of the story. He begins his narrative by writing about his initial visit to Ruby Ridge "to make sense of a . . . site of confrontation: between the u.s. government and a white separatist named Randy Weaver."[23] This view places Randy as the head of the household, the one in charge, and is in line with conservative beliefs about desirable gender roles within the family.

Yet the truth of the matter seems to be somewhat different. Randy's role during the siege was seen both by government agents and by members of the far right who were present as a failure of masculinity. Many agents involved in the standoff, like Deputy Marshal Dave Hunt, were troubled by Randy's cowardice and willingness to put his family in harm's way. And paramilitary leader Bo Gritz, whom Randy finally accepted as a mediator, implored Randy not to listen to Sara's pleas to continue, telling him, "Damn, Randall. You are the head of the family. You are the man. Make those decisions."[24] Gritz's comment to the government agents waiting outside was that "there isn't much of a man in there."[25] The Weavers' stated beliefs were quite patriarchal: Randy told an interviewer, years after the standoff, that he was fairly indifferent to his daughters' success in school because "the girls will meet men, get married, and become wonderful homemakers like their mother. . . . I'm a chauvinist, I guess. But that's their calling and that's what's best for them."[26] However, it was clear even to outside observers that the women of the family, rather than the nominal patriarch, exercised real authority. Talking later with a journalist, Rachel Weaver said of her mother and father's relationship: "She was dainty. Petite, very feminine, never burped in front of anyone. . . . She was the brains, and she just let him think he was running the show. Dad probably still doesn't know it."[27]

As its subsequent importance to militias suggests, the Ruby Ridge case encapsulated many themes of the conservative and ultraconservative movements. There was the issue of gun rights, given that Randy's initial indictment had been on weapons charges, after he had sold (or was entrapped into selling to support his family, depending on whose version one accepts) a number of sawed-off shotguns to a government informer. Every member of the family save infant Elisheba was heavily armed. After the siege, the FBI brought in reporters, via Humvee, to view the cabin and the family's arsenal, which was spread out on a sheet: seven rifles, two shotguns, five pistols, and thousands of rounds of ammunition. Then, there was the issue of a family's right to pursue an alternative way of life free from government interference: the Weavers were Christian white supremacists who looked forward to the imminent end time. Finally, there was the feeling, shared by many conservatives, that the government had engaged in a conspiracy to cover up its murderous mistakes at Ruby Ridge.

One did not have to be a member of the far right to be troubled by the facts of the case. Government agents had lured Sam Weaver's dog to where they were hiding in the woods and shot it to death in order to effect a quiet entry onto the property. In the shootout that followed, Sam was first wounded in the arm and then shot in the back while fleeing. The FBI, overestimating the violent potential of the Weavers, had changed the rules of engagement for the standoff, instructing sharpshooters to use deadly force against any male wielding a firearm while leaving the cabin. More-over, although the Weavers were white separatists, and although Randy frequented Aryan Nations gatherings, the family was described by journalists and friends as happy and functional. Their cabin was deemed "cozy," and the children were viewed as clean, well behaved, and smart.[28] They did not fit negative stereotypes of white supremacists. In fact, a jury acquitted Randy Weaver and a young friend of the family, Kevin Harris, of all charges related to the standoff, including the killing of u.s. Marshal William Degan, who was shot in the gun battle that also resulted in Sam Weaver's death. The Justice Department settled the claim filed by the Weavers, refusing to ac-knowledge any wrongdoing but awarding the three Weaver girls $1 million apiece and Randy $100,000. Eventually, Randy and Sara published an auto-biographical account of the events at Ruby Ridge,[29] which they promoted at gun shows and "preparedness expos."[30]

The siege at Ruby Ridge, while disturbing to many, became the event that launched the contemporary American militia movement. In October 1992, activists from all over the country convened at Estes Park, Colorado, for the Rocky Mountain Rendezvous. One hundred and sixty members of far-right groups, along with Larry Pratt, the executive director of Gun Owners of America, came together to discuss a possible response to the events at Ruby Ridge. While at the Rocky Mountain Rendezvous, members of Klan groups, the Aryan Nations, Christian Identity groups, and other extremist organi-zations learned to form an alliance and cloak their rhetoric. In *Gathering Storm: America's Militia Threat*, Morris Dees shows how focused the confer-ence was: "All the angry rhetoric at the Rendezvous flowed in one direction —at the federal government. Not the Jews, not the blacks, not the homo-sexuals, not the abortionists, though each group was tagged throughout the three days. The enemy was clearly defined as the federal government and the New World Order. . . . [The militia leaders] were smart this time. They borrowed a page out of David Duke's book."[31] That is, they used code words rather than blatantly racist rhetoric. More important, the Klan leaders and the members of Aryan Nations strategically emphasized the problem of government intrusions into the lives of citizens and the disempowerment of Americans by gun-control laws. In other words, they criticized the federal government rather than talking, as many of them once had, about the Zionist Occupation Government and other staples of the racist right. As Michael Barkun points out, while the still-active Michigan Militia, one of the most prominent of the paramilitary groups in the 1990s, has as its mission the protection of the constitutional rights of "all citizens regardless of race, color, religion, sex, physical characteristics, or national origin," one should be wary of such bias-free language: "The absence of explicitly anti-Semitic or anti-black motifs is often more apparent than real."[32]

Despite their extreme rhetoric and barely cloaked racism, militias found support from leaders of the religious right and from a number of prominent Republican politicians. Idaho congresswoman Helen Chenoweth, a Newt Gingrich protégée, openly expressed sympathy with militia goals. The Militia of Montana, in fact, sold a videotape by Chenoweth in which, as their description went, this "former natural resources consultant explains how environmentalists are taking public and private property from American's [sic] and placing the property in the control of the n.w.o. [New World Order]. Over 50% of America is now in their control."[33] Voicing similar views, Idaho senator Larry Craig advocated arming citizens and disarming federal agents. After the government siege of the Branch Davidians in Waco, Texas, ended in fiery catastrophe in 1993, militia groups grew both in strength and in number. Following the events at Waco, Texas representative Steve Stockman called for the arrest of Attorney General Janet Reno on charges of premeditated murder. He has appeared as an honored guest on a radio show produced by the anti-Semitic Liberty Lobby.

Even as these conservative politicians have brought militia ideas into the mainstream, there is a trend that seems still more notable: some militias have forsaken explicitly conservative rhetoric and have come to rely instead on gun-rights and antiglobalist rhetoric to gain converts. This new populism, which seems at first glance to be left-wing, is articulated most strikingly in the work of a writer and militia leader who may appear to defy categorization.

CAROLYN CHUTE AND THE PROLETARIANIZATION
OF THE MILITIA MOVEMENT

If the roles of women on the far right seem explicitly contradictory, there is perhaps no figure who encapsulates and extends the contradictions more than Carolyn Chute, a militia leader and literary novelist who coyly refuses to categorize herself as being either on the left or on the right, and who says she stands for nothing more than the defense of the working class.

The term "proletarian writer" may be outmoded these days, but one might have the impression that it applies to Carolyn Chute, who in both her literary and her political activities champions the rural white working class — the tribe, as she describes it — which she sees as having been ground down by powerful corporations. Her novels focus on poor, rural Maine residents, and she was the founder, in 1996, of the 2nd Maine Militia, an organization whose first meeting, as a journalist wrote, "marked the beginning of what [was] intended as a working-class revolution, [where] what held participants together was stronger than what divided them: The belief that corporations run the government through their influence and by buying politicians — that they value each worker about as much as a piece of equipment."[34] Chute would seem to be the kind of promoter of the working class and chronicler of working-class concerns who has been notably absent from American fiction since the 1930s, when such novelists as Josephine Herbst and Michael Gold marched on picket lines with striking coal miners and wrote novels about the struggles of the proletariat.

This first impression, however, would be misleading. In both her political and literary work, Chute uses the idea and the language of tribalism to unite the divergent rhetorics of class struggle and nativist resentment. In doing so, Chute is able to deflect concern about some of the more militant right-wing aspects of her militia. In Chute's work, tribal identity functions as if it were what we often think of as "ethnic" identity: she uses literary scholar Werner Sollors's ideas of consent and descent to underscore the idea that ethnicity, or tribalism, involves both performance (consent, or agreeing to behave as a member of a group) and genetics (descent from parents with the same ethnic identity).[35] For Chute, tribal identity is crucially linked to a region or homeland (in her case, Maine) as the sacred space. Thus, Chute uses white rural poverty structurally in her work the way other writers use ethnicity, as something both inherited and inevitable, or essential, and as something that is consensual and embraced, or constructed. Guns, and gun rights, are central to the tribe she champions. Moreover,

The novelist and Maine Militia leader Carolyn Chute, with her husband in the background.
Courtesy of David A. Rodgers.

the gun creates the conditions of possibility by which Chute reconciles her essentialist conception of womanhood to her own productivity as a writer and militia leader.

Chute's tribal vision seems to enable her, personally, to find a space within which to exist. Moving between two worlds, one of liberal intellectuals and the other of a constructed "folk," Chute creates a vision of tribalism that gives her a place in the world she writes about. Using carefully crafted sentences in novels hailed by critics, she writes about the failures of artists to solve problems and about the damaging effects of education and literacy. In some ways, one could call Chute's last two novels anti-*Künstlerromane*. For even as her vision of tribalism gives Chute the opportunity to slip out of some of the more uncomfortable political implications of her work, it also catches her in the central contradiction of a seeming revolutionary whose "folk," to stay pure, must remain forever untainted by damaging outside influences. Then again, the quest for "authenticity" seems always destined to end in failure.

Although Chute's literary work has always been focused on the working poor, she herself was not born into poverty. She grew up in a middle-class suburb of Portland, Maine, where her father was an electrical supply salesman. After dropping out of high school at age sixteen to marry a bread factory worker, she gave birth to a daughter, divorced, and ended up working in factories and on a farm.[36] The stories she wrote in creative writing classes at the University of Southern Maine became the basis for her first novel, *The Beans of Egypt, Maine* (1985), which sold a half million copies. She married her "ideal man," an illiterate junkyard worker seven years her junior whom she met at a shooting match. She lives in a house without indoor plumbing, hot water, electricity in all rooms, a clothes dryer, a dishwasher, or a computer.

Chute started the 2nd Maine Militia in 1995 with an op-ed piece in the *Maine Sunday Telegraph* in which she defended the right to own guns and called for like-minded people to get together for a target shoot and discussion at her house. "I am really sick and tired of the bad image some people are giving guns," she wrote. "I am worried sick over the way huge corporations now own our government. . . . You say the government is evil? Yes, yes, yes, yes. Because the government is not ours anymore." Chute differentiated her militia from others:

The 2nd Maine Militia is clear about where our country's problems lie. Many other militias and many individuals blame gays, blacks, Jews,

Spanish-speaking folks, welfare mums, illegal drugs, seat belts, schools without prayers, women with shoes, abortions, environmentalists, unseen communist forces and so-called liberals.

Meanwhile, the so-called liberals blame men with guns, men who whistle and wink at women, women who like whistles and winks, women who like waiting on men, unseatbelted people, and what they call "uneducated white trash."[37]

In other words, while other militias are recognizably bigoted in their racism, anti-Semitism, and homophobia, liberals reserve their prejudices for poor whites and "traditional" women. It was the objects of liberal scorn to whom Chute appealed. By February 1996 her meetings were attracting nearly one hundred people, many of them there for one reason; as one of them put it, "I love my guns. That's why I'm here. I believe in protecting what's mine."[38] Chute, after all, explicitly ties gun ownership to her self-proclaimed "redneck" identity: "Rednecks love guns, always have. It's our *culture*."[39] This is a culture that at once imagines for women a highly traditional role and allows women to step out of that role, as the case of Vicki Weaver exemplifies. In interview after interview, Chute called hers a "no-wing" militia. "To me, there is no left or right of this issue. . . . We are here today to consider doing something about what the corporations are doing to us. That is not left or right. That is corporations being way up there, and us being way down here."[40]

Chute has acknowledged to an interviewer that "some of her social values," such as her support for gay rights, the ethical treatment of animals, and Amnesty International, "may not be typical working-class ones," but she is certain that "her lifestyle, her work ethic, and the way she values people and time before corporations, government and money put her in the same culture."[41] She is in favor of solar energy and praises small communities while criticizing corporate America. The umbrella of Chute's militia is big enough to shelter lifetime union members, and the actions taken by the group include statehouse protests against lobbyists.

Yet when the progressive columnist Molly Ivins greeted Carolyn Chute's announcement of her new militia with a resounding "Yesssssss! . . . Hallelujah! That's pure, old-time populism,"[42] she may not have known about all of Chute's ideas. Although her militia is probably unique in that she founded it at an artists' colony, inspired by Noam Chomsky tapes, it attracts many whose beliefs would fit into any militia: they are motivated by fears of black helicopters, secret concentration camps across America, and the

United Nations as one of the leaders of the New World Order.[43] As Chute herself acknowledges, "The No-Wing Militia is not really separate from the Right-Wing Militia Movement. We attend each other's meetings, hang out together, do business together. We have the same values, same fears, same dreams."[44] Like many other militias, Chute's is opposed to new environmental regulations that restrict logging.[45] She describes Americans today as "house slaves (professional class) and the field slaves (working class). But," she adds, "some of us don't even make it to the auction block."[46] Unlike many other militias, Chute's is not explicitly racist or anti-Semitic; it does romanticize, however, white rural life. Chute promotes a vision of authentic folk, unsullied by education, living in a barter economy. She sidesteps accusations of bigotry by saying that "everybody hates somebody. . . . Liberals hate working-class white men, especially those who don't do dishes and whistle at women."[47] And, while denying that Timothy McVeigh was a militia member, she proposes that "a militia sentiment was what killed those people in Oklahoma. . . . The bombing of innocent people is not justified. But the rage is justified. I just wish I could induct those enraged millions into our No-Wing Militia Movement."[48]

In a 1997 interview, Chute explained that she started the militia because "I was mad. People of the tribal class have seen their interdependence disappearing, and they become dependent on the big people for everything."[49] Or, as Chute, writing in the guise of "Dear Revolutionary Abby," put it in one of the leaflets that she addressed to her militia, "Form citizens [sic] militias. Camo, jokes, food, gentleness, listening to each other, recreating a tribe, a little target shooting, patience, anger directed at THE SYSTEM, compassion for the tribe, The Tribe. The Tribe. The Tribe."[50] Thus, she celebrates the heroic guerrillas at the center of her 1994 novel, Merry Men, for their blood ties and shared roots. Chute, indeed, locates an ancient aristocracy in Maine speech, in Maine faces.

To hear of a Maine militia may surprise many people, since in recent decades militia movements and other forms of right-wing extremism have been associated primarily with the Midwest and the Northwest. In the 1970s and 1980s, Posse Comitatus, a farmers' antitax movement, was strong in Iowa and other midwestern states. Idaho and Washington have long been hotbeds of radical right activity. In the wake of the Oklahoma City bombings, Americans got accustomed to hearing about the Militia of Montana and such militia figures as "Mark from Michigan." But New England remains a region generally not associated with that type of extremism.

Perhaps the most notable agrarian uprising in Maine began before the

American Revolution and continued for some time after it, when, as Catherine McNicol Stock writes, farmers from the central counties "struggled against the economic and political power of the Great Proprietors, rich men who claimed title to the lands and refused to sell it to squatters. Calling themselves Liberty Men and White Indians, settlers terrorized local men associated with the Proprietors, including merchants and court officials."[51] These farmers, who were suspicious of aristocracy and power and believed in the importance of small production, were eventually neutralized after 1800, when political power in Maine appeared to shift out of the hands of the wealthy few and into the hands of the many. Jeffersonian leaders managed to assert the rights of small farmers, while effectively nipping their radical movements in the bud.[52]

Chute's portrayal of her white rural guerrillas suggests a resonance with the "Liberty Men and White Indians" of eighteenth-century Maine. In creating a tribal class of characters, she compares them, both implicitly and explicitly, to the people Americans think of as most clearly tribal: Indians. There are few characters in Chute's novels who are not white (a group of black characters have a cameo appearance in *Snow Man* so as to show that the life of the working poor resembles slavery). In *Merry Men*, it is an Appalachian and Indian radical minister who appears to encourage the Maine characters in their efforts to maintain their own culture. She urges them to "relearn how to move softly and with dignity like the Indians. . . . How many survival skills do your children have? How many kids today can provide for themselves food, tools, clothing, warmth . . . from the elements?"[53] Thus, Chute's tribal vision of rural white poverty spills over to include the group that, as Philip Deloria has pointed out, seems to represent the most American of Americans in popular culture.[54] The working-class hero of her 1999 novel, *Snow Man*, looks "part Indian."[55] Just before he leaves to meet his death, one of his lovers, Kristina, sees "that his family has a lot of Indian . . . maybe a grandparent . . . maybe his mother" (*Snow Man*, 203). The novel closes with a quotation from Geronimo: "I think I am a good man, but . . . all over the world they say I am a bad man."

Chute's embrace of Native American imagery accords with the beliefs of many on the racist right. Kathleen Blee has found that "some racist activist women regard American Indian ancestry to be authentically white."[56] Moreover, just as Chute's romanticization of rural white poverty echoes that of folklorists in the 1920s and 1930s, so her identification of Indians with white Anglo-Saxons echoes what certain race theorists of that period had to say. As the literary scholar Walter Benn Michaels has written, "It is

because the Indian's sun was perceived as setting that he could become . . .
a kind of paradigm for increasingly powerful American notions of ethnic
identity and eventually for the idea of an ethnicity that could be threatened
or defended, repudiated or reclaimed."[57]

Although Chute does not specifically allude to the events of two centuries ago when discussing her militia, her vision of a small-scale, producer-
based economy is reminiscent of the life on the land espoused by the Liberty Men and White Indians. Yet this vision is not simply economic. In *Snow
Man*, Chute gives what is to date the clearest expression of a theme that has
run through her work since the publication of her first novel, *The Beans of
Egypt, Maine*: that rural white poverty is as much a tribal, or ethnic, condition as an economic one. In this she follows in the footsteps not only of turn-
of-the-century folklorists who invented, and then idealized, the folk culture
of another poor, white, rural group—Appalachians—but also of a generation of sociologists, of the 1920s and 1930s, who saw in hoboes the truest
exemplars of "white primitives." Maine, in many ways, might be called the
Appalachia of New England. It is a state whose population has long been
associated in the popular imagination with poverty and with primitivism.
And, like Washington and Idaho, Maine is a state with an overwhelmingly
white population.

For Chute to describe working-class life as essentially male and "effete"
middle-class life as essentially female obviously creates a dilemma for her
as a woman writer. As I will explore further, Chute uses her relationship
with the gun in part as a way out of this problem. She is a militia leader who
bonds with her followers over target practice. In identifying herself with the
gun, rather than with, say, the writers' colony at which she first envisioned
her militia, Chute can have access to the working-class culture that would
otherwise be closed off to her as a woman and a writer. The gun, with its
links to masculinity, can offer her a way out of an identity she considers
problematic.

Chute embraces the culture of poor, white rural Maine residents, a culture that she describes as timeless and static. Her novels do not trace the
struggles of the working class to rise into the middle class. Rather, it seems
that no matter how miserable and difficult working-class life is, it is infi-
nitely preferable to upward mobility. The lives of artists are shown as cha-
otic and meaningless; the lives of the middle class and yuppies as being
built on the backs of the poor. The protagonist of *Merry Men*, Lloyd Barrington, has a master's degree in sociology but prefers to work as a gravedigger.
His nephew, Jeff Johnston, leads a dissolute, disconnected life as a success-

ful artist, and only comes into himself when he gives it up to become a well digger. Most of Chute's characters proudly eschew "white yuppie trash" culture (*Merry Men*, 594). As one of the yuppies in the novel, who has fallen in love with Lloyd Barrington, looks at a man repairing a truck, the narrator voices her reflections: "She is coming more and more to understand this oldest kind of dignity. That no matter how many aristocracies overtake the common man, no matter how they denude and molest him, there are always men like these who can never be gelded, who will always have this pageantry, this covenant, this fierce high rank, the faces of kings" (*Merry Men*, 644).

More than anything, this recalls the romanticization of Appalachian poverty common in the early years of the twentieth century, when ballad collectors and settlement workers traveled to West Virginia and Kentucky in search of signs of aristocracy among the white poor. As the most famous of them, Cecil Sharp, noted in 1917, "Their language, wisdom, manners, and the many graces of life that are theirs, are merely racial attributes which have been gradually acquired and accumulated in past centuries and handed down generation to generation."[58]

Unlike the aristocratic and apolitical Appalachians described by Sharp and other folklorists, Chute's characters are consumed by class rage and see corporate culture as the destroyer of ancient peasant ways, and thus as their enemy. In this respect, it would be tempting to think of Chute's novels as mining the proletarian literature tradition of the 1930s. Chute herself attributes the "mean reviews" of *Snow Man* to "people who say my work has too much working-class rage."[59] However, the class consciousness with which Chute's protagonists are endowed is not at all indebted to Marxism. Rather, it is class consciousness as a form of tribalism. As Jewel Grissom, the Scotch Indian organizer from West Virginia, explains, "To hell with buying American. Buy or trade with your *neighbor*! Buy from that *face* not the brand name! Do this whenever there's a choice, even when it costs a little more. What price can we put on our freedom?" (*Merry Men*, 618).

In *Merry Men*, it is a theatrical guerrilla band of men that forms the nucleus of the tribe. This group, led by Lloyd Barrington, the gravedigger with a master's in sociology, leaves a milk carton of human blood in the car of an executive, leaves caskets with papier-mâché effigies in Mercedes, drains the fuel from backhoes, and so on. Even these political actions are expressed as being tribally based. After all, the guerrillas are "synchronized, so much common tie, tied by blood and the common roots . . . the truest passion . . . the only real love" (*Merry Men*, 619). The blood that ties these men together is, thus, almost a racial condition, as nineteenth-century theories of race would have it.

When Gwen Curry, the daughter of a local doctor who has returned to Maine after the death of her CEO husband, falls in love with Lloyd, she receives a harsh shock. The barrier that exists between the Mainers and wealthy cosmopolitans is seen by Lloyd as insurmountable: for him to mate outside his tribe would be miscegenation, and thus a disaster. Lloyd's final guerrilla action is a statement about the impossibility of forming a human relationship between a rural Mainer and a yuppie.

Chute's portrait of Gwen is a caricature of the liberalism she derides in her call to action for her militia. Gwen, like all the other "goddamn white yuppie trash" (*Merry Men*, 594) in Chute's work, is artistic, rootless (she owns homes all over the world), cosmopolitan, and "politically correct." When her friends get together to eat runny cheese and hummus and pesto, their conversations are ones of "heated agreement. Sexual harassment in the workplace and colleges is unacceptable. Global warming is unacceptable" (*Merry Men*, 568).

The facile liberalism of Gwen and her friends manifests itself as ignorant condescension toward Lloyd and other rural Mainers. As rootless cosmopolitans, they cannot possibly understand the pull of the tribe. They see Lloyd as "quaint," "authentic." One remarks, "I thought he was something Gwen got at an auction to go with the colonial decor . . . some chipped but still serviceable antique" (*Merry Men*, 570). Yet while Gwen can complacently urge Lloyd to visit Italy because "Lloyd, it's *important* to see the Old World . . . to . . . to believe in humanity's ability to endure" (*Merry Men*, 642), she has failed to understand how deeply he is grounded in the past and that he and his band of merry men, and their consorts, are in fact timeless peasants. It is ironic that this insistence on Lloyd's "authenticity," which Chute caricatures as condescending, in fact mirrors her own essentialism.

Gwen gains her first understanding of Lloyd's timeless nature when she pays him a surprise visit and he takes her to meet his people. As Gwen listens to Lloyd and his friends talking, she hears the "voice of the hills, all one flowing river of voices, a mastery, a proficiency enviable and the even more enviable association of their clan" (*Merry Men*, 648). These people are more archetypes than individuals—as Gwen cannot help but notice: "Seems like practically all the men in this place are the Hercules type" (*Merry Men*, 650).

Though Gwen would love to have access to Lloyd's world and to his tribe, it is impossible. She is tainted, for him, by her association with her late husband. Although Lloyd is attracted to Gwen, she in the past "slept with the devil and looked fondly into the devil's eyes, worked to do right by him and gave him grace when he had none" (*Merry Men*, 682). Lloyd sees her husband's company as symbolic not only of a fatal homogenization in the business world but also of the corporatization of government: "The final and nearly singular corporate regimes. The future. Too near." He wonders, "What is this MATRIX BANKCORP ENERGY INTERNATIONAL? What is this squirming speck of the future, the thousands upon thousands of people who will not make it, will not keep up with hi-tech . . . the people not made for hi-tech . . . these people made by God to farm, to hunt, to fish . . . people of the earth and air?" (*Merry Men*, 683–84). Like the Appalachians whose cultural "tainting" settlement workers of the early twentieth century bemoaned, the poor white Mainers in Chute's work have a culture that can only be authentically preserved under conditions of desperate poverty. To be "made by God" to live close to the earth, to be "of the earth and air," means to be, in effect, a timeless peasant.[60]

Chute uses physical markers—hairstyles and breast shapes—to separate out the authentic characters, who adhere rigidly to traditional gender roles, from those who have become assimilated into American capitalism. For example, one of the novel's most "authentic" characters is Dottie Soule, a woman who is working class to the core and particularly fecund, a hallmark, in Chute's writing, of true womanhood. Dottie has a real working-class hairstyle: "Dottie's ponytail . . . well . . . it's a tail. Hard, tapered, supple appendage" (*Merry Men*, 183). Dottie's look is "no longer the fashion where even here in Maine, fashion has come at last. But hit or miss, there's still a lot of Dottie Soules around with their plastic-frame glasses, stoic oily little ponytails or tightly permed curls solid as knuckles. Immune. Unbending resisters. Deep as anchors in the waters of old ways" (*Merry Men*, 280).

Leaving Maine and the old ways results in gender confusion. For instance, in *Merry Men*, Jeff Johnston, who has left Maine to become a successful artist in Los Angeles, returns with a California girlfriend, acting purposeless and looking feminine: his sweater is "nothing-you'd-ever-see-on-a-Maine-man-yellow," and his hair is "long preened frizzled curls" (*Merry Men*, 290, 294). Jeff, who has left all traces of his Maine past behind when we first meet him, "busts out into many giggles" and looks "California and glitterish" (*Merry Men*, 287, 288). Chute insists on this geographical marker over and over again: he is "handsome California Jeff, his hair short wet spikes on top, long preened frizzled curls over the nape of his YELLOW sweater" (*Merry Men*, 294). Upward mobility is associated with femininity or homosexuality: Jeff, with his giggles, his narcissistic preening, and his overly colorful sweater, has clearly relinquished his manhood as the price of moving into the cosmopolitan middle class.

While Jeff is not a real man anymore, and by implication is unlikely to engage in procreative sex, his female counterpart, whom he has brought along, is less than a real woman. Jeff's girlfriend, Coti, is as Californian, and hence inauthentic, as he is. She is "a Los Angeles beautiful, too beautiful, great smoldery white smile, little doctored nose . . . Coti, whose looks would be okay on TV. But in this kitchen, her looks are an overdose" (*Merry Men*, 299). Even her breasts are hallmarks of her class and of her remove from the important things in life: her breasts have "a small tense cone shape, which is the desirable mode of breasts these days. Fun breasts. Picture-perfect breasts. Big breasts might look too work-related. Too utility. Too motherish. In these times, breasts must be preserved forever in daughter-ishness. This is the last word in femininity. The new law of the land" (*Merry Men*, 301). Coti has strayed far from her biological prerogatives. In Chute's vision, the "new law of the land" would divorce women from their child-bearing functions and liberate them from enforced maternity. This seems to be something that Chute mourns.

Like the other out-of-state characters, Coti patronizes the Mainers, telling Jeff, "What a grip your dad has, J.J.! A hand like a regular fossil or something. A real working man's hand . . . Jiminy Cricket . . . yes!" (*Merry Men*, 299). It is she, in part, who has corrupted Jeff: "Jeff's magenta sweater is soft and tight-fitting like a leotard and has many little fashion buttons close together down the front. The permed curls of his dark hair lay over the back. This is not the way Jeff dressed and wore his hair until he met Coti Pederson" (*Merry Men*, 326). Or acted, presumably: the post-California Jeff spends his time smoking pot, stealing and begging money from his parents and grandmother, dodging responsibility for his child, and making out with his girlfriend in full view of his older relatives. California and Coti have robbed him of his manhood. Coti is assertive toward him, demanding, for instance, that he get a towel for her after he calls her "Bitch" during an argument and spills water on her. When he complies, his father watches "with fascination and sad marvel this castration of his son" (*Merry Men*, 311). It is only when Jeff sends Coti back to Los Angeles, gives up painting, and becomes a well digger that he can find peace and become a real man again.

The idea that being an artist and being a real man are incompatible exemplifies the biggest problem with Chute's tribalist, primitivist literary vision. It is fitting that she developed the idea for her working-class militia while at the elite artists' colony of MacDowell. As her former writing teacher, Ken Rosen, speculating on Chute's political activities, theorized, "To her, it represents a way to get in touch with the people she writes about. They don't read books, and the militia enables her to exert some kind of leadership and be a focus for people who find life daunting."[61] Yet how can Chute reconcile her authorship of complex literary works with her primitivist perspective?

In essentializing white rural poverty, Chute reaches back to an American tradition that had its apotheosis in the 1920s and 1930s, when hoboes, the most "purely" poor Americans, were treated by sociologists and journalists as an exotic group, to whom were ascribed "authentic" qualities that had little to do with economic realities and much to do with the projected fantasies and stereotypes of their interlocutors. When the University of Chicago sociologist Nels Anderson celebrated hoboes as frontiersmen striking out for the territories, he emphasized not only the Americanness of these men but also their masculinity: they were men unfettered by female demands. They had not been assimilated into the world of middle-class domesticity, and they had retained their masculine "essence." Within this construct, working-class life, especially the life of a laborer, is masculine, and middle-class life is seen as feminine.[62]

Chute subscribes to the old dogma associated with the hobo and elaborates on it. In her novels, femininity is identified with the creation of art (in *Merry Men*, it is a gay male character and an upwardly mobile woman who are artists; in *Snow Man*, it is the senator's wife). In fact, the only artists worth respecting seem to be those untainted by education. Thus, one of the women besotted by *Snow Man*'s ultramasculine militia assassin, Robert Drummond, admiringly describes a drawing of his as being "in a style much like the primitives . . . Here is a kind of artist for which no amount of training could ever undo that powerful raw childly edge" (*Snow Man*, 133). Ironically, however, given Chute's probable readership—which is not men like the militia leader Robert Drummond but precisely the kind of well-educated, middle-class, primarily female group caricatured in her novels—one can see her as simply reinscribing a kind of primitivism. Like the Appalachian settlement workers and the folklorists who collected hobo ballads, she employs the model of a kind of Anglo-American folk culture that exists outside capitalism, is economically circumscribed, and can only be tainted by contact with the wider world. Her characters would lose their essence should they become educated and no longer have that "raw childly edge." Chute's characters are essentially poor, in much the same way that hoboes of the Depression era were stereotyped as such. Moreover, her most heroic characters' hatred of education puts her in an even more problematic political position.

In positing working men as "naturally" masculine, Chute harks back, in many ways, to the masculinized, idealized proletariat lauded by Michael Gold and other radical writers of the 1930s. Yet there is an important difference between Chute's class constructs and those of her leftist forebears. Whereas radical writers of the thirties saw education as being necessary for liberation, and wrote novels that were designed to be read by workers, Chute is strongly anti-education, as are her characters. Chute's refrigerator sports a hand-scrawled "School stinks" sign, and in a leaflet issued by "Dear Revolutionary Abby," she says, "We need to burn down the schools. These are the total institutions of industrialism and capitalism."[63] In the most extreme statement of this position, Anneka DiBias, the closest thing to a heroine in Merry Men, muses on her recent brutal rape: "I've had almost thirteen years of school. If I had to do one over again . . . school or rape, I'd pick rape. Rape only lasts about two minutes" (Merry Men, 447). Earlier generations of proletarian writers may have condemned the school system, but they certainly did not frown on workers' becoming educated by any means necessary. Marxism, after all, demands a kind of rigorous study. Yet Chute, who posits a primitivist tribe of workers, does not want them spoiled by contact with the dominant culture.

If Chute contrasts a world of "natural" working-class men with effete middle-class men and women, she is harsher still when it comes to real-world gender politics. Her novels display an unabashed longing for the most repressive forms of patriarchy. If femininity is bad, feminism, which is strongly identified with yuppiedom, is far worse. Chute's strongest critique of feminism comes in Snow Man, which is also her most clearly articulated vision of her militia views. In her author's note at the beginning of the novel, Chute remarks that Snow Man is "actually a kind of DNA" of a longer book that she has been working on since 1993, which she describes as "the 'true story' of the 'Militia Movement' in New England as I have experienced it." She goes on to comment that "Snow Man is a possible story, given the situation of most working Americans today, but it is not representative of the goals of the New England Militia Movement." It is not surprising that Chute makes this disclaimer because the book's hero is Robert Drummond, a member of a Maine-based militia, who at the novel's start has just assassinated one United States senator and is hunting for another. Wounded, Drummond collapses outside the home of the second senator (a liberal) and is taken in and nursed back to health by the senator's wife and daughter.

The senator's daughter, Kristina, is the chair of a women's studies department at a university, an "edgy, angry, rivalrous ultrafeminist" (*Snow Man*, 57). But after Robert Drummond, the militia leader, beats chess champion Kristina at the game the first time he plays it, and, then, after this seemingly barely literate backwoodsman beats her at Scrabble, she begins to see, ever so faintly, the error of her ways. She is starting to learn that, after all, winning isn't everything, and this quickly leads her to a revelation:

> Throw the men out! Grab those thrones! Claw! Scramble! Scrape. Stand erect. Someday you will rule!
> The capitalist creed. Was feminism created in the image of the big "C"? (*Snow Man*, 107)

Even more than Robert's lectures about the "big-boy fucker in the White House and his arrogant bitch broad femmie-Ms. wifey" (*Snow Man*, 126), it is masculine sexual power that finally subjugates her. When he gives her orders, "Down! Down, Ms. Bitch Bad-Loser Bitch! Sit!" (*Snow Man*, 157), she becomes even more adoring of him.

Kristy's mother, who also sleeps with Robert, responds similarly to his assertion of masculine authority: "Connie is confounded. Not by his words of sexual aggression, but at her response to it, which is nothing but a submissive wordless flush" (*Snow Man*, 128). Soon, Connie and Kristina are spending their time cooking, shopping, and sewing for Robert. Robert's own wife is adored by him for her cooking, housekeeping, and child-rearing skills; the most celebrated women in Chute's novels are those who bear many children and stand by their men.

Chute herself does not use racist rhetoric in her books or in interviews. However, in many other respects her beliefs and statements resemble those of other militia leaders, many of whom downplay the movement's origins in the racist far right. The vision that far-right militia groups have of the future of the United States is near-apocalyptic, and much of what Lloyd Barrington muses on at the end of *Merry Men* directly echoes the rhetoric of these groups. First he envisions "the helicopters. They see your skin, your wedding ring, your splintered nails . . . In this future time, you can only be one of two possibilities. A success. Or a lawbreaker" (*Merry Men*, 684). Then he foresees the proliferation of detention centers and of politically correct environmental laws:

> In this future time, drugs are against the law. Not all drugs. Just the drugs they call street drugs. Like sports. The shots have been called. They

set up some of the first camps to put the people in who committed drug crimes. Dealers. Users.

Shortly after drug camps came "opportunity centers" where the millions of untrained get trained to keep up. Mandatory job training.

Next "shelters for the homeless."

Camps and shelters of all varieties. But nobody has actually ever seen one. Well, at least nobody has come back from one to tell . . . Clean air laws are strict. Only the very successful can afford to break the clean air laws.

The new gleamy trains run between the cities where most people must live, *by law*. (*Merry Men*, 685–86)

The details of this vision echo those described by Pat Robertson in his book *New World Order* and are more generally a staple of extreme right-wing beliefs. Many far-right groups believe that dissidents will be herded into concentration camps by the government.[64] According to an Aryan supremacist interviewed by Kathleen Blee for her book *Inside Organized Racism: Women in the Hate Movement*: "In the new world order that the government is arranging, America will be reduced to a pathetic state of subservience to the powers that be. Nothing can be done at this point because they will have taken our arms [by] convincing us that it would make the country safer, and we will have coded identity cards that we will need in order to buy food or anything else. All of the UN prison camps that they are setting up all over the U.S. will be used to isolate any offenders."[65] The heroic Lloyd Barrington's musings echo throughout the far right.

Like her characters, Chute, in her position as head of the 2nd Maine Militia, espouses beliefs common to militia leaders and members of other far-right organizations. Even her insistence on the "winglessness" of the 2nd Maine Militia has its echo in a statement issued by a Militia of Montana leader, who instructed audiences that "we have to forget about right-wing, left-wing. We have good guys and bad guys, that's it."[66] As the white supremacist ideologue Louis Beam wrote in the aftermath of the protests against the World Trade Organization in Seattle in 1999, "The New American Patriot will be neither left nor right, just a freeman fighting for liberty." And, as the Southern Poverty Law Center pointed out in a 2000 newsletter, "since the 1980s, neo-Nazi Tom Metzger, leader of the California-based White Aryan Resistance, has rejected the left-right dichotomy and concentrated on labor issues he believes will draw in working-class whites."[67] This position has its roots in a European neofascist strain called the "Third Position": neither capitalism nor communism but a third way. As described by the Southern Poverty Law Center's *Intelligence Report* article, adherents of this position

> are opposed to what are seen as the homogenizing forces of globalism. They despise capitalism, with its tendency to concentrate wealth and to make people and economies more and more alike—turning the planet into what is seen as a bland and materialistic McWorld. They pine for nations of peasant-like folk tied closely to the land and to their neighbors. They fight for a pristine environment, a land unsullied by corporate agriculture and urbanization. They detest man-centered philosophies, seeing animals as no less important than humans.[68]

Robert Drummond explains to Kristy, the senator's daughter, that there is no difference between capitalism and socialism, since they are both part of the "New World Order . . . this World Government coming down" (*Snow Man*, 193). A particularly bizarre example of this working-class hero's muddy politics is his swastika tattoo, which he made in sixth grade, because "it was just fun to do," and which he declines to have removed; as Robert puts it, "'Tain't offensive. It's just a thing" (*Snow Man*, 62).

In this, as in so much else, Chute's ideology, however liberal on the subjects of animal rights, gay rights, and human rights, seems disturbingly close to that embraced by leaders of other militia movements. And it is here, in her idealization of the essentialized, tribal poor, that the paradox of her work becomes most apparent. In founding a political movement and writing about the working poor, she resembles more than perhaps any other American writer the proletarian novelists of the 1930s. But in her seeming insistence that rural poverty is not a material but a tribal, or ethnic, condition, Chute denies any real opportunity for change. As she has written, the working class is not about income but about "the tribe holy in the eyes of the working class."[69] Chute seems to say that, like the hoboes of the thirties, or the Appalachians of the first decades of the twentieth century, the working poor cannot, must not, change their condition—they can only be spoiled by education and upward mobility.

As an armed militia leader, Chute may be anomalous when considered in the context of the far-right movement as a whole. After all, it is difficult to imagine most militia leaders ensconced in their cabins at prestigious literary colonies. Yet in many ways Chute can provide a link between the two worlds she inhabits, and can thereby help illuminate the paradoxes of the armed woman of the right. After all, women on the far right often occupy explicitly contradictory positions as they debate in Web chat rooms about whether it is possible to be a race mother and a warrior at the same time. Chute embodies more contradictions than most. In doing so, she illustrates the capacity of tough women on the far right to transcend opposite images, or to exist in the creative tension between seemingly irreconcilable positions.

The gun, for Chute, makes many things possible. On a personal level, it allows her to connect with people who are not readers of literary fiction. After all, she met her husband at a shooting match. And in her fiction, as in her life, she uses guns as a shorthand for a kind of power that is concrete, as opposed to the amorphousness of MATRIX BANKCORP ENERGY INTERNATIONAL. The power of the gun is accessible to just about everyone. Guns are easy to use and easy to understand, and they are a symbol of the old frontier rather than the new, post-1989 global frontier. They are concrete in a way that the new world order is not. Finally, guns are a shorthand for a culture that Chute wants to be part of: as she says, "Rednecks love guns, always have. It's our *culture*." If the gun is truly the great equalizer, then it can erase not only the distinctions between men and women but also those between timeless peasants and authors of literary fiction.

ARMED FEMINISM OR
FAMILY VALUES? WOMEN
AND GUNS TODAY

Let's take another look at where we began: with the gun industry's embrace of the female consumer, starting in the late 1980s, and the concurrent (and closely related) interest of the National Rifle Association in promoting women's gun ownership. As we have seen in previous chapters, the gun industry had focused earlier advertising campaigns on women as shooters or potential consumers, whether as the race-building hunters of the late nineteenth century, as the competitive trapshooters of the early twentieth century, or, to a lesser degree, as the helpmate shooters of the 1940s and 1950s. However, despite or perhaps because of the sophistication of the mass-media presentations of the NRA and the firearms industry, this most recent campaign highlights more clearly than any previous efforts the contradictory nature of the models for successful womanhood, and successful citizenship, suggested by the late twentieth- or early twenty-first-century armed woman. As presented by the gun industry and its supporters, the latest version of armed womanhood must be an avatar of strength and female achievement while remaining respectable and embodying family values. In this, she resembles armed female icons from the past, such as Annie Oakley and Osa Johnson, who were attractive, strong, and extremely domestic. Yet, unlike them, she personifies, rather than rejects, a version of feminism that emphasizes female self-sufficiency. She does this, too, without alienating the politically conservative men who make up the bulk of the NRA's membership. Rather than wielding a gun to build the white race, she must understand gun ownership as a civil rights issue and gun-control advocates as heirs to a racist tradition. Although it goes without saying that this new female gun owner must abjure the violence of the gangster girls of the 1920s and 1930s or the left-wing revolutionaries of the 1960s and 1970s, she shares some of the attitudes of the militia women of the 1980s and 1990s. The new armed woman, in this construct, must be patriotic while realizing that the state has no responsibility for her protection, and may even be hostile to her interests. Above all, the new armed woman must take on the most difficult task of all: saving the gun industry from declining sales and helping protect the NRA against its antigovernment, pro-militia image.

Gun-industry spokesmen began using the language of women's rights as soon as they launched their 1980s marketing push for female consumers. As Richard Feldman of the American Shooting Sports Council, an industry group, says of gun ownership for women, "It's a very logical extension of women's lib. It's like the bumper sticker says: God didn't create men and women equal. Samuel Colt did."[1] The bumper sticker says, of course, much more than Feldman may have thought, with its implication that women can gain equal rights only through violence. This position was echoed by Laura Ingraham, a Washington attorney and activist, who opined in the pages of the *Wall Street Journal* that "Smith & Wesson and the National Rifle Association are doing more to 'take back the night' than the National Organization of Women and Emily's List."[2] In promoting gun ownership for women, Christopher Dolnack, marketing manager of Smith & Wesson, suggested that gun-owning women were feminist pioneers: "Firearms are one of the last bastions of male dominance," he pointed out. "Today, in 1992, it's OK for women to be CEOs of companies and go into space as astronauts, so why shouldn't they own guns?"[3] The feminism of the gun industry extended to the development of a new women's gun, the Smith & Wesson LadySmith handgun, introduced in 1989—a revolver designed for women's smaller hands but created to look like a serious weapon, unlike the "novelty" women's guns of the 1950s, produced by Hi-Standard, which featured pink, turquoise, and gold handles.[4] The armed woman as new feminist icon even got a big boost from Naomi Wolf. In *Fire with Fire*, the 1993 book in which she coined the term "power feminism," Wolf decried what she termed "victim feminism" (the paradox of a woman's seeking "power through an identity of powerlessness") and approvingly noted the rise of *Women & Guns* magazine as an antidote to this condition: "In the voices of women's letters to the magazine, one can hear the pioneer voices of women who know that no one will take care of them but themselves."[5] In this, Wolf seemed to be celebrating the spirit that animated so many late nineteenth-century representations of self-reliant, armed Prairie Madonnas. Were these women, and the magazine they read, just the latest iteration of this familiar rhetoric?

In fact, *Women & Guns* and *Woman's Outlook*, the women's gun magazine published by the NRA, offer the reader a wonderful opportunity to study the construction of the armed woman, or more accurately the female arms consumer. By treating women with guns as another niche market, these magazines suggest the possibility that armed women can be a self-conscious community. Thus, their publication truly marks a watershed moment for the armed American woman, both because of the extent of the audience the magazines reach and because of who makes up that audience. After all, from colonial times on, most American representations of armed women have not been directed at other armed women. From the late eighteenth-century coffeehouse patrons who listened to ballads about female soldiers in male disguise, to the early nineteenth-century readers of cheap novels masquerading as female soldiers' autobiographies, to late nineteenth-century spectators of Wild West shows, the audiences for armed women were not, by and large, women with guns. And even though these audiences grew over the years, such that a late twentieth-century action movie about an armed femme fatale could reach tens of millions, hardly any of the viewers were armed women. Until the advent of *Women & Guns* in 1989, the few pieces of literature created specifically for armed women were intended for fairly small audiences, such as radical feminists interested in forming G.C.R. (Gun Consciousness Raising) groups, as in the instance of one mid-1970s pamphlet discussed in chapter 4. Mass-media images intended for armed women have existed for over a century in the form of advertising, and this advertising does have something in common with the new magazines, in that, to succeed, it has needed to present an image with which a significant number of women interested in guns could identify. Because the goal of the advertising is to sell more guns or gun-related products to women, it has generally avoided using titillating or violent images of the armed woman. Yet there is a crucial difference between the purpose of gun advertising and the goal of the new magazines, particularly *Women & Guns*: to prosper, these magazines, although they are full of advertisements for guns, must do more than merely sell firearms products: they must create an imagined community of armed women. And they must do so efficiently, in a way that can reach as many women as possible (without, in the case of *Woman's Outlook*, alienating whatever male NRA members may live in the household).

How do the editors of these magazines, then, think that armed women might imagine themselves?

WOMEN & GUNS, OR A ROOM OF ONE'S
OWN . . . MAY BE A GUN ROOM

Women & Guns and *Woman's Outlook* are the only two magazines available today that are marketed exclusively to armed women. Their different editorial approaches reveal the tensions inherent in marketing guns to women. With eighteen thousand subscribers,[6] *Women & Guns* has the smaller circulation of the two, and a notably edgier approach to its subject. *Women & Guns*, the first magazine marketed to gun-owning women, started out in 1989 by acknowledging sexism within the gun industry and supporting some feminist initiatives. But, over time, it has become less critical, and more celebratory, moving away from a recognition of social evils and of the dangers posed by guns and toward a focus on cowgirl reenactments and celebrity shooting matches. Finally, *Women & Guns* has had to face the fact that within the conservative framework of the gun-rights movement, there is no room for a recognition of women's anger and potential violence. While it still uses feminist rhetoric, it ultimately cannot escape the political necessity of offering uncritical support to the gun industry and its most powerful lobby, the NRA.

For a short history of women's most recent courtship by the gun industry, there is no better place to go than the history page on the *Women & Guns* Website, www.womenandguns.com, authored by its executive editor, Peggy Tartaro (daughter of Joseph Tartaro, head of the nonprofit Second Amendment Foundation, which publishes the magazine). It is all in there: the development of the NRA's Refuse to Be a Victim program, which attempts to "educate" women about their self-defense options; the policy report issued in 1994 by the Violence Policy Center, titled *Female Persuasion*, which documented—and decried—the gun industry's ad campaigns aimed at women; the controversial cover story in the May/June 1994 issue of *Ms.* magazine, illustrated with a picture of a handgun under the heading "Is This Power Feminism?" (the answer, unsurprisingly, was no). On the home page, there are also the celebration of the NRA's first female officer in 125 years, elected in 1992, and a discussion of the publication of Naomi Wolf's *Fire with Fire*, which, as Tartaro puts it, "seemed to understand, if not out-right approve, of women who viewed the choice argument more totally than their sisters at Ms."

While Tartaro's narrative is informative, if unabashedly celebratory, about the history of the firearms industry's latest foray into marketing to

This August 1994 cover from *Women & Guns* illustrates the magazine's sometimes playful tone; here, a June Cleaver look-alike applies her domestic skills to the world of guns. Courtesy of *Women & Guns*.

women, and the accompanying controversy, for the purposes of this chapter what is most interesting is the way it frames the magazine's mission and describes its history. Of its founding in 1989 by Sonny Jones, Tartaro writes: "There must be a zillion clichés about mothers: all of them true and all of them false. But all the ideas about them boil down to one thing: they are the ones who give birth-life. In Sonny's case, she had an understandable mother's pride in having created something no one else had, in having it come to 'life.'"[7] In this construct, the magazine is Sonny's baby. Tartaro seems to be presenting the mother's role as being perfectly in keeping with gun ownership and gun ownership as being the most natural role for women.

While clearly no friend of *Ms.* magazine, Tartaro does not hesitate to reach back into feminist history for her references: "When talking to more thoughtful journalists, I sometimes quote Virginia Woolf's book titled, 'A Room of One's Own,' to try to give a sense of what we are about at W&G. There is room, we thought 12 years ago, and believe more strongly now, for women gunowners to have that place and to make it comfortably to their own liking." Like contemporary scholars who promote "armed feminism," such as Mary Zeiss Stange, author of *Woman the Hunter* (1997) and, with Carol K. Oyster, of *Gun Women: Firearms and Feminism in Contemporary America* (2000), Tartaro uses the rhetoric of feminism to advocate women's gun ownership. When, in 1991, *Women & Guns* premiered its first newsstand issue, the cover bore a popular image familiar to feminists: Thelma and Louise.

Although much of the feminism of the early years of *Women & Guns* was all about fighting back against male violence, it had an edge to it that the NRA-sponsored "Refuse to Be a Victim" programs lacked. The women profiled in the magazine not only deterred attackers; they often ended up killing them. Early issues of *Women & Guns* featured a regular column called "In Self-Defense," carrying accounts of women who repelled assailants with guns. "This is one lady who refuses to become a victim," read a typical story in the August 1989 edition;[8] the next month carried a story about a woman in Phoenix who turned the tables on her assailant, mortally wounding him with gunshot.[9] In an editorial criticizing "Take Back the Night" rallies, editor Sonny Jones commented that "the whole thing reminds me of a funeral procession rather than a protest march. . . . These people ask for help: form [*sic*] the legal system; from the police; and from society. They want help from everyone but themselves. . . . By apologetically asking for the violence to end, these women are missing the mark completely." Jones ended by saying, "Don't misunderstand me, I'm all for women taking back the night . . . at gun-point."[10]

In fact, Women & Guns took some surprisingly feminist stances in its early days. In an editorial supporting Joseph Biden's Violence against Women Act (though complaining that it did not go far enough), Jones asked, "How much longer can we afford to program our young people to accept and indulge in male dominance and female submission?"[11] Jones used her editorial space to support a woman's right to dress as she pleased: with regard to an Arkansas case in which a woman was found in contempt of court for appearing braless before a judge, she remarked, "If a woman, well-endowed or not, chooses to let the world view the outline of her breasts beneath a sweater, that is her business."[12] An article opened, "A Broward County jury has acquitted a Georgia drifter of kidnapping and raping a 22-year-old woman at knife point, saying she got what she deserved," because she was wearing a miniskirt. The author asked, if the drifter "was justified in raping this woman because he judged her dress to be provocative, would he also be justified in robbing someone wearing jewelry because he thought she appeared wealthy?"[13]

On many issues Jones found common ground with liberal feminists —but then often went a step further. Jones's article on the film *Thelma and Louise*, which ran in *Women & Guns*' first newsstand issue, is purely celebratory: "Thelma and Louise take action on their rage against a male-dominated, corrupt social system. . . . What is the problem here, anyway? Why do so many people, male and female alike, feel threatened by the concept of women shooting rapists?"[14] Women's rage and violence were honored and foregrounded in the early days of the magazine.

Sexism within the gun industry and the gun-rights movement also came in for criticism by the magazine. Tartaro, less militant than Jones, opined that "while the gun fraternity often seems a little behind the curve on women's rights, there's nothing like commerce to even things up."[15] Jones wrote that "Smith & Wesson has appealed to the thoughtful, logical woman interested in personal safety and a quality product. Mossberg & Sons, on the other hand, has appealed to the chauvinistic male who sees women as helpless, fearful and ineffectual Barbie dolls, and secondarily to women who see themselves the same way."[16] Early issues printed photographs of the sexist advertising used at gun shows, provoking rage from readers.[17]

Throughout its history, readers of *Women & Guns* have responded well to its editorial stance of naturalizing gun ownership for women—a stance that flies in the face of the long history of public rhetoric that has linked women's biological attributes to an incapacity for shooting, let alone owning, guns. In a letter to the editor in the November 1989 issue, a reader requested a gift subscription to *Women & Guns* for her gynecologist's waiting room, since "pregnant women feel very protective toward all life, not only the life within them. They might be especially approachable on subjects of need for self-protection, protection of their children, freedom of gun ownership, etc."[18] In other words, because women care about others and wish to protect "all life," they will embrace guns.

Yet *Women & Guns* moves beyond "mother lioness" rhetoric of the type used by contemporary firearms manufacturers. It is one thing to link maternity and gun ownership rhetorically and quite another to include articles that give practical advice on the dos and don'ts of shooting while pregnant, as an August 1995 cover story did. After discussing lead poisoning and possible fetal hearing damage, the article's author concluded, "Don't let the fact that you're pregnant or a new mother put you off shooting. Just make sure you're shooting and working outdoors or in a well-ventilated area, take the normal precautions you take for anything else while you're pregnant, and enjoy your shooting-range activities while you prepare for the arrival of your child."[19] The models for the article—a pregnant woman in hunting gear, holding a dead antelope by the horns, and a woman in frilly, flowered maternity gear, looking angelic as she examines a handgun at the shooting range—suggested a spectrum of possible roles for the pregnant shooter. This article, in its refusal to consider the idea of a pregnant woman's use of guns as shocking or even noteworthy, went far beyond the usual rhetoric aimed at normalizing the idea of women's shooting. Before the publication of this article, it was difficult to find examples of images of pregnant women with firearms: a visible pregnancy underlines women's biology in a way that the image of a slender mother who is tucking in a child at bedtime, handgun on the nearby nightstand, does not.

Ultimately, it proved impossible for *Women & Guns* to continue acknowledging any of the complexities of gun ownership, to use identifiably feminist rhetoric, or to maintain a stance critical of any aspects of the firearms industry. The firearms industry and its allies have closed ranks over time, and the editorial stances of many gun journals follow the NRA line. Groups like Feminists for the Second Amendment, profiled in the August 1992 issue of *Women & Guns*, have been replaced by the less threatening-sounding Sisters for the Second Amendment. When Sonny Jones left the editorship of the magazine in 1993, *Women & Guns* became less critical of

"Single Action Shooting Society 1994 End of Trail." Cowgirl reenactment shooting matches have become a popular way for women to reimagine themselves as historical actors. Although they ride fake horses and shoot cardboard villains, cowgirl reenactors are fully invested in their chosen historical identities. © 2004, Nancy Floyd.

the gun industry and became much more clearly a forum for domesticating the gun.

Although *Women & Guns* continues to present shooting as a means of female bonding, the magazine has always been as notable for what it omits on a chosen subject as it has been for what it includes. There are few articles on professional women who use guns as police officers or as members of the armed forces, but there are plenty of articles about how stuntwomen have learned to shoot and how mystery writers have learned to write accurately about firearms. There are almost no women of color in the pages of *Women & Guns*. The women profiled tend to be suburban rather than urban. By the 1990s, the features on gun consumerism were augmented not only by frequent articles about "celebrity shoots" but also by articles on the new sport of cowgirl reenactment shooting. Advice on how to pick a cowgirl alias and features on reenactment ranches now appear in most issues of the magazine. According to one such article, which is on a "cowboy action shooting" event called End of Trail (EOT), "Shooting, shopping, seeing old friends and enjoying the California sunshine is all part of the EOT experience."[20]

Cowgirl shooting is a perfect sport for the less controversial direction that Women & Guns is now taking. As Women & Guns writer Susan Laws notes, "Cowboy Action Shooting has given women a new forum in which to celebrate the tough, independent spirit of their 19th century sisters who worked and fought . . . and shot their way into a modern America where even the anti-gunners can lead a good life. Because reasonable people allow that 'history' and 'firearms' are intertwined, public sentiment often tolerates the legendary 'Peacemaker' where modern weaponry would be shunned. Enter the cowgirl, with her 'almost politically correct' guns, into the women's shooting arena with a chance to breathe new life into the pro-gun cause."[21]

Over a century ago, Annie Oakley created a powerful archetype of the armed western woman—skilled at using firearms yet not violent, exotically different in her western attire yet emphatically white and domestic. Today, the armed women featured in Women & Guns—who often, as Oakley did, sew their own costumes—are making guns safe and fun again. Some, like Susan Laws, who has herself become a regular on the cowgirl shooting circuit, credit the children's television show based on Oakley's life for inspiration: "Until [the show debuted], playing Cowboys and Indians was largely a pastime for little boys. TV's Annie Oakley changed all that and gave little girls like me permission to join the fun. With Annie as a role model, I not only played the game, but also earned the right to lead the posse."[22] Women's rage and power, celebrated in the early days of Women & Guns, have been tamed, and the armed woman has been made palatable for non-gun owners and conservatives alike.

WOMAN'S OUTLOOK—FAMILY CIRCLE FOR THE ARMED WOMAN?

In January 2003, the NRA launched its new monthly magazine, Woman's Outlook. The magazine has steadily gained in popularity since then; although it was initially available only to NRA members, it is now sold on newsstands, including the world's largest single newsstand, Wal-Mart. The latest figures available from the NRA peg the magazine's circulation at sixty thousand.[23] As Dana Calvo reported in 2003 in the *Boston Globe,* Wal-Mart decided to carry it because it "offers wholesome articles and emphasizes responsibility." The NRA's only disappointment with the chain, according to Calvo, was its decision to sell the magazine in the sporting section. "'I would prefer it be placed with mainstream women's magazines, which we think it is,' said head of publishing for the NRA, Joe Graham. 'It's designed to provide women's points of view on things that might be unfamiliar to women today, like selecting hunting clothes, a self-defense firearm, protecting the firearm with children in the house.'"[24]

It is hard to imagine a serious woman gun owner reading *Woman's Outlook.* In fact, it is hard to imagine a blander magazine, and perhaps that is the point: *Woman's Outlook* presents a gentle, wholesome image that seems designed to take the edge off the rhetoric of the NRA. By imitating mainstream magazines for middle-class women, *Woman's Outlook* works hard to normalize gun ownership as a choice no more controversial than a woman's favorite shade of lipstick.

Unquestionably, the NRA in recent years has felt the need to soften its image. The public statements of the organization, especially its "members-only" pronouncements, have seemed fairly alarming to people outside the organization, particularly in moments of national crisis. In the wake of the 1995 Oklahoma City bombing, for instance, the NRA came under widespread criticism for its antigovernment statements, including, most notoriously, a fund-raising letter from Executive Vice President Wayne LaPierre that discussed "jack-booted government thugs" who "take away our constitutional rights, break in our doors, seize our guns, destroy our property, and even injure and kill us. . . . In Clinton's administration, if you have a badge, you have the government's go-ahead to harass, intimidate, even murder law-abiding citizens." The letter also referred to "federal agents wearing Nazi bucket helmets and black storm trooper uniforms."[25] This letter was widely quoted in newspaper and television reports, and NRA leaders took to the weekly television talk shows to mount their defense. This effort was undercut, however, by news that NRA leader Tanya Metaksa had met two months prior to the Oklahoma City bombing with leaders of the Michigan Militia, the group with which bomber Timothy McVeigh was linked. At whose request the meeting took place—the militia group's or the NRA's—remained in dispute. News reports revealed that McVeigh had, in fact, been an NRA member from 1990 until 1994 and had sent a letter to his congressman protesting restrictive gun laws, with a sticker affixed to the back of the envelope that read, "I'm the NRA."[26] President George H. W. Bush's resignation from the NRA in protest of LaPierre's inflammatory remarks did further damage to the NRA's public image. Since then, as Osha Gray Davidson has reported, the NRA has been on the defensive: "Given the group's internal chaos, financial problems, flat or declining membership, the defection of 'big name' supporters, a string of legislative defeats and most important, the lobby's unsavory image among a growing number of Americans, doubts about the NRA's future have become something more than just the wishful thinking of the gun lobby's many enemies."[27]

Yet for many years the NRA's public rhetoric did not soften even in the face of shrinking membership. After Charlton Heston accused President Bill Clinton of lying about the dangers of guns in a series of NRA television commercials, Wayne LaPierre went even further. In an interview with Sam Donaldson on the ABC program *This Week*, in May 2000, he said, "I've come to believe that [Clinton] needs a certain level of violence in this country. He's willing to accept a certain level of killing to further his political agenda and his vice president too."[28] This was rhetoric that would be difficult for all but the extreme right wing to swallow: accusing a sitting president not only of lying but also of supporting gun deaths for his own political purposes.

The Million Mom March, which followed these incendiary remarks by just weeks, on Mother's Day, May 15, 2000, served to inject gender into the debate on guns and the NRA. An estimated 750,000 women, many of them pushing baby strollers, descended on Washington, D.C., in a demonstration that was emceed by popular TV talk-show host Rosie O'Donnell. Women demonstrated in seventy other American cities as well, making this the largest gun-control demonstration in U.S. history. The gun-rights counterdemonstration held by the Second Amendment Sisters in Washington drew only about a thousand women.

The million moms (or the "million" moms, as they are always called in *Women & Guns* magazine) created a juxtaposition that was rhetorically hard for the NRA and its allies to counter: peace-loving moms with small children in tow versus the masculinized rhetoric of the NRA. As Donna Dees-Thomases said in explaining her reasons for organizing the march, "There is nothing more powerful than a mother's drive to protect her children. Mothers across the country are harnessing that energy, and it is their passion that will have impact here."[29] Dees-Thomases, who divided her book on the march, *Looking for a Few Good Moms*, into chapters titled "Fertility," "Conception," "First Trimester," and so on, framed gun-control work as something that mothers were naturally suited to do—work that was heroic in a maternal way: the "founders of the Million Mom March were—to me—the kind of women that myths are made of; these were the women who could lift a 2-ton car off a child pinned underneath. In my mind, these MMM women were lifting an 18-wheeler off too many children pinned underneath. The massive truck was the gun lobby, and its weight was crushing our children's hope for a future free of gun violence."[30] This rhetorical strategy, which posited mothers as naturally opposed to the gun violence that could kill their children, was very powerful. The NRA clearly needed to come up with a strategy that suggested, just as powerfully, that maternity and gun ownership were compatible and that women need not be fundamentally opposed to firearms.

By this point, the NRA had already seeded women in prominent positions within the organization. However, their chief lobbyist, Tanya Metaksa, was one of the most extreme rhetoricians in the organization, the spokeswoman responsible for some of the organization's most intemperate critiques of President Clinton and the Centers for Disease Control. Although she was female, Metaksa certainly did not present the softer side of the NRA. The organization faced an important challenge: how could it fight back? One answer was to create a new magazine.

Although *Women & Guns* has occupied an uneasy territory between feminism and conservatism, *Woman's Outlook* has shown itself from its January 2002 launch onward to be relentlessly domestic. As Karen Mehall's "From the Editor" column promised in the December 2003 issue, "When we don our formal gowns or fancy party dresses for those holiday socials, we need to be ever creative when it comes to our concealed carry methods."[31] A story in that issue, called "The Perfect Present," advised parents on how to shop for their child's first gun. "And speaking of holiday shopping," Mehall remarked, "please take a few minutes to scan '23 Holiday Safety Tips' from the NRA's Refuse to Be a Victim Program for some great, easy-to-implement strategies to help enhance your personal security, when you are out shopping for that special present, driving to the mall to buy it, or sitting at home in front of the fireplace wrapping it up." In her overview of the December 2003 issue, Mehall also drew attention to a sentimental holiday story, "Angel on Call," which "introduces us to one of the angels in the ranks of women of the NRA as Tina Pattison, founder of the Hunt of a Lifetime Foundation, continues to dedicate her life to helping children with life-threatening illnesses live their hunting dreams. For more on the hunting front," Mehall added," 'Fare Game' [a regular feature of the magazine] cooks the traditional holiday goose."

Most articles in *Woman's Outlook* take a maternal slant on gun issues. For instance, in the December 2003 issue, Eileen Clarke opened her "Eye on Optics" column by reminiscing, "When my son was little, we used to play a game called 'hide the thimble,'" and used this memory to segue into the best way to focus a rifle scope.[32] Another columnist urged women gun-rights advocates to defend their viewpoints with "grace, logic and facts."[33]

Woman's Outlook resembles nothing so much as an Eddie Bauer catalog. Whereas the women featured in *Women & Guns* are often slightly overweight, casually dressed, wear glasses, and do not look like models, the women of *Woman's Outlook* have the appearance of professional models—not supermodels, but women who would be hired to represent outerwear or casual wear companies. Thus, women in the magazine often are depicted backlit, wearing pink lipstick while hunting in the woods.

Whereas *Women & Guns* employs some feminist rhetoric, *Woman's Outlook* goes out of its way to make sure that readers do not draw any feminist inferences from its articles. The focus is on family, and the articles mimic those in mainstream women's magazines—only with guns. A summer issue of the magazine may include tips on traveling with firearms and an article on a fun family vacation destination: the NRA's National Firearms Museum in Fairfax, Virginia. The message is that guns can be incorporated into almost any aspect of wholesome family life.

In fact, the family is presented as being the means of perpetuating gun culture. The gun industry as a whole has focused for the last several years on increasing the number of gun owners by getting mothers to teach gun culture to their kids. As Lisa Parsons wrote in a 1997 article in *Shooting Industry*, "There are 12.2 million female head of households in the United States. If those female head of households never introduce their children to the shooting sports, our industry will suffer greatly. The first step is to make women welcome and to let them know they are wanted. The rest will follow."[34]

Many articles in *Woman's Outlook* are devoted to the question of when and how to buy a child's first gun. In June 2003, Daniel T. McElrath offered insight into weapons and childhood development: "If you have a boy, you wonder if owning an airgun is a rite of passage into adulthood, a part of the maturation process that will result in a complete and well-rounded adult. If you have a daughter, you may be afraid that denying her will limit her potential by reinforcing gender stereotypes, preventing her from undertaking new challenges or—in the extreme—establishing a fear of arms and/or self-defense that could eventually lead her to accept victimization."

Furthermore, McElrath warned, "preventing [your children's] participation in the shooting sports will block them from a popular and potential lifelong activity, one that can help them develop self-discipline, personal responsibility, new relationships and, in some cases, lead to competitive success or even a college scholarship."[35] Thus, articles like McElrath's play on parents' anxieties about their children's development and achievements and suggest gun ownership as a means of ensuring a well-adjusted and successful child.

Although almost all of the faces shown in *Woman's Outlook* are white, an article in June 2003, titled "Girls Just Wanna Have Fun," focused on the "Sunday Sisters," two dozen women of color who got together for a day at the NRA Headquarters Range. "There were plenty of refreshments and finger foods, giving the event the feel of a sorority meeting." In other words, this was an extremely genteel and festive gathering. "After all questions were answered and participants passed the NRA Range examination, it was off to the range for some safe, clean fun. . . . At the end of the day, the participants had gained a better understanding of safe and proper firearms handling, while enjoying a Sunday afternoon with their 'sisters.'"[36] These women were not dedicated shooters; they were a group of "sorority sisters" who just happened to choose the shooting range as a site for "safe, clean fun"—fun of a kind that anyone would enjoy.

Even seemingly explicitly feminist protests are depoliticized within the magazine. In a recent issue of *Woman's Outlook*, in the "My Two Cents" column, Deborah Webbe recalled her participation in the Bayville Black Powder Club, founded by her father in 1968. In 1975, when the president of the club proposed that the author not be allowed to participate in the "Grand Bicentennial Skirmish" on account of her gender—and all twenty members except her father agreed—she appealed to the NRA. Appearing in the column were a picture of the author shooting a black powder rifle in redcoat regalia and a letter dated October 3, 1975, from the NRA's executive vice president, Maxwell E. Rich, to the president of the Bayville Black Powder Club. Rich urged the club president to reconsider because "it is the women of this country who most strongly influence our youngsters, boys and girls alike, to whom we look to carry on our traditions. . . . And I would think that the publicity gained by having a woman shoot in your Bicentennial demonstration would be of definite value to your club." In conclusion, Rich said, "while I realize you perhaps have considered the question of authenticity, may I point out that it has been historically proven that women have fought shoulder to shoulder with men in the front lines of battle."[37] Although Rich reached back into history for examples of female combatants in the military, the NRA vice president was primarily concerned with women as the bearers of tradition and as the means of perpetuating a gun culture.

The magazine highlights the ways that women can pass on gun culture, and many of its articles focus on loyal daughters of gun enthusiasts. These pieces, in fact, begin with a comment about how a woman was introduced to shooting by her father, as in the case of an article from the March 2004 issue: "Elizabeth DeMarco shot her first firearm years ago under her father's watchful eye."[38] The same issue features an article about a dad who takes his 11-year-old daughter on her first turkey shoot.[39] In yet another article from the March 2004 issue, a female hunter is quoted as saying, "Hunting is a great way to get that one-on-one time with your children that bonds the family together and creates the ties that hold the family together through the years."[40] Even an article on shotgunning (from a later issue) shows a young woman being mentored by a white-haired instructor.[41]

This patriarchal outlook permeates the magazine. In contrast to the many articles in *Women & Guns* that depict female instructors, the teachers in *Woman's Outlook* are almost all men. In this light, it is amusing to look back to an article titled "Hail the Riflewoman" published in another NRA magazine, *American Rifleman*, in January 1931. In it, an instructor of college women, W. M. Garlington, discusses his experience and his techniques. The attitude he takes toward his female students is patronizing at best: "Don't for one minute think that young women aren't just as prone to chatter in a rifle range as they are in a sorority house—for they are, brother!"[42] While he evinces no interest in producing serious riflewomen, he supports college women who want to try shooting as "a temporary proposition—a unique activity to engage in while in school." As Garlington notes, "The large majority retain interest in it just so long as they are able to turn in satisfactory scores. When they find that the going is too difficult interest wanes and they soon quit" (18). "The young college women of today are interesting personalities. They are brim full of ideas concerning everything earthly, cocksure of themselves to a marked degree, and generally sophisticated beyond their years. Most of them are but changelings undergoing the transformation from girlhood to womanhood, and destined to become the mothers of a generation yet to appear. . . . Rifle-shooting being a good clean sport it is no wonder that some of them are attracted to it. Hence when they go in for it they should be encouraged and afforded every opportunity to derive the maximum pleasure from their efforts" (26). Garlington concludes by saying, "I have always found them easy to handle and get along with, and grateful for considerations shown" (26).

What is most remarkable about *Woman's Outlook* is how traditional it is, how untouched it is by feminist considerations; many articles seem as though they might have been written sixty years ago. In the July 2003 issue, an article by Donna Robinson, wife of NRA president Kayne Robinson, asks, "So what's it like to experience the dark continent?" and offers the story of her safari. Here, she serves as helpmate to her husband: "My hunting goal was to take only one or two trophies—a Thompson's gazelle and perhaps a gerenuk or a warthog. I left the 'big stuff,' like the Cape buffalo and wildebeest, to Kayne."[43] The Africa depicted here might almost be the one described by Osa Johnson in the 1920s or 1930s.

The female readers of the magazine are assumed to be ladylike and fashion oriented, or attracted to that image. In the "Industry Spotlight" section, an article titled "The Makeup of a Huntress" focuses on half of a husband-wife team of entrepreneurs: "Both a hunter and a lady, Carman Forbes has used her feminine side to help create one of Hunters' Specialties' most-popular-selling products—the Camo-Compac."[44] The fashion column, "Woman's Wear," promotes "the softer side of Browning" by discussing how the gun manufacturer has branched out to produce women's hunting clothes: "Browning for Her will take you from a rough-and-tumble December hunting day to dining at a five-star hunting lodge."[45] The elegant appearance of the female hunter in the fancy lodge seems more important than her ability to move freely in her hunting clothes.

While *Women & Guns* focuses on danger and has many articles on events designed specifically for women, *Woman's Outlook* has as its motto "Celebrating your firearms freedom and outdoors lifestyle." The motto effectively removes the gun from any association with violence.

Unlike *Women & Guns*, *Woman's Outlook* takes for granted that its readers have little or no experience with guns and lack any interest in the technical aspects of shooting. *Women & Guns* features many articles dealing with the pros and cons of specific firearms, and it assumes that its readers have a deep familiarity with weaponry, but *Woman's Outlook* betrays its bias with a November 2003 article titled "Hot Flashes and Cold Feet: Two friends of a certain age try their hand at clay target shooting and laugh to tell about it." (One of the women says, "For my money, lifting a shotgun on a range is a lot more fun than lifting weights in a gym!" and the article concludes that clay target shooting "offers a fun-filled challenge for many.")[46] Compare that feature to the March–April 2004 issue of *Women & Guns* in which, as is typical of the magazine, a number of guns are reviewed: an author lauds the Taurus PT-24/7 for "one of my favorite features, a captive recoil spring over the guide rod," but she finds fault with the "fixed three-dot sights staked atop the 24/7's slide. They are fairly elementary, and I would feel a bit better had at least the rear sight been dovetailed to the slide for simple windage adjustments."[47] By contrast, although the "Product Showcase" in the April 2004 *Woman's Outlook* has a paragraph on the European American Arms' Witness Compact, a handgun designed for speed-shooting sports, it gives prominence to a campfire ring ("it's the cut-out shapes of moose and pine trees that really make this fire ring glow"), sheets for the hunting lodge ("Add a feminine touch while you keep that rustic feel with the True Grit linens collection from Cabela's"), and a set of steak knives ("With handles of European stag, these knives are sure to become your children's heirlooms as you pass your hunting traditions on to them").[48]

Woman's Outlook, in other words, is a gun magazine for women that manages not to talk about violence or personal danger, whose models never seem to get dirty, and in which shooting is entertainment and only mentioned in the context of good clean family fun. The cultural work that the magazine does for the NRA will be extended, the NRA hopes, by its new president, Sandra Susan Froman, who plans to promote *Woman's Outlook* as part of a larger initiative to diversify membership. According to Darren LaSorte, a lobbyist for the NRA, "Froman will soften the group's image with the general public." According to a January 2005 profile in the *Arizona Republic*, supporters of Froman "say she is friendly yet competitive, tender yet tough."[49]

Moreover, the model of citizenship that the NRA proposes for armed women through its "Refuse to Be a Victim" program, founded in 1993, is based on a privatized notion of citizenship, a refutation of so-called victim politics. If a woman is really strong, she will not entrust her safety to the hands of others and then whine when no protection is forthcoming. Rather, she will use a gun to accomplish what the state is no longer qualified to do.

Armed women seem to be everywhere in American culture today. They wield weapons in Iraq; in popular culture, beautiful and deadly women armed with automatic weapons are a Hollywood staple.[1] No matter what the gun industry and its allies do to pretend otherwise, guns remain a charged symbol of women's access to full citizenship, of women's capacity for violence, and of women's sexuality.

Most feminists have rejected the notion that gun ownership is or can be a meaningful part of women's empowerment: in 1993, Betty Friedan decried the trend of women's purchasing firearms as "a horrifying, obscene perversion of feminism"[2] and denounced the National Rifle Association's "Refuse to Be a Victim" campaign as a "false use of feminism."[3] However, a number of scholarly books and articles published since the mid-1990s have suggested the contrary, that it is time, as Mary Zeiss Stange and Carol K. Oyster put it, to start "exploring the positive feminist implications of women's gun use and ownership."[4] Stange and Oyster are even more forceful in arguing against gun control laws: "Why should we, especially those of us who are feminists, invite the state to be responsible for our personal health and safety? We don't want state interference when it comes to things like reproductive freedom or sexual orientation. If we do not trust the government and its agents with our sexual organs and appetites, why on earth should we trust them with our lives?"[5] There are, of course, a number of possible responses to this argument, which conflates the legalization of abortion, gay rights legislation, and the absence of gun control: women fought for the right to legalized abortion precisely because they wanted government regulation, rather than dangerous back-alley operations; gay rights advocates are fighting for government regulation to prohibit antigay discrimination. What is finally clear, though, is that Stange and Oyster are advocating a kind of vigilante libertarian feminism in the guise of freedom; they approvingly quote Leslie Marmon Silko's remark that "women must learn how to take aggressive action individually, apart from police and the courts."[6] In other words, rather than working to strengthen the power of the courts and police, women must accept the fact that the state will not protect them and act accordingly.

Yet armed feminism depends both on the acceptance of a martial notion of citizenship and on the idea that power ultimately comes only through violent capabilities. Armed feminism is shortcut feminism: it is an argument for using guns to obtain equal rights that leapfrogs over all of the issues—like access to day care, equal employment opportunity, and so forth—that are at the heart of true equality. A woman cannot gain equal pay for equal work by shooting her boss. Samuel Colt may have made men and women equal, but only if equality means the ability to deal death without regard to gender. While superficially somewhat similar to the feminism of self-defense courses, the armed feminism that Stange and Oyster advocate is fundamentally quite different: one can hardly compare taking a Model Mugging course and gaining a set of sophisticated physical skills to be used only against an attacker with just picking up a gun that can be fired by almost anyone, under a broad range of circumstances.

In addition to adopting the language of feminism to promote women's gun ownership, spokespeople for the gun industry and pro-gun academics have recast gun ownership as a strike against racial oppression. Whereas the women who were being promoted as gun consumers at the turn of the twentieth century were explicitly white, the gun industry and its advocates today have reframed women's gun ownership by tying it to larger issues of civil rights. The NRA's Website has a link to articles about civil rights and gun ownership. Of course, it is absolutely correct that, in the United States, laws governing gun ownership since the late seventeenth century were written to help enforce racial hierarchies.[7] As *Women & Guns* editor Peggy Tartaro notes, "Gun control is about controlling groups of people, not firearms. The first gun control laws were Jim Crow laws, passed in the South after the Civil War because they did not want the newly emancipated slaves to own firearms. When it was passed a century ago, New York City's Sullivan Act was hailed in the press because it would 'keep guns out of the hands of low-brow foreigners,' by which I assume they meant my great-grandparents."[8] This progressive language takes the conservative edge off of gun ownership by reframing it as a civil rights issue. Even as the gun lobby links gun ownership to civil rights, the NRA tends to funnel money to right-wing Republican candidates, who have traditionally been enemies of civil rights legislation.

The most effective guns are the ones that never get fired: real guns are highly destructive to women and their worlds. In studying guns in the popular imagination, we cannot lose sight of the fact that in reality guns are used not to entertain or provide sexual images but to shoot—and, in real life, women who use guns in a violent way are ostracized. Guns are perhaps the best cultural example of how the imaginary and the real cannot be conflated: there is a fatal world of difference between props in fantasies and real guns that have the power to kill.

I have chosen not to fully enter into the debates about the safety, or lack thereof, of guns; that is a topic for another book—and has already been a topic for many, many other books and articles.[9] As Stange and Oyster say, "It is possible to find, or massage, numbers that can support either a pro-gun or anti-gun stance, to pick and choose the figures that support the ideological position of your choice."[10] However, there is a great deal of evidence to suggest that a woman is much more likely to fall victim to a gun in the home than to repel a violent attack with it; that her children are even more likely to suffer as the result of a gun in the home; and that the extraordinarily high degree of violent death in the United States can be correlated with the ease with which Americans can purchase firearms. Over the course of writing this book, I have met many thoughtful gun owners—and have discovered that many women who are friends of mine in fact own guns. And yet I have been appalled by other casual discoveries I have made along the way: for example, that 85 percent of the children seen at the pediatric practice where I take my kids live in homes with guns, and that the new dress code adopted by the public school system in my home town of Richmond, Virginia, mandates that shirts be tucked in, even by kindergartners, in order to make it more difficult for children to bring concealed weapons to school. It only takes a glance inside the metro section of most urban newspapers to see the many horrific ways in which guns shape women's lives.

However much we may want to fantasize about women with guns, reality is something very different. The popular fiction, autobiographies, movies, magazines, and tabloid stories discussed in these pages may make women intelligible to men. But while the armed woman stands in for citizenship, it really is a poor substitution of image for reality. Our fascination with the armed woman is an expression of our societal ambivalence about women's equality with men: we are titillated, but we are afraid.

As I have noted in the introduction, it is very difficult to pin down how many new female gun owners there are in the United States. Yet there is every reason to believe that in the American imagination the armed woman will continue to confound, arouse, and scare us. It is only by unpacking her often contradictory meanings that we can begin to untangle the relationships between race, gender, and the violent mythologies that have shaped this nation.

The first armed women to become the subjects of popular ballads and fiction were female soldiers, and it was the woman in combat who became a litmus test for both feminists and antifeminists as they discussed the suitability of women for full citizenship. Today the terms of the debate about women and guns may be changing as it becomes more widely understood that the policy of the u.s. armed services banning female soldiers from combat is essentially meaningless: the war in Iraq has blurred the experiences of front-line and support troops beyond all recognition.

For example, in April 2005 the *New York Times* ran a front-page article profiling two women soldiers who had been maimed while fighting in Iraq. One of them, Dawn Halfaker, reflecting on her military career, told the reporter that "in what she calls her worst moments, she had to kill insurgents." However, this article also illustrates that even a female soldier who kills may end up as a poster child both for conservatives and for the weapons industry. Halfaker, a white West Point graduate who joined the military police upon graduation and "jumped at the chance to test her leadership when the war began," was "proud of her time in Iraq" and remained uncritical of the u.s. war effort. In addition, she was reluctant to wear a "scary"-looking prosthesis and wondered whether men would still find her attractive. She was traditionally feminine and very concerned with her self-presentation. The other subject of the profile, Danielle Green, was a black woman from the projects who joined the army after a romantic disappointment. About her prosthesis, she said, "I don't care what it looks like, as long as it works." She told the reporter for the *Times* that "she has 'never been patriotic' and is conflicted about American involvement in Iraq: she is against the war but supports the troops." After a number of false starts, Green went back to school to become a school counselor. In the view of the two women's occupational therapist, "Dawn was more political. She was groomed to be responsive to people and kept her pain inside." Green, on the other hand, "could be in a bad mood and felt it was O.K. to show that." While still in the Walter Reed Army Medical Center, recuperating from her injuries, Halfaker landed an internship with Representative Duncan Hunter (R-Calif.) and received "lucrative job offers from the defense industry."[11]

In their differences, these women who used guns as soldiers, and who lost limbs in combat, suggest the limits of any efforts to see guns as inherently transformative. The two women's backgrounds, not their weapons or their wounds, shaped their outlooks: one adjusted to a future supporting the war effort and the arms industry, while maintaining her traditional gender role, and the other continued to express pain and loss.

Although Dawn Halfaker and Danielle Green appeared on the front page of the *New York Times*, their story quickly faded from public view. The only female soldier to emerge thus far as an icon in the Iraq war is Lynndie England; photographs of her — grinning as she holds a leashed Iraqi prisoner, playfully pointing her fingers like guns at the genitals of naked Iraqi soldiers — have been published in newspapers around the world and have become staples of the Internet. England, who also had herself photographed having sex with her commanding officer, embodies a nightmare version of the female soldier: violent, sexually out of control, and amoral.

Americans have only begun to think about armed women as professional soldiers, rather than as Prairie Madonnas or doting wives or criminals or performers. It was one thing for audiences to enjoy Annie Oakley's staged performance depicting the settling of the West or Pauline Cushman's theatrical reenactment of her Civil War adventures. And while many of the best-known armed women of the twentieth century, from Bonnie Parker to Patty Hearst, were not professional entertainers, they certainly became celebrities as criminals or as revolutionaries. It is a very different matter to read about women who have lost limbs, or lost their lives, in war. As the bloody realities of the twenty-first century are starting to sink in, the questions about citizenship, rights, power, and violence raised by the armed woman remain just that: questions. Perhaps because this is a moment when armed women have become ordinary soldiers, and are no longer treated as icons, there is no better time to look at how the woman with a gun has shaped our national identity. In a nation where gun ownership and citizenship are often considered to be closely connected, and where masculinity and guns are also linked, the armed woman continues to provoke and perhaps to haunt us.

NOTES

INTRODUCTION

1. Ian Katz, "Firearms Industry Woos Women Who Dress to Kill," *Guardian*, May 21, 1986. This article in a British newspaper focuses on the United States.
2. Jeff Wu, "Guns Aren't Just for Boys: More Women Buying, Shooting Pistols," *San Francisco Chronicle*, August 28, 1991.
3. Quoted in Barbara Carton, "Arms and the Woman: Gun Manufacturer Aims New Revolver at Growing Market of Female Customers," *Boston Globe*, February 16, 1989.
4. Kelly, *Blown Away*, 210.
5. Susan Paynter, "Magazine Shoots for Equality," *Seattle Post-Intelligencer*, August 26, 1991.
6. Kevin Goldman, "NRA Is Defending as Educational Its Campaign Targeting Women," *Wall Street Journal*, 28 September 1993.
7. Joan Wenner, "Targeting a New Market for Firearms (Women Buyers)," *Shooting Industry*, January 1, 1992, 19.
8. Lisa Parsons, "Get the Inside Track on the Fastest Growing Market! (Women in the Shooting Sports)," *Shooting Industry*, April 1, 1997, 20.
9. Smith and Smith, "Changes in Firearms Ownership." The National Science Foundation has also disputed the NRA's claims about the increase in female firearms ownership. See Colleen O'Connor, "Women's Self-Defense: Big Business; Sales of Everything from Firearms to Garter-Belt Holsters Are Up," *Dallas Morning News*, October 24, 1993.
10. Bruce Horovitz, "Firearms Sellers Increasingly Target Women," *Chicago Sun-Times*, September 2, 1992.
11. "Stevens Special Fire Arms" (ad), *Forest and Stream*, February 12, 1891.
12. Stevens firearms ad, *Outing*, January 1890.
13. Marlin repeater ad, *Forest and Stream*, July 23, 1898.
14. Iver Johnson Sporting Goods poster, 1903, in Strauss and Strauss, *American Sporting Advertising*, 2: n.p.
15. Winchester Repeating Arms Company poster, 1909, in Strauss and Strauss, *American Sporting Advertising*, 1: n.p.
16. Winchester ad, *Leslie's Illustrated Weekly Newspaper*, July 29, 1915.
17. Stevens firearms ad, *National Sportsman*, September 1905.

18. Union Metallic Cartridge Co. calendar, 1891, in Strauss and Strauss, *American Sporting Advertising*, 1: n.p.
19. Iver Johnson ad, *McClure's Magazine*, July 1903.
20. Ithaca Guns ad, *National Sportsman*, October 1921.
21. Ithaca Guns ad, *Outdoor America*, August 1929.
22. Ithaca Guns ad, *Outdoor Life*, February 1929.
23. Winchester firearms ad, *Sports Afield*, May 1953.
24. There are exceptions. For example, a 1907 ad in the *Outing Magazine* for the Savage featherweight sporting rifle shows an Indian maiden dressed in buckskin crouching on her knees and holding her gun.
25. The *Harper's Weekly* cover is from the issue of October 13, 1877.

    To be fair, Annie Oakley's biographies always emphasized her work as a young girl supporting her family by hunting. However, her role in Buffalo Bill's Wild West show was much more focused on making Western conquest seem fun.
26. "Women Catching Up with Men in One More Field: Crime," *U.S. News & World Report*, September 23, 1974, 45–48.
27. Gibson, *Warrior Dreams*, 98.
28. *Dred Scott v. Sandford*, 60 U.S. 393, 417 (1856).
29. The civil rights movement of the 1950s and 1960s produced a number of memoirs and images that detailed black women's gun use—as well as the resistance of men in the movement to women's use of firearms. The famous photograph of civil rights leader Robert F. Williams teaching his wife to shoot (reproduced in this book) is counterbalanced by Williams's memory that although women "wanted to fight . . . we kept them out of it." Tyson, *Radio Free Dixie*, 91.
30. "Indian Heroines in Peasant Armed Revolutionary Struggle," *Red Star: Organ of the Red Women's Detachment*, August 1970, n.p.
31. *Woman's Outlook* Staff, "Photo Essay: Women of War," *Woman's Outlook*, June 2003, 36.
32. See, for instance, Leonard, *All the Daring of the Soldier*, 155–57; De Pauw, *Battle Cries and Lullabies*, 126–31.
33. De Pauw, *Battle Cries and Lullabies*, 126.
34. Oral histories quoted in ibid., 130.
35. See Nelson, *National Manhood*; Nelson and Castronovo, *Materializing Democracy*; Berlant, *Queen of America Goes to Washington City*; Kerber, *No Constitutional Right to Be Ladies*. Some of these authors have looked specifically at the ways that members of marginalized groups, such as Jewish immigrants in the early part of the twentieth century, have moved into a more secure re-

lationship with the state and with national identity by participating in racialized performances. See, for instance, Lott, *Love and Theft*; Roediger, *Wages of
Whiteness*; Rogin, *Blackface, White Noise*.

36. The membership total is the official NRA estimate, as of April 2005. As with
    most other things in the highly fractious world of guns, even such a seem-
    ingly clear-cut matter as the number of NRA members is contested. It may be
    worth noting Osha Gray Davidson's skepticism about the NRA's own figures.
    As Davidson points out, the NRA's 1998 membership figures of 2.7 million
    included not only people with trial memberships but also over a million life
    members; "the problem is that some unknown portion of that life member
    group is, to put it bluntly, dead." Davidson, *Under Fire*, 306.

37. Quoted in ibid., 294.

38. Hemenway, *Private Guns, Public Health*, 5, 6. For the higher percentage, see
    the National Rifle Association's Website: <www.nraila.org/Issues/FAQs/De
    fault.aspx?/Section=70>.

39. A notable example of this is the furor that erupted over Michael Bellesiles's
    Arming America: The Origins of a National Gun Culture. For a discussion of
    the Bellesiles controversy, see Ventello, "Violence Engendered," 153–63. See,
    as well, the forum on the book in *William and Mary Quarterly* 59, no. 1 (May
    2002).

CHAPTER 1

1. Kerber, *No Constitutional Right to Be Ladies*, 240.

2. *New York Herald*, September 14, 1852, quoted in Isenberg, *Sex and Citizenship*, 42.

3. "Male Impersonation," *National Anti-Slavery Bugle*, April 28, 1853, quoted in
   ibid., 48.

4. L.S.M., "Woman and Her Needs," *De Bow's Southern and Western Review* 1,
   no. 3 (September 1852): 279–80.

5. Isenberg, *Sex and Citizenship*, 151.

6. *Proceedings of the Woman's Rights Convention*, 44.

7. Mott, *Discourse on Woman*, 5.

8. Isenberg, *Sex and Citizenship*, 144.

9. Hosley, *Colt*, 67.

10. Legends of women in battle date back for centuries, as do documented ex-
    amples. See De Pauw, *Battle Cries and Lullabies*; Dugaw, *Warrior Women and
    Popular Balladry*; Wheelwright, *Amazon Women and Military Maids*.

11. Dugaw, *Warrior Women and Popular Balladry*, 43.

12. George Carey, *A Sailor's Songbag: An American Rebel in an English Prison, 1777–*

79 (Amherst: University of Massachusetts Press, 1976), quoted in Dugaw, *Warrior Women and Popular Balladry*, 63.

13. C. B. Brown, *Ormond*, 202.

14. Deborah Sampson Gannett began life as "Deborah Samson" and seems to have changed the spelling of her maiden name to "Sampson" following her service in the Continental army as "Robert Shurtliff." See Young, *Masquerade*, 18.

15. Gannett, *Addrss* [*sic*], 6–7.

16. Mann, *The Female Review*, vi.

17. Casper, *Constructing American Lives*, 2.

18. Young, *Masquerade*, 14.

19. Tappan, introduction, iv.

20. As Alfred E. Young points out, the volume of *Beadle's Dime Tales* featuring "Deborah Sampson, the Maiden Warrior," circa 1862, was illustrated with an image of Sampson standing by a cannon, Molly Pitcher–style. Young, *Masquerade*, 280–81.

21. See, for instance, L. Merrill, *When Romeo Was a Woman*.

22. Cohen, *Female Marine and Related Works*, 25.

23. Lucy Brewer's memoir stands in contrast to another "autobiography" written and published by Coverly in 1816, *The Surprising Adventures of Almira Paul*. Paul, a Nova Scotian mother of two, went to sea disguised as a man in order to avenge the death of her husband, a sailor on a British privateer who was killed in an engagement with an American privateer. After three years on board British ships—"to convince the world that the capacities of *women* were equal to that of the *men*, there was not a piece of rigging on board a ship, but what I could name, and no duty but what I could perform" (13)—she musters out, but finds that she misses the company of sailors: "I had become so habituated to their customs and manners, that I must indeed acknowledge, I even yet felt a disposition to associate with them." Therefore, "I took board at a house of ill-fame on Fells-Point (Baltimore) where I rather invited than objected to the company of such as are in the habit of spending their cash, much easier than what they earn it" (22). While Lucy Brewer found that the life of a sailor promoted virtue and cleansed her of sin, Almira Paul ended up writing her memoir in prison, where she had ended up following her arrest for prostitution.

24. Billings, *Female Volunteer*, 67.

25. Even during the Civil War, the public could feast on patently inauthentic "autobiographies" such as *The Lady Lieutenant: A Wonderful, Startling and Thrilling Narrative of the Adventures of Miss Madeline Moore, who, in order to be near her lover, joined the Army, was elected Lieutenant, and fought in Western Virginia under the renowned General McClellan: and afterwards at the Great Battle of Bull Run*

(1862). Moore's story was much more romantic than it was patriotic. However, such narratives must be regarded as throwbacks to what had become an outmoded style; in vogue were such fiercely partisan works as Alexander's.

26. Bradshaw, *Picket Slayer*, 26.
27. Bradshaw, *General Sherman's Indian Spy*, 21.
28. Bradshaw, *Pauline of the Potomac*, 33.
29. Bradshaw, *Maud of the Mississippi*, 48.
30. Ellet, *Women of the American Revolution*, 122.
31. Nurse Mary Livermore, in *My Story of the War*, 119–20, while noting that many contemporary observers "stated the number of women soldiers known to the service as little less than four hundred," says she was "convinced that a larger number of women disguised themselves, and enlisted in the service, for one cause or another, than was dreamed of."
32. De Pauw, *Battle Cries and Lullabies*, 151. See also Leonard, *All the Daring of the Soldier*, 310–11.
33. "A Rejected Recruit," *Liberator*, August 22, 1862, 135. For a discussion of reporting on female soldiers during the Civil War, see Blanton and Cook, *They Fought Like Demons*, 145–62.
34. *Savannah (Ga.) Republican*, June 5, 1861, quoted in "Women Soldiers, Spies and Vivandieres: Articles from Civil War Newspapers," <http://www.uttyl.edu/vbetts/women_soldiers.htm> (September 13, 2005).
35. Quoted in Whites, *Civil War as a Crisis in Gender*, 40.
36. Mrs. Forrest T. Morgan, "'Nancy Harts' of the Confederacy," *Confederate Veteran*, December 1922, 465–66.
37. Quoted in Faust, *Mothers of Invention*, 20.
38. Brockett and Vaughn, *Woman's Work*, 25, 21.
39. Cross-dressing soldiers and spies continued to be written about throughout the postbellum period. Recent years have seen a marked surge of publications on the subject, ranging from studies such as Leonard's *All the Daring of the Soldier* to the reissue of many of these women's autobiographies with scholarly introductions, including Boyd's *Belle Boyd in Camp and Prison*, Edmonds's *Memoirs of a Soldier, Nurse and Spy*, and Velazquez's *Woman in Battle*. In addition, the wartime correspondence of one such soldier, Sarah Rosetta Wakeman, has recently been published (Burgess, *Uncommon Soldier*).
40. There is only one known memoir of a black woman's service in the Civil War, Susie King Taylor's *A Black Woman's Civil War Memoirs*. Taylor worked as a laundress and nurse attached to her regiment; while she was in danger a great deal of the time, she did not actually serve as a soldier. Her memoir is well worth reading for its descriptions of antebellum life near Savannah, Georgia,

her often hair-raising experiences with her regiment, her ingenious solutions to nursing problems, and her life as a teacher and household worker after the war.

41. See, for instance, Varon, *We Mean to be Counted*; DuBois, *Woman Suffrage and Women's Rights*; Gustafson, *Women and the Republican Party*; Parker and Cole, *Women and the Unstable State*.

42. Isenberg, *Sex and Citizenship*, 44.

43. See Fox-Genovese, *Within the Plantation Household*; Faust, *Mothers of Invention*; Lebsock, *Free Women of Petersburg*; Whites, *Civil War as a Crisis in Gender*; Clinton and Silber, *Divided Houses*; Bardaglio, *Reconstructing the Household*.

44. George Fitzhugh, "The Conservative Principle, or Social Evils and Their Remedies," *De Bow's Review*, April 1857, 422, 424.

45. Boyd, *Belle Boyd in Camp and Prison*, 82.

46. See Kennedy-Nolle, introduction to *Belle Boyd in Camp and Prison*, 40–48.

47. Schechner, "What Is Performance Studies Anyway?" 361.

48. Cushman, *Romance of the Great Rebellion*, 15.

49. Sarmiento, *Life of Pauline Cushman*, 27.

50. Velazquez, *Woman in Battle*, 37.

51. Jubal Early to William H. Slemons, May 22, 1978, Tucker Family Papers, Collection 2605, Folder 41, Southern Historical Collection, Wilson Library, University of North Carolina at Chapel Hill; Alemán, "Authenticity," xix; Hall, *Patriots in Disguise*, 207–8.

52. Early to Slemons, May 22, 1978. Early was thoroughly sanctimonious about *The Woman in Battle*: "I should be sorry to believe that either of the Southern members of Congress, who have signed Madame Velazquez's credentials, after having read her book carefully, be willing to place it in the hands of their wife or daughter, with a commendation of its morality."

53. Evans, *Macaria*, 302.

54. Edward Edgeville's *Castine* is a pulpy romance in which female militarism is downplayed. Although the title character has gone to war to avenge her sister's ill treatment at the hands of an intemperate suitor, she spends very little time on the battlefield. The play *The Confederate Vivandière*, performed in 1862 by an amateur company for the benefit of the first regiment of the Alabama Cavalry, features a vivandière—that is, a girl whose job it is to minister to the wounded and the dying rather than to fight in battle. Though struck dumb by watching her mother murdered at Harpers Ferry, Clara Brandon is still able to render valuable assistance to the Confederacy by dressing as a gypsy and acting as a spy. She almost, but not quite, gets to kill a Yankee with a sword; she

remains throughout "Clara Brandon, the dumb beauty of Baltimore," and is not even mentioned in the final stage directions when "the stage bursts into flames, and the whole country becomes illuminated." Hodgson, *Confederate Vivandière*, 20.

55. Southworth, *Fair Play*, 439; subsequent citations in the text are identified as *FP*.

56. Southworth, *How He Won Her*, 50; subsequent citations in the text are identified as *HHWH*.

57. At one point the narrator editorializes, "Take it home to yourself, my manly reader, if I have the honor of possessing one" (*FP*, 633).

CHAPTER 2

1. Ingram, *Centennial Exposition*, 648.
2. DeConde, *Gun Violence in America*, 21.
3. Ibid., 39.
4. K. Brown, "Nathaniel Bacon and the Dilemma of Colonial Masculinity," 46.
5. *Dred Scott v. Sandford*, 60 U.S. 393, 417 (1857).
6. DeConde, *Gun Violence in America*, 75. See also Kramer, "Racist Roots of Gun Control"; I retrieved this article from the Gun Owners of America Website, <http://www.keepandbeararms.com> (January 23, 2003).
7. Quoted in DeConde, *Gun Violence in America*, 73.
8. Slotkin, *Fatal Environment*, 465.
9. Dartt, *On the Plains*, 5. Dartt was Maxwell's half sister.
10. Quoted in Benson, *Martha Maxwell*, 199.
11. Reviews quoted in *A Suitable Book for Holiday Presents. Just Published. On the Plains, and Among the Peaks*, a leaflet from Claxton, Remsen and Haffelfinger, in Martha Maxwell Collection, MSS 762, box 3, file folder 99, Colorado Historical Society (CHS), Denver, Colo.
12. Dartt, *On the Plains*, 171.
13. *Daily News* (Denver, Colo.), in Martha Maxwell scrapbook, pp. 51–52, Martha Maxwell Collection, CHS.
14. "Mrs. Maxwell's Rocky Mountain Museum," *Harper's Bazaar*, November 11, 1876, 730.
15. "Centennial Correspondence," *Lynn (Mass.) City Item*, October 21, 1876.
16. *Forest and Stream*, Maxwell scrapbook, p. 61.
17. Olive Harper, "The Colorado Huntress' Display of Birds and Animals," *Weekly Alta California and San Francisco Times*, undated, in Maxwell scrapbook, p. 50.
18. *The New Century for Women*, n.p.

19. *Advance*, in Maxwell scrapbook, pp. 71–72.

20. "The Museum of Mrs. Maxwell, of Boulder, Colorado," *Philadelphia Times*, in Maxwell scrapbook, p. 59.

21. *Truth for the People*, in Maxwell scrapbook, p. 73.

22. *People's Journal* (New York), October 2, 1876, in Maxwell scrapbook, n.p.

23. For an account of the origins of the NRA, see Leddy, *Magnum Force Lobby*, 55–67. See also Gilmore, "Crack Shots and Patriots"; Sugarmann, *National Rifle Association*; J. Anderson, *Inside the NRA*; DeConde, *Gun Violence in America*.

24. Colonel William F. Church, editor of the *United States Army and Navy Journal*, was the other.

25. George W. Wingate, "Early Days of the NRA," reprinted in *American Rifleman*, May 1951, 32.

26. Quoted in Sugarmann, *National Rifle Association*, 25.

27. Trefethen, *Americans and Their Guns*, 104–5.

28. DeConde, *Gun Violence in America*, 62.

29. As Russell Stanley Gilmore notes, "The ladies' contest used a lance swinging on wires and paid off in parasols, combs, and gewgaws." Gilmore, "Crack Shots and Patriots," 24.

30. Ibid., 23.

31. Ibid., 34.

32. Ibid., 96.

33. Wm. J. Sutor, letter to the editor, *Rifle*, October 1886, 219.

34. "Ladies' Day at the Rifle Range," *Rifle*, May 1888, 519.

35. Williamson, *Winchester*, 185–86.

36. "Coming the Famous Topperweins" (Winchester pamphlet), undated, Winchester Arms Collection Archives, McCracken Research Library, Buffalo Bill Historical Center, Cody, Wyo.

37. Undated, Winchester Arms Collection Archives.

38. American Powder Mills ad, *Outdoor Life*, May 1907, McCracken Research Library.

39. Henry Brewer to Major Leonard A. Horner, September 6, 1917, file 67.1, Winchester Arms Collection Archives.

40. L. A. Horner to Henry Brewer, September 8, 1917, file 67.1, Winchester Arms Collection Archives.

41. Interestingly, Annie Oakley did tour a number of army camps in 1918 under the auspices of the YMCA and War Camp Community Service (Kasper, *Annie Oakley*, 216). Perhaps a private enterprise like Winchester was more concerned about public relations; clearly, the U.S. government was able to accept a woman in an army camp.

42. *Diana of the Traps*, 1.

43. Christensen, "Gun in Her Hands," 62.

44. *Developing a Broader Interest in Trapshooting*, n.p.

45. Daniel Justin Herman, *Hunting and the American Imagination*, 227, 228.

46. "The Publisher's Basket," *Outing*, July 1896.

47. See Trachtenberg, *Incorporation of America*, chap. 1.

48. "Monster Buck Trophy of Pueblo Huntress," *Denver Post*, October 3, 1903, Dawson scrapbooks, vol. 72, 537, CHS.

49. "Bear Hunting as a Sport for Women," *St. Louis Globe Democrat*, April 30, 1905, Dawson scrapbooks, vol. 72, 537, CHS.

50. Mrs. F. T. Miller, "The American Tendency to Dwarf Life," *Outdoor Life*, January 1904, 14.

51. Oakley was much admired by members of rifle clubs. "During the past month," an article in the *Rifle* noted, "Miss Annie Oakley was kind enough to show a large number of ladies and gentlemen about Boston how proficient a lady could become in handling rifle and gun." "Ladies' Day at the Rifle Range."

52. Newman, *White Women's Rights*, 15.

53. A. Stott, "Prairie Madonnas and Pioneer Women," 302.

54. Fowler, *Woman on the American Frontier*, 37.

55. Etulain, "Calamity Jane: Creation of a Western Legend," 150.

56. Jordan, "When Women Ruled the West," 26.

57. Buntline, *Bob Woolf*, 8.

58. Wheeler, "Captain Crack-Shot," 4.

59. Coomes, "Rambling Dick," 1.

60. Buntline, "Merciless Ben the Hair-Lifter," 1.

61. Quoted in Shirley, *Belle Starr*, 14.

62. Quoted in ibid., 17. In 1898 Samuel W. Harman expressed a dissenting view, claiming that Starr was the daughter of a slave-owning judge and that her girlhood experiences during the Civil War turned her into a hater of the United States. Harman, *Hell on the Border*, 59.

63. Harman, *Hell on the Border*, 58.

64. Ibid., 68.

65. Sollid, *Calamity Jane*, xxv.

66. For example, Edward L. Wheeler's *Deadwood Dick on Deck; or, Calamity Jane, the Heroine of Whoop-Up* (1878).

67. Jane Cannary, "Life and Adventures of Calamity Jane," reprinted in Sollid, *Calamity Jane*, 125.

68. Bederman, *Manliness and Civilization*, 25.

69. For instance, May Lillie, the wife of Wild West show entrepreneur Major Gor-

don W. Lillie, a.k.a. Pawnee Bill, was featured in Paul Braddon's *Pawnee Bill's Shadow; or, May Lillie, the Girl Dead Shot* (1891).

70. Quoted in Shirley, *Pawnee Bill*, 117.

71. Clark, "Doing What Comes Naturally," 5.

72. Pawnee Bill's Wild West courier, undated, Western History Collection, Denver Public Library, Denver, Colo.

73. Shirley, *Pawnee Bill*, 117.

74. Belleisles, *Arming America*, 442.

75. Kasper, *Annie Oakley*, 12.

76. Pawnee Bill's Wild West courier, undated.

77. See Kasper, *Annie Oakley*, 36; Moses, "Wild West Shows." See also Moses, *Wild West Shows*, 21.

78. Kasson, *Buffalo Bill's Wild West*, 112–13.

79. Rydell, *All the World's a Fair*, 4.

80. Riley, *Life and Legacy*, 116.

81. Kasper, *Annie Oakley*, 213.

82. Annie Oakley, "The Story of My Life," *Daily News* (Dayton, Ohio), November 24, 1926, Annie Oakley scrapbooks, McCracken Research Library, Buffalo Bill Historical Center. See also Riley, *Life and Legacy*, 20.

83. Faragher, *Women and Men on the Overland Trail*, 97.

84. *St. Louis Globe Democrat*, May 9, 1886, Buffalo Bill Cody scrapbooks, Wild West Shows, Western History Collection, Denver Public Library.

85. Kasper, *Annie Oakley*, 12.

86. Wallis, *Real Wild West*, 311.

87. Kasper, *Annie Oakley*, 60.

88. "Good Shooting," *Republican*, May 13, 1886, Buffalo Bill Cody scrapbooks.

89. *Brick Pomeroy's Democrat*, 1886, 3.

90. Wallis, *Real Wild West*, 309.

91. Kasper, *Annie Oakley*, 22.

92. Riley, *Life and Legacy*, 35–36.

93. The *Daily Chronicle* of London noted that when Smith was called up by the Prince of Wales to the royal box, she "proceeded with perfect self-possession to explain and show [the prince] the working of the weapon in her hand." Quoted in Kasper, *Annie Oakley*, 73.

94. Letter from C. L. Daily, Neuilly, France, 22nd/89, Western History Collection, Denver Public Library.

95. Kasper, *Annie Oakley*, 101.

96. Smith did not always take her new identity entirely seriously. A 1902 article in the *Kansas City Star* represented her as having been adopted into the Sioux

tribe; the article also claimed that "her makeup was so good that it deceived most people, and a number of the society women of Buffalo entertained her, thinking she was an Indian princess." "Women Who Can Shoot," *Kansas City Star*, April 2, 1902.

97. Obituary for Wenona, *Billboard*, February 15, 1930, 95.

98. "Pawnee Bill's Wild West and Great Far East," Courier, Watertown, July 4, 1907, from the collection of the Circus World Museum, Baraboo, Wis.

99. Wallis, *Real Wild West*, 309.

100. Oakley, "Story of My Life." A "non-descript" is someone who is not of a defined race.

101. Kasper, *Annie Oakley*, 25–27.

102. Ibid., 91.

103. *Weekly Dispatch*, July 19, 1887, quoted in Kasper, *Annie Oakley*, 86.

104. Wallis, *Real Wild West*, 308.

105. Oakley, "Story of My Life."

106. The book was ghostwritten entirely by a radio scriptwriter, Winifred Dunn. See Imperato and Imperato, *They Married Adventure*, 209.

107. Johnson, *I Married Adventure*, 106.

108. Imperato and Imperato, *They Married Adventure*, 102.

109. "Beauty and the Beast," *New York World*, May 21, 1923, quoted in Imperato and Imperato, *They Married Adventure*, 113.

110. Quoted in K. Stott, *Exploring*, 44.

111. K. Stott, *Exploring*, 145.

112. Johnson, *I Married Adventure*, 239.

113. Ibid., 252. In fact, Osa Johnson was named one of the twelve best-dressed women in the United States in 1940. See Imperato and Imperato, *They Married Adventure*, x.

114. Cameron, *Africa on Film*, 196.

CHAPTER 3

1. Although women did serve in the U.S. Navy and the Marine Corps during World War I, and were trained in the use of arms, they never fired their weapons. However, they were important to the service for the purposes of publicity and participated in many recruiting parades. As Lettie Gavin reports, "In Yakima, WA, startled residents saw the Yeoman (F) contingent come marching down the main street carrying light rifles—while enlisted men followed carrying the luggage." Gavin, *American Women in World War I*, 8. These female soldiers could thus emphasize their ladylike status at the same time that they wielded their (purely ornamental) arms.

2. Mabel Potter Daggett, "Women Wanted" (1918), quoted in Moynihan, Russett, and Crumpacker, *Second to None*, 148.

3. Ruth, *Inventing the Public Enemy*, 13.

4. D'Emilio and Freedman, *Intimate Matters*, 241.

5. Perrett, *America in the Twenties*, 398.

6. Lait, *Gangster Girl*, 1.

7. E. Parker Levy, "The Lady from Castle-Bar," *Gangster Stories*, December 1929, 359.

8. Lothrop Stoddard, *The Rising Tide of Color against White World-Supremacy* (New York: Scribner, 1920), 220, quoted in Dijkstra, *Evil Sisters*, 249.

9. Dijkstra, *Evil Sisters*, 249.

10. Burns, *One-Way Ride*, 241.

11. Reeve, *Golden Age of Crime*, 148.

12. Mabel Abbott, "Is Dread Bob-Haired Bandit Female Dr. Jekyll–Mr. Hyde? Former Gangster Has Theory," *New York World*, April 13, 1924.

13. "Girl Held as Lure for Robber Band," *New York World*, April 15, 1924.

14. Abbott, "Is Dread Bob-Haired Bandit Female Dr. Jekyll–Mr. Hyde?"

15. "Bobbed Bandit Confesses Shooting Clerk in Hold-Up; on Way Here with Husband," *New York World*, April 22, 1924.

16. "Girl Bandit Here; Wants No Lawyer; Crowds Greet Her," *New York World*, April 23, 1924.

17. Walter Lippmann, "Cecilia Cooney," *New York World*, May 8, 1924, quoted in Broylan, *World and the Twenties*, 172.

18. Ibid., 173.

19. George J. Brenn, "Man-Killer," *Greater Gangster Stories*, April 1933, 95.

20. R. Sampson, *Yesterday's Faces*, 3:153.

21. Tyler, *Quality Bill's Girl*, 18.

22. Quoted in Server, *Danger Is My Business*, 82.

23. Cowley, *Dream of the Golden Mountain*, 22.

24. Hobsbawm, *Bandits*, 142.

25. In this chapter, I rely heavily on the autobiographies of criminals, gun molls, and the families of criminals. Like slave narratives and nineteenth-century Native American autobiographies, these are all edited by professional writers and given recognizable generic form.

26. Foreword to Audett, *Rap Sheet*, 9; Audett's book is hereafter cited in the text.

27. Karpis, *Alvin Karpis Story*, 124.

28. Hoover, *Persons in Hiding*, 95.

29. Purvis, *American Agent*, 150.

30. Hoover, *Persons in Hiding*, 94.

31. For a fuller discussion of Americanism in the 1930s, see L. Browder, *Rousing the Nation*. On the direction of the American Communist Party in the 1930s, see Isserman, *Which Side Were You On?* 9.

32. Cowley, *Dream of the Golden Mountain*, 94.

33. Gordon, *Woman's Body, Woman's Right*, 317.

34. Ware, *Holding Their Own*, 27.

35. Scharf, *To Work and to Wed*, 79.

36. Ibid., 78, 111; Ware, *Beyond Suffrage*, 91.

37. "Women in Business, II," *Fortune*, July 1935, 50.

38. J. Carter, *Hour before Daylight*, 60.

39. Quoted in Gentry, *J. Edgar Hoover*, 179.

40. Corey, *Farewell, Mr. Gangster!* 37.

41. Madison Grant, *The Passing of the Great Race* (1916; repr., New York: Scribner's, 1922), 27, quoted in Dijkstra, *Evil Sisters*, 349.

42. Cooper, *Here's to Crime!* 194.

43. Robert W. Chambers, *The Crimson Tide: A Story of Bolshevism in New York* (New York: D. Appleton, 1919), 245, quoted in Dijkstra, *Evil Sisters*, 253.

44. Gentry, *J. Edgar Hoover*, 179.

45. Glueck and Glueck, *Five Hundred Delinquent Women*, 300.

46. Cooper, *Here's to Crime!* 208. Although "Machine Gun" is now the usual rendering of George Kelly's nickname, Hoover and Cooper evidently favored "Machine-gun."

47. Hoover, *Persons in Hiding*, 147.

48. Purvis, *American Agent*, 151.

49. Waller, *Feud*, 232.

50. Blee and Billings, "Where 'Bloodshed Is a Pastime,'" 131.

51. E. Carl Litsey, "Kentucky Feuds and Their Causes," *Frank Leslie's Popular Monthly*, January 1902, 292, quoted in Blee and Billings, "Where 'Bloodshed Is a Pastime,'" 131.

52. Karpis, *Alvin Karpis Story*, 80.

53. Hoover, *Persons in Hiding*, 21.

54. Karpis, *Alvin Karpis Story*, 81. In this paragraph the parenthetical citations refer to either Karpis's autobiography or to Hoover's *Persons in Hiding*.

55. The characterization of Barker as a hillbilly whose criminality was traceable to her mountain identity has persisted in the literature about her. For instance, Lew Louderback's popular 1968 work, *The Bad Ones*, describes her as "typical of the mountain breed: tough, fierce in her affections and loyalties, suspicious of outsiders. . . . Slowly Kate Barker began to change. Criticism of her offspring had triggered some indefinable shift in her chemistry. Her mountain-

eer's touchy pride, her fierce resentment of outside authority became more pronounced." Louderback, *Bad Ones*, 14–15.

56. Hoover, *Persons in Hiding*, 10.

57. Karpis, *Alvin Karpis Story*, 91.

58. Quoted in Edge, *Run the Cat Roads*, 20.

59. Burrough, *Public Enemies*, 508.

60. *New York Evening Journal* magazine, March 3, 1935, quoted in Burrough, *Public Enemies*, 508.

61. Karpis, *Alvin Karpis Story*, 74.

62. Treherne, *Strange History of Bonnie and Clyde*, 94.

63. Milner, *Lives and Times of Bonnie and Clyde*, 101.

64. Potter, *War on Crime*, 76.

65. E. Anderson, *Thieves Like Us*, 69.

66. Fortune, *Fugitives*, iv.

67. Burrough, *Public Enemies*, 360.

CHAPTER 4

1. S. Stern, *With the Weathermen*, 243.

2. Alpert, *Growing Up Underground*, 235.

3. There is an enormous theoretical literature on autobiography. See, for instance, Olney, *Studies in Autobiography*; Olney, *Autobiography*; Benstock, *Private Self*; Adams, *Telling Lies in Modern American Autobiography*; Eakin, *Fictions in Autobiography*; Eakin, *How Our Lives Become Stories*. For a discussion of radical women's autobiography, see Perkins, *Autobiography as Activism*.

4. Davis was charged as complicit in the 1970 Marin County Courthouse shootout in which Jonathan Jackson, two other prisoners, and a judge were killed in Jackson's attempt to free his brother George Jackson, author of *Soledad Brother* (New York: Coward-McCann, 1970).

5. Beal and friends, *Safe House*, 130.

6. Meyer, *Creating G.I. Jane*, 2. The Women's Army Auxiliary Corps, or WAAC, established in May 1942, was replaced in September 1943 by the Women's Army Corps, which had the more familiar acronym WAC.

7. Ibid., 86.

8. Cpl. Vic Herman, *Winnie the WAC*, n.p.

9. Barsis, *They're All Yours, Uncle Sam!* n.p.

10. Eleanor Dunn, "More Women!" *American Rifleman*, December 1945, 38.

11. Quoted in Daniels, *Wonder Woman*, 22.

12. In the armed services, African American WACs were generally housed in seg-

regated facilities; except in black publications, they were not in great evidence in popular culture.

13. Quoted in Beal and friends, *Safe House*, 111.

14. Quoted in McWhorter, *Carry Me Home*, 22.

15. Branch, *Parting the Waters*, 759.

16. Hill, *Deacons for Defense*, 2.

17. Van Deburg, *New Day in Babylon*, 44.

18. Gentry, *J. Edgar Hoover*, 602.

19. Although Hoover eventually nixed an FBI plan to poison food and donate it to the Panthers' "Breakfast for Children" program, it was only because he was afraid that someone *other* than a Panther or child might eat it—the idea, he wrote, "has merit." Gentry, *J. Edgar Hoover*, 623.

20. Ibid., 620–21.

21. Ibid., 622.

22. Hilliard and Cole, *This Side of Glory*, 201.

23. Robert Justin Goldstein, *Political Repression in Modern America from 1870 to the Present* (Boston: G. K. Hall, 1978), 474–75, quoted in Churchill and Vander Wall, *COINTELPRO Papers*, 222. One FBI and Seattle police informer lured Larry Eugene Ward into planting a bomb at a Seattle real estate office in 1970 "by paying Ward $75, providing him with the bomb and giving him transportation to the bombing scene. Ward, a twenty-two-year-old veteran who had twice been wounded and decorated three times for service in Vietnam, was shot and killed by waiting Seattle police as he allegedly fled after the bombing attempt, although he was unarmed, on foot and boxed in by police cars." Goldstein, *Political Repression*, 473, quoted in Churchill and Vander Wall, *COINTELPRO Papers*, 222.

24. Wallace, *Black Macho*, 53.

25. K. Cleaver, "Women, Power, and Revolution," 125.

26. On the matter of "collective manhood," see Van Deburg, *New Day in Babylon*, 52.

27. Foner, *Black Panthers Speak*, xix.

28. Quoted in Hilliard and Cole, *This Side of Glory*, 122.

29. *Black Panther*, April 25, 1970, anthologized in Foner, *Black Panthers Speak*, 19.

30. As Lance Hill writes, "Many blacks in the South in the early 1960s believed that while they could possess a weapon in their home, they could not legally carry weapons on their person or in their vehicle." Hill, *Deacons of Defense*, 61. This belief may have been mistaken, technically speaking, but it was based on centuries of laws intended to keep blacks disarmed in the South. And cer-

tainly, during this period, few southern sheriffs felt strictly bound by the rule of law when it came to issues involving race.

31. A. F. Alexander, *Race Man*, 42.

32. D. Carter, *Politics of Rage*, 179.

33. Van Deburg, *New Day in Babylon*, 156–57.

34. Shakur, *Assata*, 222.

35. E. Brown, *Taste of Power*, 107.

36. Beale, "Civil Rights and Women's Liberation," 148.

37. Murray, "Liberation of Black Women," 186.

38. La Rue, "Black Movement and Women's Liberation," 164.

39. Weathers, "Argument for Black Women's Liberation," 160.

40. E. Brown, *Taste of Power*, 3.

41. As Ruth Rosen has documented, Carmichael's comment, which he made to a group of close friends within SNCC, seemed initially intended as a harmless in-joke about all of the sexual shenanigans that occurred during Freedom Summer. However, Carmichael kept repeating the comment to audiences ranging from Mississippi to London—and most female listeners in those audiences did not find the joke funny at all. Rosen, *World Split Open*, 108–10.

42. E. Brown, *Taste of Power*, 189.

43. Mailer, *Advertisements for Myself*, 339.

44. E. Brown, *Taste of Power*, 319.

45. Zwerman, "Women on the Lam," 44.

46. Daley, *Target Blue*, 430.

47. Shakur, *Assata*, 250.

48. Ibid., 65.

49. For a New York police officer's recent account of the BLA murders of cops, see Conlon, *Blue Blood*, 276–79.

50. Castellucci, *Big Dance*, 135.

51. O'Reilly, *Racial Matters*, 321.

52. Umoja, "Repression Breeds Resistance," 12.

53. Reginald Major, *A Panther Is a Black Cat* (New York: William Morrow, 1971), quoted in Doss, "Revolutionary Art," 179.

54. Shakur, *Assata*, 185.

55. Perkins, *Autobiography as Activism*, 18.

56. Shakur, *Assata*, 227.

57. Hinds, foreword to *Assata*, x.

58. Shakur, *Assata*, 66.

59. Castellucci, *Big Dance*, 137; Shakur, *Assata*, 246.

60. Williams, *Inadmissible Evidence*, 222–26.

61. S. Stern, *With the Weathermen*, 243.

62. Cummins, *Rise and Fall*, 100.

63. Wallace, *Black Macho*, 65.

64. Mailer, *Advertisements for Myself*, 348.

65. E. Cleaver, *Soul on Ice*, 26.

66. Hoberman, *Dream Life*, 173.

67. Ibid., 175.

68. Melinda Gebbie, cover to *Wimmen's Comix*, no. 7 (1976), in Robbins and Yronwode, *Women and the Comics*, 88.

69. *Dragon*, November 1975, 9.

70. Alpert, *Growing Up Underground*, 275.

71. Quoted in Beal and friends, *Safe House*, 132.

72. Beal and friends, *Safe House*, 81.

73. *Dragon*, August 1975, 22; *Dragon*, November 1975. The journal was published by the Bay Area Research Collective.

74. *Plexus*, November 1975, quoted in *Dragon*, November 1975, 3.

75. John Sinowski, "Liberal Trash" [letter to the editor], *Ramparts*, January 1974, 6.

76. Gitlin, *Sixties*, 374.

77. Women's Press Collective, *Woman's Gun Pamphlet*, 1.

78. Untitled poem, *Rat*, January 17–23, 1969, 15.

79. *Rat*, January 24–30, 1969, 3.

80. *Argus*, June 19–July 3, 1969, 17.

81. Jay Kinney and Ned Sonntag, *Young Lust*, no. 2 (1971), reprinted in Estren, *History of Underground Comics*, 151.

82. *Berkeley Tribe*, September 19–25, 1969.

83. *Berkeley Tribe*, August 15–21, 1969.

84. Otis Oakland, "Guns for Sale," *Berkeley Tribe*, January 16–23, 1970, 6.

85. Peck, *Uncovering the Sixties*, 233.

86. Leamer, *Paper Revolutionaries*, 111–12.

87. In fact, one of the Hollywood Ten, John Howard Lawson, published an essay criticizing the new left's embrace of Bonnie and Clyde and of "criminal," rather than "socially motivated," violence. Lawson, "Our Film and Theirs," 111–13.

88. "Kim Il Sung," "Learn to Shoot: School for Traitors," *Berkeley Tribe*, January 16–23, 1970, 21.

89. Stew Albert, "Piece Now," *Berkeley Tribe*, January 24–30, 1970.

90. "An Armed People," *Berkeley Tribe*, April 10–17, 1970, 8.

91. "Armed People," *Berkeley Tribe*, May 8–15, 1970, 14.

92. Annie Oakely, "Street Daughter," *Berkeley Tribe*, May 15–22, 1970, 19.

93. See George Prosser's columns in *Black Politics*, January 1968, March 1968, Summer 1968, September–October 1968.

94. Debray, *Revolution in the Revolution?*

95. Quoted in Varon, *Bringing the War Home*, 57.

96. R. Jacobs, *Way the Wind Blew*, 75.

97. Quoted in ibid., 43.

98. Susan Stern uses the term "macho mamas" liberally throughout her autobiography.

99. Payne, *Deep Cover*, 223.

100. Originally, Stern had included a chapter on her marriage to Robby and one on her childhood in the memoir, but took them out before publication. Many years later, Stern's editor, Tom Congdon, could not "recall whether our lawyers found it a legal necessity for reasons of libel, or whether we editors felt they were a different order of thing and didn't work in the book, or whether Susan herself decided not to publish them, perhaps because she was reconciling with her parents (if she was)." E-mail communication with Tom Congdon, May 17, 2005.

101. S. Stern, *With the Weathermen*, 11.

102. Peck, *Uncovering the Sixties*, 213.

103. Morgan, "Goodbye to All That," 362.

104. Susan Brownmiller, "With the Weathermen," *New York Times Book Review*, June 15, 1975, 6.

105. "Honky Tonk Women," reprinted in H. Jacobs, *Weatherman*, 319.

106. Bread and Roses collective, "Weatherman Politics and the Women's Movement," excerpted from *Women*, Winter 1970, and reprinted in H. Jacobs, *Weatherman*, 334.

107. Peter S. Prescott, "Stormy Weather," *Newsweek*, June 30, 1975, 64–65.

108. S. Stern, *With the Weathermen*, 45.

109. "With the Weathermen," *WIN* magazine, October 16, 1975, 21–22.

110. S. Stern, *With the Weathermen*, 76.

111. Quoted in Peck, *Uncovering the Sixties*, 217.

112. S. Stern, *With the Weathermen*, 277–78.

113. Stern's autobiography, in addition to documenting her go-go dancing and street-fighting, includes wonderfully detailed accounts of daily life in a Weather collective house as well as accounts of her participation in a number of key Weather actions.

114. Taussig, *Nervous System*, 120.

115. S. Alexander, *Anyone's Daughter*, 215.

116. Although Nancy Isenberg has recently made a case for the Symbionese Liberation Army as a serious political organization, it is a hard case to make. See Isenberg, "Not 'Anyone's Daughter.'"

117. Hearst, *Every Secret Thing*, 109.

118. Quoted in Cummins, *Rise and Fall*, 228. In early 1970, following the death of three Weathermen who accidentally blew up a Manhattan townhouse while making bombs, the group went underground and renamed itself the Weather Underground Organization.

119. McLellan and Avery, *Voices of Guns*, 308.

120. "S.L.A.'s Field Marshal Cinque: Revolutionary or Police Agent?" *Black Panther*, April 13, 1974, 3.

121. Varon, *Bringing the War Home*, 295.

122. "Women Catching Up with Men in One More Field: Crime," *U.S. News & World Report*, September 23, 1974, 45–48.

123. Hearst, *Every Secret Thing*, 211.

124. "SLA Communique," *Dragon*, November 1975, 17–20.

125. Zwerman, "Women on the Lam," 45.

126. Adler, *Sisters in Crime*, 1.

127. Baker, *Exclusive!* 22–23.

128. "Case Closed," *Nation*, December 11, 1976, 612.

129. S. Alexander, *Anyone's Daughter*, 156.

130. Hearst, *Every Secret Thing*, 74.

131. S. Alexander, *Anyone's Daughter*, 175.

132. Hearst, *Every Secret Thing*, 47.

133. S. Alexander, *Anyone's Daughter*, 531.

CHAPTER 5

1. Farai Chideya, "Women Who Love to Hate," *Mademoiselle*, August 1994, 134–37, 186.

2. Kathy Dobie, "Long Day's Journey into White," *Village Voice*, April 28, 1992, 22–32.

3. Amy Benfer, "Salon Mothers Who Think: Nazi Family Values," *Salon.com*, July 15, 1999, <http://www.salon.com/mwt/hot/1999/07/15/aryan_compound/index.html>.

4. "Cookbooks and Combat Boots," *Klanwatch Intelligence Report* (Southern Poverty Law Center), June 1991, 7.

5. These popular articles echoed a trend in academia that challenged received notions of femininity, including books on female Nazis (Koonz, *Mothers in the Fatherland*) and Klanswomen of the 1920s (Blee, *Women of the Klan*).

6. Floyd Cochran, "Sisterhood of Hate: Women in the Racist Movement" (privately published pamphlet, 1993), posted at Education and Vigilance Network, <http://www.evnetwork.org/sister/html> (January 2001).

7. Blee, *Inside Organized Racism*, 7.

8. Ibid., 112–13.

9. For instance, ibid., 132.

10. Rachel Pendergraft, "Dear Sisters . . . ," <http://www.kukluxklan.org/women.htm> (January 24, 2001).

11. Unsigned letter from spider-ti062.proxy.aol.com-152.163.194.202, November 6, 2000, on <http://www.saram.net/ws_forum/sexuality/messages/141346.html>

12. Warrior Woman, "The Role of the Childless White Woman in the Aryan State," <http://ourhero.com/library/Discourse/ahmk881.txt> (January 24, 2000).

13. Kaplan and Weinberg, *Emergence of a Euro-American Radical Right*, 68.

14. Benfer, "Salon Mothers Who Think," 2.

15. For background on far right movements, I have relied on K. Stern, *Force upon the Plain*; Dees, *Gathering Storm*; Hamm, *Apocalypse in Oklahoma*; Mulloy, *American Extremism*.

16. As D. J. Mulloy notes, militia leaders and members, on their Websites and in their newsletters, frequently invoke the history of the American Revolution and tie their aims to those of the founding fathers. "It is this connection that modern militia members seek to exploit by linking themselves not only with the famed Minutemen but also with the origins of the American nation itself, and by suggesting that both are intimately bound up with the colonists' defense of their right to keep and bear arms." Mulloy, *American Extremism*, 49.

17. K. Stern, *Force upon the Plain*, 48.

18. Walter, *Every Knee Shall Bow*, 232.

19. Weaver had refused to appear in court to answer weapons charges stemming from his sale of a sawed-off shotgun to an undercover informant. The sting operation had been intended as a way to recruit Weaver as an informant against the Aryan Nations; it was a complete failure.

20. Walter's *Every Knee Shall Bow* is the definitive account of the events at Ruby Ridge. I have relied on it as the basis of my factual discussion.

21. Aho, *This Thing of Darkness*, 58.

22. Walter, *Every Knee Shall Bow*, 129.

23. Bock, *Ambush at Ruby Ridge*, xv.

24. Quoted in Walter, *Every Knee Shall Bow*, 236.

25. Quoted in ibid., 238.

26. Quoted in ibid., 367.

27. Ronson, *Them*, 69. As Jack McLamb, head of an organization called Police against the New World Order, told Jon Ronson, "You know why they shot Vicki Weaver? They knew Vicki was the strongest member of the family. This is what you learn in military training. Take out the head." Ibid., 79.

28. Aho, *This Thing of Darkness*, 59.

29. Weaver and Weaver, *Federal Siege at Ruby Ridge*.

30. See 1999 Preparedness Shows ad on <http://www.icimedia.com/prepared nessmall/boocat.html> (October 10, 2002). Randy Weaver continues, at the time of this writing, to make a living touring gun shows and offering people a chance to have their picture taken with him for five dollars.

31. Dees, *Gathering Storm*, 58–59.

32. Barkun, "Conspiracy Theories," 59.

33. Quoted in K. Stern, *Force upon the Plain*, 77–78.

34. David Connerty-Marin, "Led by Chute, Militia Attracts Diverse Crowd," *Maine Sunday Telegram*, February 11, 1996.

35. Sollors, *Beyond Ethnicity*.

36. Peter Carlson, "Ask Questions First: Novelist Carolyn Chute's Militia Aims to Be Different," *Washington Post*, January 3, 2000.

37. Carolyn Chute, "Making Government Ours Again," *Maine Sunday Telegraph*, December 24, 1995.

38. Connerty-Marin, "Led by Chute."

39. Carolyn Chute, "Interview with Carolyn Chute," *New Democracy Newsletter*, March–April 2000, posted at <http://newdemocracyworld.org/chute.htm> (January 2006).

40. Connerty-Marin, "Led by Chute."

41. David Connerty-Marin, "Author Hopes 'Militia' Will Lead to Change," *Portland Press Herald*, January 24, 1996.

42. Molly Ivins, "Of Bad Jokes and True Populism," *Atlanta Constitution*, February 21, 1996.

43. Carlson, "Ask Questions First."

44. Chute, "Interview with Carolyn Chute."

45. Carlson, "Ask Questions First."

46. Carolyn Chute, "How Can You Create Fiction When Reality Comes to Call?" *New York Times*, September 27, 1999.

47. Chute, "Interview with Carolyn Chute."

48. Ibid.

49. Jules Crittenden, "Author Leads Crusade vs. 'Bad Government,'" *Boston Herald*, June 1, 1997.

50. Carlson, "Ask Questions First."

51. Stock, *Rural Radicals*, 50–51.

52. Ibid., 51–52.

53. Chute, *Merry Men*, 618.

54. Deloria, *Playing Indian*.

55. Chute, *Snow Man*, 23.

56. Blee, *Inside Organized Racism*, 60.

57. Michaels, *Our America*, 38.

58. Quoted in Whisnant, *All That Is Native and Fine*, 120.

59. Chute, "How Can You Create Fiction When Reality Comes to Call?"

60. As Janet Biehl writes of the recent German ecofascist movement, "Conceptions of one's region as one's homeland, or *Heimat*, can be perverted into a nationalistic regionalism when a region's traditions and language are mystically tied to an 'ancestral' landscape." Biehl, "'Ecology' and the Modernization of Fascism," 35.

61. Quoted in Carlson, "Ask Questions First."

62. N. Anderson, *The Hobo*. For an elaboration of this argument, see Browder, *Slippery Characters*, chap. 6.

63. Carlson, "Ask Questions First."

64. K. Stern, *Force upon the Plain*, 14; Robertson, *New World Order*, 215–16.

65. Blee, *Inside Organized Racism*, 94.

66. Quoted in K. Stern, *Force upon the Plain*, 79.

67. "'Neither Left Nor Right,'" *Intelligence Report* (Southern Poverty Law Center), Winter 2000, 40–41.

68. Ibid., 42.

69. Quoted in Alicia Anstead, "Just Who Is Carolyn Chute?" *Bangor Daily News*, August 7, 1999.

CHAPTER 6

1. Quoted in Ian Katz, "Firearms Industry Woos Women Who Dress to Kill," *Guardian*, May 21, 1996.

2. Quoted in Katz, "Firearms Industry."

3. Quoted in Bruce Horovitz, "Firearms Sellers Increasingly Target Women," *Chicago Sun-Times*, September 2, 1992.

4. McKellar, "Guns," 72–73.

5. Wolf, *Fire with Fire*, 135, 217.

6. Circulation figure supplied by the magazine on October 25, 2005; personal communication.

7. Peggy Tartaro, "Women & Guns Magazine Part of Long History of Women

Gun Owners," <http://www.womenandguns.com/history.html>, 1 (January 23, 2003).

8. "Alert to Danger," *Women & Guns*, August 1989, 5.

9. "Phoenix Woman Fights Back, Survives: Attacker Dies from Gunshot Wounds," *Women & Guns*, September 1989, 5.

10. Sonny Jones, "From the Editor," *Women & Guns*, September 1989, 6.

11. Sonny Jones, "From the Editor," *Women & Guns*, August 1990, 6.

12. Sonny Jones, "From the Editor," *Women & Guns*, June 1990, 6.

13. "Florida Jury Acquits Drifter of Armed Rape Because 'She Asked for It,'" *Women & Guns*, November 1989, 5. (The author of the article is not identified.)

14. Sonny Jones, "Thelma & Louise: Reality Meets Movie Myth," *Women & Guns*, September 1991, 15.

15. Peggy Tartaro, "Gun Shows," *Women & Guns*, October 1989, 17.

16. Sonny Jones, "1990: Year in Review," *Women & Guns*, December 1990, 6.

17. For instance, the February 1990 issue.

18. Patsy, letter to the editor, *Women & Guns*, November 1989, 4.

19. Carolee Boyles-Sprenkle, "Shooting and Pregnancy: Do They Mix?" *Women & Guns*, August 1995, 4.

20. Susan Laws, "End of Trail Just the Beginning for Cowgirl Action Shooters," *Women & Guns*, July–August 2003, 35.

21. Susan Laws, "Cowgirl Action Shooting: A Portfolio of Pistoleras," *Women & Guns*, January–February 1998, 24.

22. Laws, *Cowgirl Action Shooting*, 1.

23. Phone interview with Wendy LeFever, April 12, 2005.

24. Dana Calvo, "NRA Still on Target with Gun Magazine Aimed at Women," *Boston Globe*, November 28, 2003.

25. Undated NRA fund-raising letter, Spring 1995, quoted in Davidson, *Under Fire*, 294.

26. Davidson, *Under Fire*, 295, 296.

27. Ibid., 310.

28. Quoted in DeConde, *Gun Violence in America*, 291–92.

29. Quoted in Brown and Abel, *Outgunned*, 240.

30. Dees-Thomases, *Looking for a Few Good Moms*, 19–20.

31. Karen Mehall, "'Tis the Season," *Woman's Outlook*, December 2003, 6.

32. Eileen Clarke, "Eye on Optics: What You See Is What You Get," *Woman's Outlook*, December 2003, 14.

33. J. R. Labbe, "My Two Cents: Grace, Logic and Fact," *Woman's Outlook*, December 2003, 26.

34. Lisa Parsons, "Get the Inside Track on the Fastest Growing Market! (Women in the Shooting Sport)," *Shooting Industry*, April 1, 1997, 20.

35. Daniel T. McElrath, "The Gateway Gun," *Woman's Outlook*, June 2003, 45.

36. Percy Bennett, "Girls Just Wanna Have Fun," *Woman's Outlook*, June 2003, 52–53.

37. Deborah Webbe, "My Two Cents," *Woman's Outlook*, July 2003, 19.

38. Joe Kerper, "Clang! The Sweet Sound of Silhouette," *Woman's Outlook*, March 2004, 32.

39. Tim Christie, "Rite of Passage," *Woman's Outlook*, March 2004, 47–70.

40. John E. Phillips, "Industry Spotlight," *Woman's Outlook*, March 2004, 71.

41. Bob Brister, "Shortcuts to Shotgunning," *Woman's Outlook*, April 2004, 33–69.

42. W. M. Garlington, "Hail the Riflewoman," *American Rifleman*, January 1931, 18.

43. Donna Robinson, "Donna Robinson's Africa," *Woman's Outlook*, July 2003, 20–21.

44. John E. Phillips, "The Makeup of a Huntress," *Woman's Outlook*, March 2004, 22.

45. Marilyn Stone, "Woman's Wear," *Woman's Outlook*, September 2003, 12.

46. Linda Hoff, "Hot Flashes and Cold Feet," *Woman's Outlook*, November 2003, 44–45.

47. Gila Hayes, "Reliable, Affordable, Comfortable: Taurus PT-24/7 Is Able to Shine," *Women & Guns*, March–April 2004, 15–16.

48. "Product Showcase," *Woman's Outlook*, April 2004, 16–17.

49. Chip Scutari, "Tucson Resident Will Lead NRA: Froman Aims to Change Its Image," *Arizona Republic*, January 2, 2005.

CONCLUSION

1. See Birch, *Moving Targets*. Popular as well are videos of naked women firing automatic weapons. As Chuck Traynor, the manufacturer of the first of such videos, explained, "Guns and tits and ass all mix." Gibson, *Warrior Dreams*, 98.

2. Quoted in Ann Japenga, "Gun Crazy: Women Are Buying Firearms Like Never Before. But Do Handguns Really Make Them Safer?" *San Francisco Chronicle*, April 3, 1994.

3. Quoted in Peter H. Stone, "Showing Holes: The Once-Mighty NRA Is Wounded—but Still Dangerous," *Mother Jones*, January/February 1994.

4. Stange and Oyster, *Gun Women*, 3. Other books supportive of women's gun ownership, and (generally speaking) of Oyster and Stange's argument, include Kohn, *Shooters*, and Kelly, *Blown Away*. See also Stange, *Woman the Hunter*. For a celebratory history of women and guns, see Wilson, *Silk and Steel*.

5. Stange and Oyster, *Gun Women*, 53.

6. Leslie Marmon Silko, "In the Combat Zone," *Hungry Mind Review*, Fall 1995, 45, quoted in ibid., 53.

7. See Cottrol and Diamond, "The Second Amendment"; and Cramer, "The Racist Roots of Gun Control."

8. Quoted in Michael Levy, "The Gun Lady: Peggy Tartaro's Women & Guns Magazine Preaches the Gospel of Self-Defense," *Buffalo News*, November 5, 1995.

9. For an overview of the gun-control and gun-rights arguments, see McClurg, Kopel, and Denning, *Gun Control and Gun Rights*. See also Dizard, Muth, and Andrews, *Guns in America*.

10. Stange and Oyster, *Gun Women*, 68.

11. Juliet Macur, "Two Women Bound by Sports, War and Injuries," *New York Times*, April 10, 2005.

BIBLIOGRAPHY

PERIODICALS CONSULTED

American Rifleman
Berkeley Tribe
Billboard
Boston Globe
Chicago Sun-Times
Confederate Veteran
Dallas Morning News
De Bow's Review
Forest and Stream
Fortune
Guardian
Harper's Bazaar
Kansas City Star
Leslie's Illustrated Weekly Newspaper
Liberator
Lynn (Mass.) City Item
McClure's Magazine

Mother Jones
National Sportsman
New York Times
New York World
Outdoor America
Outdoor Life
Outing
Rifle
San Francisco Chronicle
Seattle Post-Intelligencer
Shooting Industry
Sports Afield
U.S. News & World Report
WIN
Woman's Outlook
Women & Guns

BOOKS, JOURNAL ARTICLES, DISSERTATIONS

Adams, Timothy Dow. *Telling Lies in Modern American Autobiography.* Chapel Hill: University of North Carolina Press, 1990.

Adler, Freda. *Sisters in Crime: The Rise of the New Female Criminal.* New York: McGraw-Hill, 1975.

Aho, James A. *This Thing of Darkness: A Sociology of the Enemy.* Seattle: University of Washington Press, 1994.

Alemán, Jesse. "Authenticity, Autobiography, and Identity: *The Woman in Battle* as a Civil War Narrative." In *The Woman in Battle: The Civil War Narrative of Loreta Janeta Velazquez, Cuban Woman and Confederate Soldier,* edited by Jesse Alemán. Madison: University of Wisconsin Press, 2003.

Alexander, Ann Field. *Race Man: The Rise and Fall of the "Fighting Editor," John Mitchell Jr.* Charlottesville: University of Virginia Press, 2004.

Alexander, Shana. *Anyone's Daughter: The Times and Trials of Patty Hearst.* New York: Viking, 1979.

Alpert, Jane. *Growing Up Underground*. New York: Morrow, 1981.

Anderson, Edward. *Thieves Like Us*. 1937. Reprint, New York: Avon, 1974.

Anderson, Jack. *Inside the NRA: Armed and Dangerous*. Beverly Hills: Dove Books, 1996.

Anderson, Nels. *The Hobo: The Sociology of the Homeless Man*. 1923. Reprint, Chicago: University of Chicago Press, 1961.

Audett, Blackie [James Henry Audett]. *Rap Sheet: My Life Story*. With a foreword by Gene Lowall. New York: William Sloane Asociates, 1954.

Baker, Marilyn. *Exclusive! The Inside Story of Patricia Hearst and the SLA*. With Sally Brompton. New York: Macmillan, 1974.

Bardaglio, Peter. *Reconstructing the Household: Families, Sex, and the Law in the Nineteenth-Century South*. Chapel Hill: University of North Carolina Press, 1995.

Barkun, Michael. "Conspiracy Theories as Stigmatized Knowledge: The Basis for a New Age Racism?" In *Nation and Race: The Developing Euro-American Racist Subculture*, edited by Jeffrey Kaplan and Tore Bjørgo. Boston: Northeastern University Press, 1998.

Barsis, Max. *They're All Yours, Uncle Sam!* New York: Stephen Daye, 1943.

Beal, M. F., and friends. *Safe House: A Casebook Study of Revolutionary Feminism in the 1970's*. Eugene, Ore.: Northwest Matrix, 1976.

Beale, Frances. "Double Jeopardy: To Be Black and Female." In *Words of Fire: An Anthology of African-American Feminist Thought*, edited by Beverly Guy-Sheftall. New York: New Press, 1995.

"Bear Hunting as a Sport for Women." *St. Louis Globe Democrat*, April 30, 1905.

Bederman, Gail. *Manliness and Civilization: A Cultural History of Gender and Race in the United States, 1880–1917*. Chicago: University of Chicago Press, 1995.

Bellesiles, Michael. *Arming America: The Origins of a National Gun Culture*. New York: Alfred A. Knopf, 2000.

Benson, Maxine. *Martha Maxwell: Rocky Mountain Naturalist*. Lincoln: University of Nebraska Press, 1986.

Benstock, Shari, ed. *The Private Self: Theory and Practice of Women's Autobiographical Writings*. Chapel Hill: University of North Carolina Press, 1988.

Berlant, Lauren. *The Queen of America Goes to Washington City*. Durham: Duke University Press, 1997.

Biehl, Janet. "'Ecology' and the Modernization of Fascism in the German Ultra-Right." In *Ecofascism: Lessons from the German Experience*, by Janet Biehl and Peter Staudenmaier. San Francisco: AK Press, 1995.

Billings, Eliza Allen. *The Female Volunteer; or, The Life and Wonderful Adventures of Miss Eliza Allen, a Young Lady of Eastport, Maine*. Ohio, 1851.

Birch, Helen, ed. *Moving Targets: Women, Murder and Representation*. Berkeley: University of California Press, 1994.

Blanton, Deanne, and Lauren M. Cook. *They Fought Like Demons*. New York: Vintage, 2002.

Blee, Kathleen M. *Inside Organized Racism: Women in the Hate Movement*. Berkeley: University of California Press, 2002.

———. *Women of the Klan: Racism and Gender in the 1920s*. Berkeley: University of California Press, 1991.

Blee, Kathleen M., and Dwight B. Billings. "Where 'Bloodshed Is a Pastime.'" In *Confronting Appalachian Stereotypes: Back Talk from an American Region*, edited by Dwight B. Billings, Gurney Norman, and Katherine Ledford. Lexington: University Press of Kentucky, 1999.

Bock, Alan W. *Ambush at Ruby Ridge: How Government Agents Set Randy Weaver Up and Took His Family Down*. Irvine, Calif.: Dickens Press, 1995.

Bouricius, Clara Maria. "'A Happier Ending Than Is Warranted by the Facts'; or, How E. D. E. N. Southworth Created Sentimental Capitalism, 1849–1886." Ph.D. diss., Harvard University, 1997.

Boyd, Belle. *Belle Boyd in Camp and Prison*. With a new introduction by Sharon Kennedy-Nolle. Baton Rouge: Louisiana State University Press, 1998.

Braddon, Paul. *Pawnee Bill's Shadow; or, May Lillie, the Girl Dead Shot*. New York: Frank Tousey, 1891.

Bradshaw, Wesley. *General Sherman's Indian Spy*. Philadelphia: C. W. Alexander, 1865.

———. *Maud of the Mississippi*. Philadelphia: C. W. Alexander, 1863.

———. *Pauline of the Potomac; or, General McClallan's Spy*. Philadelphia: Barclay, 1862.

———. *The Picket Slayer: The Most Thrilling Story of the War*. Philadelphia: C. W. Alexander, 1863.

Branch, Taylor. *Parting the Waters: America in the King Years, 1954–63*. New York: Simon and Schuster, 1988.

Brockett, L. P., and Mary C. Vaughn. *Woman's Work in the Civil War: A Record of Heroism, Patriotism and Patience*. Philadelphia: Ziegler, McCurdy, 1867.

Browder, Laura. *Rousing the Nation: Radical Culture in Depression America*. Amherst: University of Massachusetts Press, 1998.

———. *Slippery Characters: Ethnic Impersonators and American Identities*. Chapel Hill: University of North Carolina Press, 2000.

Brown, Charles Brockden. *Ormond; or, The Secret Witness*. 1799. Reprint, Kent, Ohio: Kent State University Press, 1982.

Brown, Elaine. *A Taste of Power*. New York: Doubleday, 1992.

Brown, Kathleen. "Nathaniel Bacon and the Dilemma of Colonial Masculinity." In *Gender and the Southern Body Politic*, edited by Nancy Bercaw. Jackson: University Press of Mississippi, 2000.

Brown, Peter Harry, and Daniel G. Abel. *Outgunned: Up against the NRA*. New York: Free Press, 2003.

Broylan, James, ed. *The World and the Twenties*. New York: Dial Press, 1973.

Buntline, Ned. *Bob Woolf, the Border Ruffian; or, The Girl Dead-Shot*. New York: Beale and Adams, 1878.

———. "Merciless Ben the Hair-Lifter: A Story of the Far South-West." *Street and Smith's New York Weekly*, March 6, 1882, 1–20.

Burgess, Lauren Cook, ed. *An Uncommon Soldier: The Civil War Letters of Sarah Rosetta Wakeman, alias Private Lyons Wakeman, 153rd Regiment, New York State Volunteers*. Pasadena, Md.: Minerva Center, 1994.

Burghart, Devin, and Robert Crawford. *Guns and Gavels: Common Law Courts, Militias, and White Supremacy*. Portland, Ore.: Coalition for Human Dignity, 1996.

Burns, Walter Noble. *The One-Way Ride: The Red Trail of Chicago Gangland from Prohibition to Jake Lingle*. Garden City, N.Y.: Doubleday, Doran, 1931.

Burrough, Bryan. *Public Enemies*. New York: Penguin Press, 2004.

Cameron, Kenneth. *Africa on Film: Beyond Black and White*. New York: Continuum, 1994.

Cannary, Jane. *Life and Adventures of Calamity Jane*. 1896. Reprint, Fairfield, Wash.: Ye Galleon Press, 1979.

Carter, Dan. *The Politics of Rage: George Wallace, the New Conservatism, and the Transformation of American Politics*. 2nd ed. Baton Rouge: Louisiana State University Press, 2000.

Carter, Jimmy. *An Hour before Daylight*. New York: Simon and Schuster, 2001.

Casper, Scott E. *Constructing American Lives: Biography and Culture in Nineteenth-Century America*. Chapel Hill: University of North Carolina Press, 1999.

Castellucci, John. *The Big Dance: The Untold Story of Kathy Boudin and the Terrorist Family That Committed the Brink's Robbery Murders*. New York: Dodd, Mead, 1986.

Cawelti, John, ed. *Focus on Bonnie and Clyde*. Englewood Cliffs, N.J.: Prentice-Hall, 1973.

Christensen, Maureen. "A Gun in Her Hands: Women in Firearms Advertising,

1900–1920." *ARMAX: The Journal of the Cody Firearms Museum* 5 (1995): 7–89.

Churchill, Ward, and Jim Vander Wall. *The COINTELPRO Papers: Documents from the FBI's Secret Wars against Domestic Dissent.* Boston: South End Press, 1990.

Chute, Carolyn. *Merry Men.* New York: Harcourt Brace, 1994.

———. *Snow Man.* New York: Harcourt Brace, 1999.

Clark, Sarah Wood. "Doing What Comes Naturally: From Stunt Riding to Bronc Busting." *Kansas Heritage* 3, no. 1 (Spring 1995): 4–8.

Cleaver, Eldridge. *Soul on Ice.* New York: Dell, 1968.

Cleaver, Kathleen. "Women, Power, and Revolution." In *Liberation, Imagination, and the Black Panther Party: A New Look at the Panthers and Their Legacy*, edited by Kathleen Cleaver and George Katsiaficas. New York: Routledge, 2001.

Clinton, Catherine, and Nina Silber, eds. *Divided Houses: Gender and the Civil War.* New York: Oxford University Press, 1992.

Cohen, Daniel A., ed. *The Female Marine and Related Works: Narratives of Cross-Dressing and Urban Vice in America's Early Republic.* Amherst: University of Massachusetts Press, 1997.

Conlon, Edward. *Blue Blood.* New York: Riverhead Books, 2004.

Coomes, Oll. "Rambling Dick, the Boy Mountaineer; or, Wild Jeannette, the Maid of the Gold Hills." *Street and Smart and Smith's New York Weekly*, September 12–October 17, 1881.

Cooper, Courtney Ryley. *Here's to Crime!* Boston: Little, Brown, 1937.

Corcoran, James. *Bitter Harvest: The Birth of Paramilitary Terrorism in the Heartland.* New York: Viking, 1990.

Corey, Herbert. *Farewell, Mr. Gangster! America's War on Crime.* New York: D. Appleton-Century, 1936.

Cottrol, Robert J., and Raymond T. Diamond. "The Second Amendment: Toward an Afro-Americanist Reconsideration." *Georgetown Law Journal* 80 (1991): 309–61.

Cowley, Malcolm. *The Dream of the Golden Mountain: Remembering the 1930s.* New York: Penguin Books, 1981.

Cramer, Clayton E. "The Racist Roots of Gun Control." *Kansas Journal of Law and Policy* 4 (1995): 17–25.

Cummins, Eric. *The Rise and Fall of California's Radical Prison Movement.* Stanford: Stanford University Press, 1994.

Cushman, Pauline. *The Romance of the Great Rebellion; the Mysteries of the Secret Service; a Genuine and Faithful Narrative of the Thrilling Adventures, Daring Enterprises, Hairbreadth Escapes, and Final Capture and Condemnation to Death*

by the Rebels, and Happy Rescue by the Union Forces, of Miss Major Pauline
Cushman. New York: Press of Wynkoop and Hallenbeck, 1864.

Daley, Robert. *Target Blue: An Insider's View of the N.Y.P.D.* New York: Delacorte
Press, 1973.

Daniels, Les. *Wonder Woman: The Complete History.* San Francisco: Chronicle
Books, 2000.

Dartt, Mary. *On the Plains, and Among the Peaks; or, How Mrs. Maxwell Made Her
Natural History Collection.* 2nd ed. Philadelphia: Claxton, Remsen and
Haffelfinger, 1879.

Davidson, Osha Gray. *Under Fire: The NRA and the Battle for Gun Control.*
Expanded ed. Iowa City: University of Iowa Press, 1998.

Davis, Angela. *With My Mind on Freedom: An Autobiography.* New York: Bantam
Books, 1974.

Debray, Régis. *Revolution in the Revolution? Armed Struggle and Political Struggle in
Latin America.* New York: Monthly Review Press, 1967.

DeConde, Alexander. *Gun Violence in America: The Struggle for Control.* Boston:
Northeastern University Press, 2001.

Dees, Morris. *Gathering Storm: America's Militia Threat.* New York: HarperCollins,
1996.

Dees-Thomases, Donna. *Looking for a Few Good Moms: How One Mother Rallied a
Million Others against the Gun Lobby.* With Alison Hendrie. New York: Rodale
Press, 2004.

Deloria, Philip J. *Playing Indian.* New Haven: Yale University Press, 1998.

D'Emilio, John, and Estelle B. Freedman. *Intimate Matters: A History of Sexuality
in America.* New York: Harper and Row, 1988.

De Pauw, Linda Grant. *Battle Cries and Lullabies: Women in War from Prehistory to
the Present.* Norman: University of Oklahoma Press, 1998.

Developing a Broader Interest in Trapshooting. New York: Interstate Trapshooting
Association, 1918.

Diana of the Traps. Wilmington, Del.: E. I. Du Pont de Nemours Powder Co., 1915.

Dijkstra, Bram. *Evil Sisters: The Threat of Female Sexuality and the Cult of
Manhood.* New York: Alfred A. Knopf, 1996.

Dizard, Jan E., Robert Merrill Muth, and Stephen P. Andrews Jr., eds. *Guns in
America: A Reader.* New York: New York University Press, 1999.

Doss, Erika. "Revolutionary Art Is a Tool for Liberation: Emory Douglas and
Protest Aesthetics at the *Black Panther.*" In *Liberation, Imagination, and the
Black Panther Party: A New Look at the Panthers and Their Legacy,* edited by
Kathleen Cleaver and George Katsiaficas. New York: Routledge, 2001.

Dred Scott v. Sandford, 60 U.S. 393, 417 (1857).

DuBois, Ellen Carol. *Woman Suffrage and Women's Rights*. New York: New York University Press, 1998.

Dugaw, Dianne. *Warrior Women and Popular Balladry, 1650–1850*. Cambridge: Cambridge University Press, 1989.

Dyer, Joel. *Harvest of Rage: Why Oklahoma City Is Only the Beginning*. Boulder, Colo.: Westview, 1997.

Eakin, Paul John. *Fictions in Autobiography: Studies in the Art of Self Invention*. Princeton: Princeton University Press, 1985.

———. *How Our Lives Become Stories: Making Selves*. Ithaca: Cornell University Press, 1999.

Eastman, George. *Chronicles of a Second African Trip*. 1928. Reprint, Rochester, N.Y.: Friends of the University of Rochester Libraries, 1987.

Edge, L. L. *Run the Cat Roads*. New York: Dembner Books, 1981.

Edgeville, Edward. *Castine*. Raleigh, N.C.: W. B. Smith, 1865.

Edmonds, Sarah Emma. *Memoirs of a Soldier, Nurse, and Spy: A Woman's Adventures in the Civil War*. Introduced and annotated by Elizabeth D. Leonard. DeKalb: Northern Illinois University Press, 1999.

Ellet, Elizabeth. *The Women of the American Revolution*. Vol. 2. Williamstown, Mass.: Corner House Publishers, 1980.

Enloe, Cynthia. *Does Khaki Become You? The Militarization of Women's Lives*. Boston: South End Press, 1983.

———. *Maneuvers: The International Politics of Militarizing Women's Lives*. Berkeley: University of California Press, 2000.

Estren, Mark Jay. *A History of Underground Comics*. San Francisco: Straight Arrow Books, 1974.

Etulain, Richard. "Calamity Jane." In *By Grit and Grace: Eleven Women Who Shaped the American West*, edited by Glenda Riley and Richard Etulain. Golden, Colo.: Fulcrum Publishing, 1997.

———. "Calamity Jane: Creation of a Western Legend." Afterword to *Calamity Jane: A Study in Historical Criticism*, by Roberta Beed Sollid. Helena: Montana Historical Society Press, 1995.

Evans, Augusta Jane. *Macaria; or, Altars of Sacrifice*. Edited by Drew Gilpin Faust. Baton Rouge: Louisiana State University Press, 1992.

Faragher, John Mack. *Women and Men on the Overland Trail*. New Haven: Yale University Press, 1979.

Faust, Drew Gilpin. *Mothers of Invention: Women of the Slaveholding South in the American Civil War*. Chapel Hill: University of North Carolina Press, 1996.

Fitzhugh, George. "The Conservative Principle, or Social Evils and Their Remedies." *De Bow's Review*, April 1857, 422, 424.

Foner, Philip S., ed. *The Black Panthers Speak*. Philadelphia: J. B. Lippincott, 1970.

Fortune, Jan. *Fugitives: The Story of Clyde Barrow and Bonnie Parker as told by Bonnie's Mother and Clyde's Sister*. Dallas: Ranger Press, 1934.

Fowler, William W. *Woman on the American Frontier: A Valuable and Authentic History of the Heroism, Privations, Captivities, Trials, and Noble Lives and Deaths of the "Pioneer Mothers of the Republic."* 1878. Reprint, Detroit: Gale Research, 1974.

Fox, Richard. *Bella Starr, the Bandit Queen*. New York: R. K. Fox, 1889.

Fox-Genovese, Elizabeth. *Within the Plantation Household: Black and White Women of the Old South*. Chapel Hill: University of North Carolina Press, 1988.

Gannett, Deborah Sampson. *Addrss [sic], Delivered with Applause, at the Federal Street Theater, Boston, Four Successive Nights of the Different Plays, Beginning March 22, 1802*. Dedham, Mass.: Printed and sold by H. Mann, for Mrs. Gannet [sic], at the Minerva Office, 1802.

Gavin, Lettie. *American Women in World War I: They Also Served*. Boulder: University Press of Colorado, 1997.

Gentry, Curt. *J. Edgar Hoover: The Man and the Secrets*. New York: W. W. Norton, 1991.

Gibson, James William. *Warrior Dreams: Paramilitary Culture in Post-Vietnam America*. New York: Hill and Wang, 1994.

Gilmore, Russell Stanley. "Crack Shots and Patriots: The National Rifle Association and America's Military-Sporting Tradition, 1871–1929." Ph.D. diss., University of Wisconsin, 1974.

Gitlin, Todd. *The Sixties: Years of Hope, Days of Rage*. New York: Bantam Books, 1987.

Glueck, Sheldon, and Eleanor Glueck. *Five Hundred Delinquent Women*. New York: Alfred A. Knopf, 1934.

Goldstein, Robert Justin. *Political Repression in Modern America from 1870 to the Present*. Boston: G. K. Hall, 1978.

Gordon, Linda. *Woman's Body, Woman's Right: A Social History of Birth Control in America*. New York: Viking Press, 1976.

Gustafson, Melanie Susan. *Women and the Republican Party, 1854–1924*. Urbana: University of Illinois Press, 2001.

Guy-Sheftall, Beverly, ed. *Words of Fire: An Anthology of African-American Feminist Thought*. New York: New Press, 1995.

Halberstam, Judith. *Female Masculinity*. Durham: Duke University Press, 1998.

Hall, Richard. *Patriots in Disguise*. New York: Paragon House, 1993.

Hamm, Mark S. *Apocalypse in Oklahoma: Waco and Ruby Ridge Revenged*. Boston: Northeastern University Press, 1997.

Harman, S. W. *Hell on the Border: He Hanged Eighty-Eight Men*. 1898. Reprint,
edited by Jack Gregory and Rennard Strickland. Muskogee, Okla.: Indian
Heritage Publications, 1971.

Hearst, Patricia Campbell. *Every Secret Thing*. New York: Doubleday, 1982.

Hemenway, David. *Private Guns, Public Health*. Ann Arbor: University of
Michigan Press, 2004.

Herman, Daniel Justin. *Hunting and the American Imagination*. Washington:
Smithsonian Institution Press, 2001.

Herman, Cpl. Vic. *Winnie the WAC: A Cartoon Visit with Our Gals in the Army*.
Philadelphia: David McKay, 1945.

Hill, Lance. *The Deacons for Defense: Armed Resistance and the Civil Rights
Movement*. Chapel Hill: University of North Carolina Press, 2004.

Hilliard, David, and Lewis Cole. *This Side of Glory: The Autobiography of David
Hilliard and the Story of the Black Panther Party*. Boston: Little, Brown, 1993.

Hinds, Lennox S. Foreword to *Assata: An Autobiography*, by Assata Shakur.
Chicago: Lawrence Hill Books, 1987.

Hoberman, J. *The Dream Life: Movies, Media, and the Mythology of the Sixties*. New
York: New Press, 2003.

Hobsbawm, Eric. *Bandits*. New York: New Press, 2000.

Hodgson, Joseph. *The Confederate Vivandière; or, The Battle of Leesburg: A Military
Drama in Three Acts*. Montgomery, Ala.: John M. Floyd, 1862.

Hoover, J. Edgar. *Persons in Hiding*. Boston: Little, Brown, 1938.

Hosley, William. *Colt: The Making of an American Legend*. Amherst: University of
Massachusetts Press, 1996.

Hudock, Amy Elizabeth. "No Mere Mercenary: The Early Life and Fiction of
E. D. E. N. Southworth." Ph.D. diss., University of South Carolina, 1993.

Imperato, Pascal James, and Eleanor M. Imperato. *They Married Adventure: The
Wandering Lives of Martin and Osa Johnson*. New Brunswick, N.J.: Rutgers
University Press, 1992.

Ingram, J. *The Centennial Exposition, Described and Illustrated*. 1876. Reprint, New
York: Arno Press, 1976.

Inness, Sherrie A. *Tough Girls: Women Warriors and Wonder Women in Popular
Culture*. Philadelphia: University of Pennsylvania Press, 1999.

Isenberg, Nancy. "Not 'Anyone's Daughter': Patty Hearst and the Rise of the
Postmodern Legal Subject." *American Quarterly* 52, no. 4 (December 2000):
639–81.

———. *Sex and Citizenship in Antebellum America*. Chapel Hill: University of
North Carolina Press, 1998.

Isserman, Maurice. *Which Side Were You On? The American Communist Party during the Second World War*. 1982. Reprint, Urbana: University of Illinois Press, 1993.

Jacobs, Harold, ed. *Weatherman*. Berkeley: Ramparts Press, 1970.

Jacobs, Ron. *The Way the Wind Blew: A History of the Weather Underground*. London: Verso, 1997.

Johnson, Osa. *I Married Adventure: The Lives and Adventures of Martin and Osa Johnson*. New York: Lippincott, 1940.

Jordan, Teresa. "When Women Ruled the West: Tales of Calamity Jane, Hurricane Nell, Bowie Knife Bessie and Stella the Girl Ranger." *Denver Post Magazine*, April 24, 1983, 26ff.

Kaplan, Jeffrey, and Leonard Weinberg. *The Emergence of a Euro-American Radical Right*. New Brunswick, N.J.: Rutgers University Press, 1998.

Karpis, Alvin. *The Alvin Karpis Story*. With Bill Trent. New York: Coward, McCann and Geoghegan, 1971.

Kasper, Shirl. *Annie Oakley*. Norman: University of Oklahoma Press, 1992.

Kasson, Joy S. *Buffalo Bill's Wild West: Celebrity, Memory, and Popular History*. New York: Hill and Wang, 2000.

Kelly, Caitlin. *Blown Away: American Women and Guns*. New York: Pocket Books, 2004.

Kennedy-Nolle, Sharon. Introduction to *Belle Boyd in Camp and Prison*, by Belle Boyd. Baton Rouge: Louisiana State University Press, 1998.

Kerber, Linda K. *No Constitutional Right to Be Ladies: Women and the Obligations of Citizenship*. New York: Hill and Wang, 1998.

Kohn, Abigail A. *Shooters: Myths and Realities of America's Gun Cultures*. New York: Oxford University Press, 2004.

Koonz, Claudia. *Mothers in the Fatherland: Women, the Family, and Nazi Politics*. New York: St. Martin's, 1987.

Lait, Jack. *Gangster Girl*. New York: Grosset and Dunlap, 1930.

La Rue, Linda. "The Black Movement and Women's Liberation." In *Words of Fire: An Anthology of African-American Feminist Thought*, edited by Beverly Guy-Sheftall. New York: New Press, 1995.

Laws, Susan [Aimless Annie, pseud.]. *Cowgirl Action Shooting: Women of the Single Action Shooting Society*. Wimberly, Tex.: Aimless Enterprises, 2000.

Lawson, John Howard. "Our Film and Theirs." 1968/69. Reprinted in *Focus on Bonnie and Clyde*, edited by John Cawelti. Englewood Cliffs, N.J.: Prentice-Hall, 1973.

Leamer, Laurence. *The Paper Revolutionaries: The Rise of the Underground Press*. New York: Simon and Schuster, 1972.

Lebsock, Suzanne. *The Free Women of Petersburg: Status and Culture in a Southern Town, 1784–1860*. New York: Norton, 1984.

Leddy, Edward F. *Magnum Force Lobby: The National Rifle Association Fights Gun Control*. Lanham, Md.: University Press of America, 1987.

Leonard, Elizabeth D. *All the Daring of the Soldier: Women of the Civil War Armies*. New York: W. W. Norton, 1999.

Livermore, Mary. *My Story of the War*. Hartford, Conn.: A. D. Worthington, 1889.

Lott, Eric. *Love and Theft: Blackface Minstrelsy and the American Working Class*. New York: Oxford University Press, 1993.

Louderback, Lew. *The Bad Ones: Gangsters of the '30s and Their Molls*. Greenwich, Conn.: Fawcett, 1968.

MacDonald, Linda R. "The Discarded Daughter of the American Revolution: Catharine Sedgwick, E. D. E. N. Southworth, and Augusta Evans Wilson." Ph.D. diss., University of Colorado, 1992.

Mailer, Norman. *Advertisements for Myself*. New York: G. P. Putnam's Sons, 1959.

Mann, Herman. *The Female Review; or, Memoirs of an American Young Lady*. Dedham, Mass.: Printed by Nathaniel and Benjamin Heaton for the author, 1797.

McCaughey, Martha. *Real Knockouts: The Physical Feminism of Women's Self-Defense*. New York: New York University Press, 1997.

McClurg, Andrew J., David B. Kopel, and Brannon P. Denning, eds. *Gun Control and Gun Rights: A Reader and Guide*. New York: New York University Press, 2002.

McKellar, Sussie. "Guns: The 'Last Frontier on the Road to Equality'?" In *The Gendered Object*, edited by Pat Kirkham. Manchester: Manchester University Press, 1996.

McLellan, Vin, and Paul Avery. *The Voices of Guns*. New York: G. P. Putnam's Sons, 1977.

McWhorter, Diane. *Carry Me Home: Birmingham, Alabama: The Climactic Battle of the Civil Rights Movement*. New York: Simon and Schuster, 2001.

Merrill, Ann Adelia. "The Novels of E. D. E. N. Southworth: Challenging Gender Restrictions and Genre Conventions." Ph.D. diss., Emory University, 1993.

Merrill, Lisa. *When Romeo Was a Woman: Charlotte Cushman and Her Circle of Female Spectators*. Ann Arbor: University of Michigan Press, 1999.

Meyer, Leisa D. *Creating G.I. Jane: Sexuality and Power in the Women's Army Corps during World War II*. New York: Columbia University Press, 1996.

Michaels, Walter Benn. *Our America: Nativism, Modernism, and Pluralism*. Durham: Duke University Press, 1995.

Miller, Mrs. Francis Trevelyan Miller. "The American Tendency to Dwarf Life."
   Outdoor Life, January 1904, 14–16.

Milner, E. R. *The Lives and Times of Bonnie and Clyde*. Carbondale: Southern
   Illinois University Press, 1996.

"Mrs. Maxwell's Rocky Mountain Museum." *Harper's Bazar*, Saturday
   November 11, 1876, 730.

Moore, Jack. *Skinheads Shaved for Battle: A Cultural History of American Skinheads*.
   Bowling Green, Ohio: Bowling Green University Popular Press, 1993.

Morgan, Robin. "Goodbye to All That." 1970. Reprinted in *The American
   Sisterhood: Writings of the Feminist Movement from Colonial Times to the Present*,
   edited by Wendy Martin, ed. New York: Harper and Row, 1972.

Moses, L. G. *Wild West Shows and the Images of American Indians, 1883–1933*.
   Albuquerque: University of New Mexico Press, 1996.

———. "Wild West Shows, Reformers and the Image of the American Indian,
   1887–1914." *South Dakota History* 14, no. 3 (1984): 193–221.

Mott, Lucretia. *Discourse on Woman Delivered at the Assembly Buildings,
   December 17, 1849*. Philadelphia: T. B. Peterson, 1850.

Moynihan, Ruth Barnes, Cynthia Russett, and Laurie Crumpacker, eds. *Second to
   None: A Documentary History of American Women*. Vol. 2. Lincoln: University of
   Nebraska Press, 1993.

Mulloy, D. J. *American Extremism: History, Politics and the Militia Movement*.
   London: Routledge, 2004.

Murray, Pauli. "The Liberation of Black Women." In *Words of Fire: An Anthology of
   African-American Feminist Thought*, edited by Beverly Guy-Sheftall. New York:
   New Press, 1995.

Nelson, Dana D. *National Manhood: Capitalist Citizenship and the Imagined
   Fraternity of White Men*. Durham: Duke University Press, 1998.

Nelson, Dana D., and Russ Castronovo, eds. *Materializing Democracy: Toward a
   Revitalized Cultural Politics*. Durham: Duke University Press, 2002.

The New Century for Women. Philadelphia: Women's Centennial Committee,
   Woman's Building, International Exhibition, 1876.

Newman, Louise Michelle. *White Women's Rights: The Racial Origins of Feminism
   in the United States*. New York: Oxford University Press, 1999.

Olney, James, ed. *Autobiography: Essays Theoretical and Critical*. Princeton:
   Princeton University Press, 1980.

———, ed. *Studies in Autobiography*. New York: Oxford University Press, 1988.

O'Reilly, Kenneth. *Racial Matters: The FBI's Secret File on Black America, 1960–
   1972*. New York: Free Press, 1989.

Parker, Alison M., and Stephanie Cole, eds. *Women and the Unstable State in*

Nineteenth-Century America. College Station: Texas A&M University Press, 2000.

Parsons, Lisa. "Get the Inside Track on the Fastest Growing Market! (Women in the Shooting Sports)." *Shooting Industry*, April 1, 1997, 20.

Payne, Cril. *Deep Cover: An FBI Agent Infiltrates the Radical Underground*. New York: Newsweek Books, 1979.

Peck, Abe. *Uncovering the Sixties: The Life and Times of the Underground Press*. New York: Pantheon Books, 1985.

Perkins, Margo V. *Autobiography as Activism: Three Black Women of the Sixties*. Jackson: University Press of Mississippi, 2000.

Perrett, Geoffrey. *America in the Twenties: A History*. New York: Simon and Schuster, 1982.

Phillips, John Neal. *Running with Bonnie and Clyde: The Ten Fast Years of Ralph Fults*. Norman: University of Oklahoma Press, 1996.

Potter, Claire Bond. *War on Crime: Bandits, G-Men, and the Politics of Mass Culture*. New Brunswick: Rutgers University Press, 1998.

The Proceedings of the Woman's Rights Convention Held at Worcester, October 23 and 24, 1850. Boston: Prentiss and Sawyer, 1851.

Purvis, Melvin. *American Agent*. Garden City, N.Y.: Doubleday, Doran, 1936.

Quigley, Paxton. *Armed and Female*. New York: Dutton, 1989.

Reeve, Arthur B. *The Golden Age of Crime*. New York: Mohawk Press, 1931.

Riley, Glenda. *The Life and Legacy of Annie Oakley*. Norman: University of Oklahoma Press, 1994.

Robbins, Trina, and Catherine Yronwode. *Women and the Comics*. Eclipse Books, 1985.

Roediger, David. *The Wages of Whiteness: Race and the Making of the American Working Class*. London: Verso, 1991.

Rogin, Michael. *Blackface, White Noise: Jewish Immigrants and the Hollywood Melting Pot*. Berkeley: University of California Press, 1996.

Ronson, Jon. *Them: Adventures with Extremists*. New York: Simon and Schuster, 2002.

Rosen, Ruth. *The World Split Open: How the Modern Women's Movement Changed America*. New York: Viking, 2000.

Ruth, David E. *Inventing the Public Enemy: The Gangster in American Culture, 1918–1934*. Chicago: University of Chicago Press, 1996.

Rydell, Robert W. *All the World's a Fair: Visions of Empire at American International Expositions, 1876–1913*. Chicago: University of Chicago Press, 1984.

Sampson, Robert. *Yesterday's Faces: A Study of Series Characters in the Early Pulp*

Magazines. Vol. 3, *From the Dark Side.* Bowling Green, Ohio: Popular Press, 1983.

Sarmiento, F. L. *Life of Pauline Cushman: The Celebrated Union Spy and Scout.* Philadelphia: John E. Potter, 1865.

Scharf, Lois. *To Work and to Wed: Female Employment, Feminism, and the Great Depression.* Westport, Conn.: Greenwood Press, 1980.

Schechner, Richard. "What Is Performance Studies Anyway?" In *The Ends of Performance,* edited by Peggy Phelan and Jill Lane. New York: New York University Press, 1998.

Server, Lee. *Danger Is My Business: An Illustrated History of the Fabulous Pulp Magazines, 1896–1953.* San Francisco: Chronicle Books, 1993.

Shakur, Assata. *Assata: An Autobiography.* Chicago: Lawrence Hill Books, 1987.

Shirley, Glenn. *Belle Star: The Literature, the Facts, and the Legend.* Norman: University of Oklahoma Press, 1982.

———. *Pawnee Bill.* Lincoln: University of Nebraska Press, 1971.

Slotkin, Richard. *The Fatal Environment: The Myth of the Frontier in the Age of Industrialization, 1800–1890.* 1985. Reprint, New York: HarperPerennial, 1994.

Smith, Tom W., and Robert J. Smith. "Changes in Firearms Ownership among Women, 1980–1994." *Criminal Law and Criminology* 86, no. 1 (22 September 1995): 133–49.

Sollid, Roberta Beed. *Calamity Jane: A Study in Historical Criticism.* Helena: Montana Historical Society Press, 1995.

Sollors, Werner. *Beyond Ethnicity: Consent and Descent in American Culture.* New York: Oxford University Press, 1986.

Southworth, Emma D. E. N. *Fair Play; or, The Test of the Lone Isle.* Philadelphia: T. B. Peterson and Brothers, 1868.

———. *How He Won Her.* Philadelphia: T. B. Peterson and Brothers, 1869.

Stange, Mary Zeiss. *Woman the Hunter.* Boston: Beacon Press, 1997.

Stange, Mary Zeiss, and Carol K. Oyster. *Gun Women: Firearms and Feminism in Contemporary America.* New York: New York University Press, 2000.

Stern, Kenneth. *A Force upon the Plain: The American Militia Movement and the Politics of Hate.* New York: Simon and Schuster, 1996.

Stern, Susan. *With the Weathermen: The Personal Journal of a Revolutionary Woman.* New York: Doubleday, 1975.

Stock, Catherine McNichol. *Rural Radicals: Righteous Rage in the American Grain.* Ithaca: Cornell University Press, 1996.

Stott, Annette. "Prairie Madonnas and Pioneer Women: Images of Emigrant Women in the Art of the Old West." In *Prospects: An Annual of American Cultural Studies,* 299–325. New York: Cambridge University Press, 1996.

Stott, Kenhelm W., Jr. *Exploring with Martin and Osa Johnson*. Chanute, Kans.: Martin and Osa Johnson Safari Museum Press, 1978.

Strauss, Bob, and Beverly Strauss. *American Sporting Advertising*. Vol. 1. Jefferson, Maine: Circus Promotions Corporation, 1987.

———. *American Sporting Advertising*. Vol. 2. Jefferson, Maine: Circus Promotions Corporation, 1990.

Strum, Philippa. *Women in the Barracks: The VMI Case and Equal Rights*. Lawrence: University Press of Kansas, 2002.

Sugarmann, Josh. *National Rifle Association: Money, Firepower and Fear*. Washington, D.C.: National Press Books, 1992.

The Surprising Adventures of Almira Paul, a Young Woman, Who, Garbed as a Male, Has for Three of the Last Preceding Years, Actually Served as a Common Sailor on Board of English and American Armed Vessels without a Discovery of Her Sex Being Made. Boston: Printed for N. Coverly, 1816.

Tappan, Eugene. Introduction to *An address delivered in 1802 in various towns in Massachusetts, Rhode Island and New York, by Mrs. Deborah Sampson Gannett*. Boston: H. M. Hight, 1905.

Taussig, Michael. *The Nervous System*. New York: Routledge, 1992.

Taylor, Susie King. *A Black Woman's Civil War Memoirs: Reminiscences of My Life in Camp with the 33rd Colored Troops, Late 1st South Carolina Volunteers*. New York: Arno Press, 1968.

Toland, John. *Dillinger Days*. New York: Random House, 1963.

Trachtenberg, Alan. *The Incorporation of America: Culture and Society in the Gilded Age*. New York: Hill and Wang, 1982.

Trefethen, James. *Americans and Their Guns*. Harrisburg, Pa.: Stackpole Books, 1967.

Treherne, John. *The Strange History of Bonnie and Clyde*. New York: Stein and Day, 1984.

Tyler, Charles W. *Quality Bill's Girl*. New York: Chelsea House, 1925.

Tyson, Timothy B. *Radio Free Dixie: Robert F. Williams and the Roots of Black Power*. Chapel Hill: University of North Carolina Press, 1999.

Umoja, Akinyele Omowale. "Repression Breeds Resistance: The Black Liberation Army and the Radical Legacy of the Black Panther Party." In *Liberation, Imagination, and the Black Panther Party: A New Look at the Panthers and Their Legacy*, edited by Kathleen Cleaver and George Katsiaficas. New York: Routledge, 2001.

Van Deburg, William L. *New Day in Babylon: The Black Power Movement and American Culture, 1965–1975*. Chicago: University of Chicago Press, 1992.

Varon, Elizabeth. *We Mean to Be Counted: White Women and Politics in Antebellum Virginia*. Chapel Hill: University of North Carolina Press, 1998.

Varon, Jeremy. *Bringing the War Home: The Weather Underground, the Red Army Faction, and Revolutionary Violence in the Sixties and Seventies*. Berkeley: University of California Press, 2004.

Velazquez, Loreta. *The Woman in Battle*. Introduction by Jesse Alemán. Madison: University of Wisconsin Press, 2003.

Ventello, Gregg Primo. "Violence Engendered: The American Rifleman Identity." Ph.D. diss., University of Kansas, 2003.

Wallace, Michele. *Black Macho and the Myth of the Superwoman*. New York: Warner Books, 1978.

Waller, Altina L. *Feud: Hatfields, McCoys, and Social Change in Appalachia, 1860–1900*. Chapel Hill: University of North Carolina Press, 1988.

Wallis, Michael. *The Real Wild West: The 101 Ranch and the Creation of the American West*. New York: St. Martin's Press, 1999.

Walter, Jess. *Every Knee Shall Bow: The Truth and Tragedy of Ruby Ridge and the Randy Weaver Family*. New York: HarperCollins, 1995.

Ware, Susan. *Beyond Suffrage: Women in the New Deal*. Cambridge, Mass.: Harvard University Press, 1981.

———. *Holding Their Own: American Women in the 1930s*. Boston: Twayne, 1982.

Weathers, Mary Ann. "An Argument for Black Women's Liberation as a Revolutionary Force." In *Words of Fire: An Anthology of African-American Feminist Thought*, edited by Beverly Guy-Sheftall. New York: New Press, 1995.

Weaver, Randy, and Sara Weaver. *The Federal Siege at Ruby Ridge: In Our Own Words*. Marion, Mont.: Ruby Ridge, 1998.

Wheeler, Edward L. *Bob Woolf, the Border Ruffian; or, The Girl Dead-Shot*. Cleveland: Westbrook, 1899.

———. "Captain Crack-Shot, the Girl Brigand; or, Gipsy Jack from Jimtown." *Beadle and Adams Half-Dime Library* 9, no. 217 (September 20, 1881).

———. *Deadwood Dick on Deck; or, Calamity Jane, the Heroine of Whoop-Up*. New York: Beadle and Adams, 1878.

———. *Pawnee Bill's Great Fight; or, May Lillie, the Rifle Queen*. New York: Diamond Dick Library, Street and Smith, 1896.

Wheelwright, Julie. *Amazon Women and Military Maids: Women Who Dressed as Men in Pursuit of Life, Liberty and Happiness*. London: Pandora Press, 1989.

Whisnant, David. *All That Is Native and Fine*. Chapel Hill: University of North Carolina Press, 1983.

Whites, Lee Ann. *The Civil War as a Crisis in Gender: Augusta, Georgia, 1860–1890*. Athens: University of Georgia Press, 1995.

Williams, Evelyn. *Inadmissible Evidence*. Brooklyn, N.Y.: Lawrence Hill Books, 1993.

Williamson, Harold F. *Winchester: The Gun That Won the West*. Washington, D.C.: Combat Forces Press, 1952.

Wilson, R. L. *Silk and Steel: Women at Arms*. New York: Random House, 2003.

Wister, Owen. *The Virginian*. New York: Grosset and Dunlap, 1904.

Wolf, Naomi. *Fire with Fire: The New Female Power and How It Will Change the 21st Century*. New York: Random House, 1993.

Women's Press Collective. *The Woman's Gun Pamphlet*. Oakland, Calif.: Women's Press Collective, 1975.

Wood-Clark, Sarah. "Doing What Comes Naturally." *Kansas Heritage* 3, no. 1 (Spring 1995): 4–8.

Young, Alfred F. *Masquerade: The Life and Times of Deborah Sampson, Continental Soldier*. New York: Alfred A. Knopf, 2004.

Zwerman, Gilda. "Women on the Lam." *Feminist Review* 47 (Summer 1994): 33–56.

INDEX